BLOOD
AND
WATER

SOLVING THE MYSTERY OF
HOW JESUS DIED BY SCRIPTURE
AND MEDICAL SCIENCE

GARY C. HASSMANN, M.D.

Copyright © 2018 Gary C. Hassmann, M.D.

All rights reserved. No part of this book may be used or reproduced by any means, graphic, electronic, or mechanical, including photocopying, recording, taping or by any information storage retrieval system without the written permission of the author except in the case of brief quotations embodied in critical articles and reviews.

Unless otherwise cited, scripture quotations taken from the New American Bible® (NAB), Copyright © 1960, 1962, 1963, 1968, 1971, 1972, 1973, 1975, 1977, 1995 by The Lockman Foundation. Used by permission.

Scripture quotations marked (NLT) are taken from the Holy Bible, New Living Translation, copyright ©1996, 2004, 2007, 2013, 2015 by Tyndale House Foundation. Used by permission of Tyndale House Publishers, Inc., Carol Stream, Illinois 60188. All rights reserved.

Scripture taken from the New King James Version®. Copyright © 1982 by Thomas Nelson. Used by permission. All rights reserved.

Scripture quotations marked (NIV) are taken from the Holy Bible, New International Version®, NIV®. Copyright © 1973, 1978, 1984, 2011 by Biblica, Inc.™ Used by permission of Zondervan. All rights reserved worldwide. www.zondervan.com The "NIV" and "New International Version" are trademarks registered in the United States Patent and Trademark Office by Biblica, Inc.

Scripture quotations are from the Revised Standard Version of the Bible, copyright © 1946, 1952, and 1971 the Division of Christian Education of the National Council of the Churches of Christ in the United States of America. Used by permission. All rights reserved.

WestBow Press books may be ordered through booksellers or by contacting:

WestBow Press
A Division of Thomas Nelson & Zondervan
1663 Liberty Drive
Bloomington, IN 47403
www.westbowpress.com
1 (866) 928-1240

Because of the dynamic nature of the Internet, any web addresses or links contained in this book may have changed since publication and may no longer be valid. The views expressed in this work are solely those of the author and do not necessarily reflect the views of the publisher, and the publisher hereby disclaims any responsibility for them.

Any people depicted in stock imagery provided by Getty Images are models, and such images are being used for illustrative purposes only.
Certain stock imagery © Getty Images.

ISBN: 978-1-9736-2959-7 (sc)
ISBN: 978-1-9736-2960-3 (hc)
ISBN: 978-1-9736-2958-0 (e)

Library of Congress Control Number: 2018906657

Printed in the United States of America.

WestBow Press rev. date: 10/29/2018

Contents

Medical and Miscellaneous Abbreviations vii
Biblical Abbreviations xi
Index of Charts xiii
Index of Figures xiv
Photographic Credits xv
Preface xvii
Prologue xxiii

Part 1: Basic Science

Chapter 1   The Sacred Scriptures 1
Chapter 2   The Human Cell 10
Chapter 3   Homeostasis 15
Chapter 4   Psychopathology 20
Chapter 5   Pathophysiology 32
Chapter 6   The Shroud of Turin 50

Part 2: Charts and Figures

Charts 61
Figures 97

Part 3: The Passion and Death

Chapter 7   Introduction of the Blood and Water 111
Chapter 8   The Blood Covenants 135
Chapter 9   My Challenges and Objectives 144
Chapter 10 Fear, Horror, and Terror.. 169
Chapter 11 The Journey and the Way 179
Chapter 12 The Preliminary Traumas and Sufferings 189
Chapter 13 The Stations of the Lord's Passion............................ 198

Epilogue 223
Glossary 233

Medical and Miscellaneous Abbreviations

A-A-B-C	**A**rterial bleeding–**A**irway–**B**reathing–**C**irculation
ABGs	arterial blood gases
ACTH	adrenocorticotropic-stimulating hormone
ADH	antidiuretic hormone
ANS	autonomic nervous system
ARDS	acute respiratory distress syndrome
ASR	acute stress reaction
ASRPD	acute stress reaction with psychosomatic disease
ATP	adenosine triphosphate
B&W	blood and water
BF	blood flow
BFT	blunt-force trauma
BG	blood glucose
BOL	blow of the lance
BP	blood pressure
BUN	blood urea nitrogen
BV	blood volume
BW	body weight
Ca^{++}	calcium
CHO	carbohydrate
Cl^-	chloride
CNS	central nervous system
CO	cardiac output
CO_2	carbon dioxide
CPR	cardiopulmonary resuscitation
CRH	corticotropin-releasing hormone
CT	computed tomogram
CVS	cardiovascular system
DAI	diffuse axonal injury
DIC	disseminated intravascular coagulopathy
dL	deciliter
DNA	deoxyribonucleic acid
DSM-IV-R	*Diagnostic and Statistical Manual of Mental Disorders*, 4th text revision
DVT	deep-vein thrombosis

ECF	extracellular fluid
EKG	electrocardiogram
EMS	emergency medical services
epi	epinephrine
ES	endocrine system
FFP	fresh frozen plasma
Fig.	figure
fMRI	functional MRI
GAS	general adaptation syndrome
GIS	gastrointestinal system
Gr.	Greek
g/dL	gram per deciliter
GUS	genitourinary system
Hb	hemoglobin
HCO_3^-	bicarbonate
Hct	hematocrit
Heb.	Hebrew
H-P-A axis	hypothalamus-pituitary-adrenal axis
HR/P	heart rate/pulse
HS	hematologic system
ICD-10	*International Classification of Disease*, 10th edition
ICF	intracellular fluid
ICP	intracranial pressure
IL	interleukin
in.	inch
IS	integumental system
IU	international units
IV	intravenous
K^+	potassium
lbs.	pounds
Lat.	Latin
L	liter
mg/dL	milligram per deciliter
mL	milliliter
mmHg	millimeters of mercury
MODS	multiple organ dysfunction syndrome
MRI	magnetic resonance image

MSS	musculoskeletal system
Na^+	sodium
ng/dL	nanograms per deciliter
NAB	New American Bible
nepi	norepinephrine
NES	neuroendocrine system
NIV	New International Version
NKJV	New King James Version
NLT	New Living Translation
NPO	nothing by mouth
NS	nervous system
OT	Old Testament
O_2	oxygen
O_2^-	reactive oxygen specie (free radical)
OH^-	hydroxyl radical specie (free radical)
P&D	passion and death
$PaCO_2$	arterial carbon dioxide pressure
PAF	platelet activating factor
PaO_2	arterial oxygen pressure
PE	pulmonary embolism
PET	positron-emission tomography
PG	prostoglandin
pH	acid/base level
PNS	parasympathetic nervous system
PTS	preliminary traumas and sufferings
PTSD	post-traumatic stress disorder
PvO_2	venous oxygen pressure
RBC	red blood cell
RNA	ribonucleic acid
ROS	radical oxygen species
RR	respiratory rate
RS	respiratory system
RSV	Revised Standard Version
SFT	sharp-force trauma
SNS	sympathetic nervous system
STURP	Shroud of Turin Research Project
T	temperature

TBSA	total body surface area
TBW	total body water
TNF	tumor necrosis factor
TSH	thyroid stimulating hormone
U	unit of whole blood
ug/dL	microgram per deciliter
WBC	white blood cell
VV	ventilatory volume (lungs)

Biblical Abbreviations

Old Testament

Genesis	Gen	Exodus	Ex
Leviticus	Lev	Numbers	Nb
Deuteronomy	Dt	Joshua	Josh
Judges	Judg	Ruth	Ruth
1 Samuel	1 Sam	2 Samuel	2 Sam
1 Kings	1 Kgs	2 Kings	2 Kgs
1 Chronicles	1 Chr	2 Chronicles	2 Chr
Ezra	Ezr	Nehemiah	Neh
Esther	Est	1 Maccabees	1 Mac
2 Maccabees	2 Mac	Job	Job
Psalms	Ps	Proverbs	Prv
Ecclesiastes	Eccl	Song of Solomon	SOS
Isaiah	Isa	Jeremiah	Jer
Lamentations	Lam	Ezekiel	Ezek
Daniel	Dan	Hosea	Hos
Joel	Joel	Amos	Amos
Obadiah	Obad	Jonah	Jon
Micah	Mic	Nahum	Nah
Habakkuk	Hab	Zephaniah	Zeph
Haggai	Hag	Zechariah	Zec
Malachi	Mal		

Biblical Abbreviations

New Testament

Matthew	Mat	Mark	Mk
Luke	Lk	John	Jn
Acts of the Apostles	Acts	Romans	Rom
1 Corinthians	1 Cor	2 Corinthians	2 Cor
Galatians	Gal	Ephesians	Eph
Philippians	Phil	Colossians	Col
1 Thessalonians	1 Thes	2 Thessalonians	2 Thes
1 Timothy	1 Tim	2 Timothy	2 Tim
Titus	Tit	Philemon	Phlm
Hebrews	Heb	James	Jm
1 Peter	1 Pete	2 Peter	2 Pete
1 John	1 Jn	2 John	2 Jn
3 John	3 Jn	Jude	Jude
Revelation	Rev		

Index of Charts

Chart I	Estimated Blood and Water Losses	62
Chart II-A	Normal Water Balance	63
Chart II-B	Water Balance in the Passion	63
Chart III	Comparison—Survival Time on a Roman Cross	64
Chart IV-A	General Adaptation Syndrome	65
Chart IV-B	Acute Stress Reaction with Psychosomatic Disease	66
Chart V	Multifactorial Shock Syndrome and Death	67
Chart VI-A	Estimated Wounds of the Passion	68
Chart VI-B	The 255 Wounds—Acute Inflammatory Response	69
Chart VII-A	Causes of Multifactorial Shock	70
Chart VII-B	Hemorrhagic Shock—Classification	70
Chart VII-C	Shock Syndrome—Clinical Manifestations	71
Chart VII-D	Hemorrhagic Shock—"Lethal Triad"	72
Chart VIII-A	Acute Respiratory Failure in the Passion	73
Chart VIII-B	Acute Cardiac Failure in the Passion	74
Chart IX	Prophetic Scripture and the Passion	75
Chart X	The 10 Pillars of the Blood and Water	91
Chart XI	The Human Cell during the Passion	94
Chart XII	Estimated Laboratory Values in the Passion	95

Index of Figures

Figure I-A, I-B, I-C	The Blood and the Water	98
Figure II	The Human Cell—The Fundamental Unit of Life	99
Figure III	The Human Brain during the Passion	100
Figure IV	Mortality Peaks after Severe Trauma	101
Figure V	Survey: "What Caused the Death of Jesus Christ?"	102
Figure VI	The Cycle of Death in the Passion	103
Figure VII	Multiple Organ Dysfunction (MDS) in the Passion	104
Figure VIII-A	Shroud of Turin—Frontal Image	105
Figure VIII-B	Shroud of Turin—Dorsal Image	106
Figure IX	Space of Destot—X-Ray of the Left Wrist	107
Figure X	The Blow of the Lance Pierced the Heart	108

Photographic Credits

Fig. I-A	Copyright stock photos, 123rf.com
Fig. I-C	Copyright Argosy Publishing, visibleimage.com
Fig. II	Copyright stock photos, 123rf.com
Fig. III	Copyright stock photos, 123rf.com
Fig. IV	Copyright Wolters Kluwer: *Greenfield's Surgery*, 5th edition (2011)
Fig. VII	Copyright illustrations, gettyimages.com
Fig. VIII-A	Copyright 1978, Barrie M. Schwortz Collection, STERA. All Rights Reserved
Fig. VIII-B	Copyright 1978, Barrie M. Schwortz Collection, STERA. All Rights Reserved
Fig. X	Copyright stock photos, 123rf.com

Cover design copyright 2017, Word and Spirit Publishing, P.O. Box 701403, Tulsa, OK 74170

PREFACE

Destiny often taps you on the shoulder in the most unlikely places. Odd or simply ordinary events can carry the nucleus from which other significant dots emerge that you connect later in the composite design of your life's purpose. It was like that for me one day in 1962 while I was studying with my friend and math tutor, Bob Swaffar, so I could be accepted into medical school.

At the time, I was a driven and talented basketball star whose future in that sport abruptly ended when I blew out my knee. Academics were of little interest to me because athletics had become my life. In fact, I had not graduated from high school, but suddenly, I was forced to channel my overachieving energy in another direction, and medicine fascinated me. I was intrigued as I read case studies concerning impossible situations that had been turned around through innovative surgical techniques.

On that fateful evening in the field house laundromat while I was working on a math problem, my friend Bob was washing and drying his jeans in a huge water extractor. When Bob casually reached inside, his right arm was caught, twisted, and amputated in a split second about three inches below his shoulder joint. I heard his deafening scream and looked up. To my complete amazement, he was standing in shock and without his arm.

I had read about a similar tragedy at Harvard: surgeons had

reimplanted a young man's arm by first stabilizing the humerus (the bone in the upper arm) and then sewing the veins and arteries together to reestablish circulation. The nerves were repaired at a later date, and they regenerated very slowly—less than a millimeter a day.

This medical emergency was much more than a fascinating medical procedure—it was a real-life crisis. I attempted to remain calm as I jumped into action. I placed Bob's detached arm in a laundry bucket filled with ice while my teammates called a doctor, who transported Bob and his severed arm to a hospital in Stillwater, Oklahoma.

At the University of Oklahoma Medical Center, a surgical team had been performing limb reimplantation surgery in their animal lab, so they risked performing the experimental procedure on Bob. That saved his arm. His reimplantation was the third recorded case in medical history.

Today, more than fifty years later, he has good sensory and motor function in his right arm and hand! This landmark case, a breakthrough in trauma surgery, made news around the world. Walter Cronkite did a news feature, and various magazines interviewed me and even offered me money to tell my story. As a result, numerous doors were opened for me. With my new focus on academics, I became a Rhodes Scholar finalist and later received a surgical residency appointment at Johns Hopkins Hospital.

From Hopkins, I went to Columbia Presbyterian Hospital, a receiving center for trauma and orthopedic patients from around the world. These two training centers prepared me to be a good trauma surgeon and to undertake several research projects.

Later, my military experience at Ford Hood, Texas, offered me invaluable experience with many patients who suffered from shock-trauma and massive blood and water losses. I learned to calculate the losses of blood and water and studied exactly how much transfused blood and IV fluids would make the difference between life and death; these were life-threatening situations in which each drop of blood loss and every second mattered.

When I finally entered my private practice in orthopedic surgery, I became very successful financially. I should have returned to Columbia and become a teacher, no question about it, but I did not. Honestly, I got a little bit too big for my pants. I now find it comical that back then, I had a stretch limo with a British chauffeur. Can you imagine the absurdity of a physician driving up and down Interstate 35 to different hospitals wearing a cape, smoking a cigar, and saying, "I'm ready to perform surgery"?

As the Bible warns us, "Pride goes before disaster and a haughty spirit before a fall" (Proverbs 16:18). In the end, I found myself caught up in a drug situation and spent a couple of years in "Club Fed." Like Paul on the Damascus road, I too was knocked off my high horse, which ultimately led to the most powerful experience of my life: I was born again through the influence of Chuck Colson's prison ministries.

I had been a Roman Catholic most of my life, and I didn't know very much about the Bible or my faith. However, I have learned it now. I experienced a rebirth of my faith and a rekindling of my passion for my area of expertise: trauma surgery. I came to Tulsa, where I attended Catholic Mass daily and taught Bible study at the First Baptist Church for about fifteen years.

One day while teaching an abdominal training class, a student asked me something that ultimately propelled me into a three-decade-long quest to find the answer to his question—*How did Jesus Christ really die?* Clearly, that young man had recognized as I had that it must have required more than a thorn-pierced scalp and a beaten back for death to have resulted after only three hours.

The combination of my biblical insights and trauma training prompted me to probe deeper for the truth. I discovered that the accepted theories on how the crucifixion actually led to Christ's death ranged from the *ridiculous* (a broken heart secondary to sorrow and grief or divine intervention) to the *incorrect* (the German death-camp asphyxiation theory or three Roman nails). I wondered, *Wasn't Jesus born to die as a sacrificial lamb? And what about His shed blood and broken body?*

The more I studied, the more I discovered how completely Jesus had suffered mental and physical afflictions to purchase our salvation. In the process, I discovered that my experiences—whether tragic or triumphal—connected like dots and revealed the outline of my purpose in this season of my life. From the supposed pinnacle of notoriety and sweeping success to the pit of poor choices and the slammer and even a post-conversion, near-death experience, I finally discovered the power of the blood and water of Jesus Christ concerning my transformation and new creation in Him.

Moses spent forty years on the backside of the desert after what seemed to be a plummet from prominence. Joseph spent time in prison but never lost his zeal to exercise his skills. The great apostle Paul redirected his rash and injurious passion away from murdering followers of Jesus Christ to making converts and building the kingdom of God he had once sought to destroy.

Our sovereign Lord often takes the characteristics that could throw us over the edge in one area, graciously channels them in His direction, and makes a positive impact for eternity.

When Paul encountered the glorified Christ and acknowledged His lordship, he redirected his passionate focus by devoting fourteen years to hearing directly from the Lord. During that time, Paul received a revelation that would transform the world through the knowledge of what Jesus Christ had accomplished by His shed blood (*blood loss* and severe shock) and His broken body (*water loss* and severe dehydration).

I believe the sovereign Lord has called me to utilize the talents and attributes He has given me—the grace of teaching the Word of God, the grace of the medical and surgical sciences, and the grace to seek the truth and solve the mystery of how Jesus suffered and died, a mystery no one else has comprehensively solved.

I have concluded that Jesus Christ's sacrificial shed blood (blood loss) and broken body (water loss) fulfilled and perfected the prophetic scriptures and satisfied the twenty-first-century medical sciences. I am confident that *Blood and Water* will teach, bless, and inspire you to grow in the grace and the knowledge of how the Lord Jesus personally identified with you, suffered and died for your sins, and granted you eternal life and heavenly bliss (2 Peter 3:17–18). For it is by His stripes that you are forgiven and healed mentally, physically, and spiritually (1 Peter 2:24).

Through our friendship and teamwork, Bob Swaffar (right) and I triumphantly raise his reimplanted arm during the fiftieth reunion of the Oklahoma State championship basketball team (1965).

Regarding Bob's "miracle" arm, he has regained about 60 percent of its function. This unprecedented surgical achievement inspired and motivated me to specialize in orthopedic and trauma surgery.

Prologue

Solving the Mystery of How Jesus Died

The passion and sacrificial death of the incarnate Son of God is the most sacred and cherished event in history, but the exact cause of His death remains a mystery no one has comprehensively deciphered and solved.

After nearly three decades of research and pilgrimages to Jerusalem and Rome, I discovered the unexpected—that solving and deciphering the mystery of how Jesus died would necessitate modern medical science and demand the fulfillment of prophetic scripture, the theological effects of the Christ event such as redemption and reconciliation, the transcendent participation of blood and water, and the sovereignty of our Lord and Great Physician.

Blood and Water is not another medical discussion about the grisly carnage of Roman crucifixion but rather an extensive scriptural and scientific investigation introducing original scientific thought and a fresh light on God's words. The collection of twenty-one specific prophecies along with exhaustive research of the twenty-first century medical sciences have made it possible to solve the mystery of how Jesus died (chart IX; chapter 5). Furthermore, it will become obvious to you—the reader—exactly why the blood and water are such important biblical concepts (chapters 1, 7).

As an experienced trauma surgeon, I began my investigation with a vigorous review of the recent medical, psychiatric, surgical, and traumatologic literature. During my several pilgrimages to the Holy Land and Rome, I meditated in the presence of the Lord to gain a deeper understanding of His sovereignty, the fulfillment of prophetic scripture, the transcendent nature of the blood and water, and the theological effects of the Christ event.

As my scriptural and medical research progressed, I developed a deeper trust and appreciation for the beauty and grace involved in the incarnation, passion, and sacrificial death of Jesus Christ (John 3:16; Romans 8:32, 35–39; Ephesians 3:17–19; 1 John 3:16, 4:9–10). I began abiding in the effects of the Christ event that grant my eternal salvation (Hebrews 5:9), my unlimited access to God (Hebrews 4:16, 6:19–20, 10:19–22), and my gracious sharing in the divine nature (2 Peter 1:4).

Second, I understood why Jesus had been sent in human flesh (70 percent water) and human blood (93.5 percent water)— "like His brothers in every way except sin" (John 1:14; Hebrews 2:14, 17, 4:15). The miraculous incarnation—the first step of the passion—made it possible for the Son to identify with every member of the human race and fulfill the prophetic scriptures (Genesis 3:15; Matthew 5:17–18; Mark 14:49; Luke 18:31–33, 24:44; Romans 5:15–21; chart IX).

In His foreknowledge, the sovereign Lord and Great Physician perfectly directed Jesus's *mental* afflictions of fear, conflict, sorrow, and anguish and His *physical* shock-trauma including the multiple wounds and fatal losses of blood and water (Acts 2:23; 2 Timothy 1:9;

1 Peter 1:20). Almighty God coordinated each episode of the passion and sacrificial death to fulfill the prophetic scriptures and satisfy modern medical science. These included the acute stress reaction (1CD-10) in Gethsemane that was complicated by hematidrosis (blood and water losses) and adrenal fatigue (↓cortisol; chart IV-B) and the savage and excessive scourging in the Roman court that resulted in multiple wounds (chart VI-A; figures VIII-A, VIII-B), severe losses of blood and water (charts I, II-B), decompensated multifactorial shock (charts I, V, VII-A, VII-D), and internal injuries (charts VIII-A, VIII-B).

During the Passover meal with His twelve apostles, Jesus boldly proclaimed the shocking revelation that He—the Son of Man, and not a sacrificial lamb—would cut, seal, and memorialize the new blood covenant of grace for the forgiveness of sin: "My shed blood" (blood loss → acute hemorrhagic shock → death) and "My broken body" (water loss → severe dehydration → death; Matthew 26:26–28; John 6:53–56; 1 Corinthians 10:16, 11:23–26; Hebrews 9:22, 10:5, 10, 19–22; charts I, V, VI-A; figure VI).

As part of my research, I randomly questioned Christians of various denominations what they thought caused the death of Jesus Christ. I received the following responses (figure V).

1. the tetany/asphyxiation theory—death by suffocation
2. the broken/ruptured heart theory—death caused by excessive grief and sorrow resulting in massive internal bleeding and cardiac arrest
3. the divine-intervention theory—out of His infinite love and compassion, the Father ended His Son's incomprehensible pain and suffering

4. the piercings by Roman nails and lance—death from severe pain and blood loss

My research in the *Blood and Water* discusses each *incorrect* cause of death listed above (chapters 4, 5, 9, 12; epilogue). In particular, the most troubling—tetany/asphyxiation—continues to be favored in many notable publications: Barbet (1950), the *Ignatius Study Bible* (2010), the *MacArthur Study Bible* (1997), the *Life Application Study Bible* (2007), Edwards (1986), Renner (2008), and O'Reilly (2013).

My fundamental challenge and objective is for the *Blood and Water* to be your teacher, consulting physician, and surgeon as we investigate the sacred scriptures and the modern medical sciences to solve the mystery of how Jesus died.

The Pauline "scandal of the cross"—the unthinkable *paradox* that the Jewish Messiah was executed on a Roman cross—illustrates the confusion and errors that result when humanity struggles against the sovereignty, wisdom, and power of God: "There is a way that seems right to a man, but ends in destruction" (Proverbs 16:25 NLT). Jews and Gentiles believed that the crucifixion of the Jewish Messiah was impotent, foolish, and absurd. The Jews demanded a heavenly sign, whereas the Greeks insisted that wisdom alone could provide the required evidence that Jesus of Nazareth was in fact the Messiah of God. The apostle Paul wrote these penetrating words: "To those who are perishing it is foolishness, but to those of us being saved, it is the wisdom and the power of God" (1 Corinthians 1:18–20).

Generally speaking, the Roman establishment also considered the execution of the Jewish Messiah King to be outrageous, even humorous. An archeological sketch was recently discovered on the walls of an affluent Roman villa (dated AD 150) that revealed the crucifixion of a donkey with the inscription, "Alexandrea, is this the god you worship?"

By His preset plan, the sovereign Lord—our Great Physician and Surgeon—effortlessly coordinated every detail of the Son's passion by His fulfillment of the prophetic scriptures and perfect knowledge of the medical sciences (Acts 2:23; 2 Timothy 1:9–10; 1 Peter 1:20). During the years of my research and meditation,[8] I have listened for that still, small voice, "the whisper from God" (1 Kings 19:12–13 NKJV). My instructors were the Holy Spirit of truth and the inspired Word of God who accompanied me on my amazing journey—from the mystery of how Jesus suffered and died (medical science), to how Jesus *must* have suffered and died (sacred scripture), and finally, *mystery solved* (science and scripture)!

I felt the necessity to collect the specific prophetic scriptures that would reveal the strongest evidence, and the divine truth that would solve and unravel the mystery of how Jesus died (Matthew 5:17–18; Mark 14:49; Luke 18:31–33, 24:44; John 19:24, 28, 36–37; chart IX; chapters 1, 9, 12).

1. Almighty God effortlessly created blood as "the life of the flesh for atonement on the altar" (Leviticus 17:11). He revealed that the blood of every living creature was "sacred" and the "seat and center of life" (Genesis 9:4–6; Leviticus 17:11–14; Deuteronomy 12:23–25). He created the water of life (70 percent of the human body and 85 percent of the earth's surface) as the major component of animal and plant life—the preeminent nutrient essential for life. Life-giving rivers of water are representative of the Holy Spirit, the washing by the Word, eternal life, and Christian water baptism.

2. The lifesaving waters of the flood delivered Noah and his family from "the great evil and wickedness of the world" (Genesis 6:5–7, 8:1–19; Hebrews 11:7; 1 Peter 2:20–21). The powerful living waters of the Red Sea destroyed Pharaoh and his mighty charioteers, which rescued the Israelites from the oppression of Egyptian slavery (Exodus 14:22–31, 15:3–5). Life-giving, spiritual water "gushed out in abundance from the rock" saving the Israelites—"that Rock was Christ" (Numbers 20:7–11; 1 Corinthians 10:4–5).

   A wondrous stream of living water will again flow from the threshold of the Jerusalem temple, and "wherever it flows, every sort of living creature shall live" (Ezekiel 47:9).

3. In preparation for Passover—the most renowned event in the Old Testament—the sovereign Lord gave Moses specific instructions concerning sacrificial blood: the shed blood of unblemished Passover lambs was sprinkled with hyssop on the Hebrew doorframes: "Seeing the *blood*, I will pass over you" (Exodus 12:13). By their act of faith, almighty God delivered, freed, and redeemed His chosen people from Egyptian slavery (Exodus 12:5–7, 21–27, 20:2).

   On the annual Day of Atonement, the shed blood of a sacrificial goat was sprinkled on the mercy seat in the holy of holies. The blood of sacrificial animals only imperfectly covered the sins of Israel and only temporarily restored their fellowship with God (Leviticus 16:12–17; Hebrews 10:1–4, 11–14).

4. The prophetic scriptures revealed a future Jewish Messiah, a Redeemer who would be the sacrificial Lamb of God (Genesis 3:15; Job 19:25; Isaiah 41:14, 43:14, 49:7, 53:7; Jeremiah 12:19; Hebrews 11:24–27; Revelation 5:9–12; chart IX). But the Redeemer's shed blood (blood loss) and broken body (water loss) infinitely, perfectly, and eternally purchased humanity from the bondage of sin and death (Romans 6:22, 8:1–2; Hebrews 9:12; Revelation 5:9), the curse of the law (Galatians 3:13), the devil (1 John 3:8; Revelation 12:11), and the wrath of God against sin and unbelief (John 3:36; Romans 5:9).

5. The shed blood of the Levitical animal sacrifices—cattle, goats, and sheep—was imperfect, temporary, and finite and required repetitive offerings (Leviticus 1–7; Hebrews 9:11–15, 22, 10:1–5). The covenants of the Old Testament were cut and ratified with the shed blood of animals representing the life of the human participants (Genesis 15:9–11; Exodus 24:3–8). Each Jewish feast, for example, the Passover, was celebrated by offering the shed blood of unblemished sacrificial lambs—perfect animals without fracture, dislocation, blindness, or other defects (Exodus 12:21–27, 46; John 19:36).

6. The sin and guilt of the Hebrew people were temporarily covered by the shed blood of the Levitical sacrificial system. Furthermore, these sacrifices were officiated by imperfect and temporary human priests (Hebrews 8:1–2, 10:1–5, 19–20).

The Mosaic blood covenant of law was fulfilled and perfected by the new blood covenant of grace—cut, sealed, and memorialized by Jesus Christ, the eternal and perfect great High Priest (1 Corinthians 11:23–26; Hebrews 8:1–2, 9:11–15) and the sinless and willing Victim (John 10:17–18).

The shed blood, broken body, and torn flesh of Jesus Christ graciously merits infinite mercy (Ephesians 2:4), eternal redemption (Hebrews 9:12), and every spiritual blessing in Him (Ephesians 1:3).

7. Jesus revealed to his disciples that the Messiah must fulfill the Old Testament prophetic scriptures that included the following examples (Matthew 5:17–18; Mark 14:49; Luke 18:31–33, 24:25–27, 44; chart IX).

- The protoevangelion or first gospel—the glorious victory of the "offspring of the woman" over the devil (Genesis 3:15).
- The murder of Abel—blunt-force trauma and shock-trauma—was the result of blood and water loss (Genesis 4:8–11).
- Abraham offered the bloody sacrifice of a ram provided by the sovereign Lord as the substitute for Isaac—the son of promise (Genesis 22:11–14).
- The murder of Eleazar resulted by the excessive scourging of an innocent Jewish scribe who by faith refused to eat the meat of a pig (2 Maccabees 6:28–31 NAB).
- The Levitical blood sacrifices (Leviticus 1–7).
- The unblemished Passover lambs (Exodus 12:1–10).
- The Old Testament blood covenants (chapter 8).
- The psalmist's Abandoned/Righteous One was afflicted with fear, horror, terror, severe dehydration, and piercings (Psalm 22:1–18).

- The Suffering Servant sustained a balance of mental afflictions and physical shock-trauma. He was crushed, bruised, pierced, and wounded to "justify many" (Isaiah 50:6, 52:13–53:12).
- The Pierced One prefigured the Jewish Messiah lifted up, pierced, and mourned by the inhabitants of Jerusalem (Zechariah 12:10).

The Old Testament prophetic scriptures firmly establish that the Jewish Messiah would sustain mental afflictions such as fear, sorrow, stress, anguish, and terror and the physical traumas of scourging, battery, piercings, blood and water losses, and shock (chart IX, see 3, 10, 12, 15, 16, 19; chapters 1, 7, 10). Shed blood (external hemorrhage) was an absolute requirement for the remission of sins (Leviticus 17:11–14; Hebrews 9:22). In addition, severe cellular dehydration, cellular dysfunction, and cellular death resulted in Jesus's broken body and torn flesh (charts I, II-B, V).

My groundbreaking investigation into the mysterious, sacrificial death and passion of Jesus Christ reveals solid evidence from each of the following.

1. The sovereignty, foreknowledge, and set plan of the Lord and Great Physician (Acts 2:23)
2. The fulfillment of God's prophetic Word (Luke 18:31–33, 24:44; chart IX)
3. The fresh light of the modern medical sciences (charts I, III, V; figures VI, VII)
4. The transcendency of the blood and water (chart X; figures I-A, I-B, I-C)
5. The theological effects of the Christ event such as the eternal redemption by His blood (Hebrews 9:12) and the perfect

sacrifice by His broken body and shed blood (Matthew 26:26–28; John 6:51–58; Hebrews 10:11–22)

Nevertheless, you may ask, "Why is this new truth so important? How does this fresh version of the gospel change my salvation? Does it really matter how Jesus died albeit He died for my family and me?"

Our heavenly Father has revealed the truth of His gospel to us—His adopted children—so we might be "consecrated by his word of truth" and "grow in grace and in the knowledge of our Lord and savior Jesus Christ" (John 17:17–19; 2 Peter 3:18). Furthermore, the scriptures instruct us to "stand fast" (Ephesians 5:8) and "trust in the word of *truth*, the gospel of your salvation" (Ephesians 1:13 NKJV, 5:8).

During the upper-room discourse in the fourth gospel, Jesus proclaimed His salvation formula: "I am the Way and the *Truth* and the Life. No one comes to the Father except through me" (John 14:6; chapter 11). In other words, the incarnate Son is the truth who offers a new and living way to access the presence of almighty God (Hebrews 4:16, 7:19, 10:19–22). Further, Jesus revealed that "the *Spirit of truth* will testify of me" (John 15:26) and will teach us to "worship the Father in spirit and truth" (John 4:23–24).

Jesus told Pilate He had "come into the world to testify to the truth of His Kingdom." However, Pilate's response, "What is truth?" reflected a cynical view of Roman truth and justice. Such disputes between the Lord Jesus and the political and religious establishments make it clear why the Christian faithful must maintain their trust in the absolute truth of the gospel (John 18:37–38).

The truth of how Jesus died is also significant since His passion and sacrificial death was repeatedly foreshadowed in the Old Testament and fulfilled in the New—the sacred unity of the scriptures must be preserved (chart IX). In addition, the prophetic scriptures and their fulfillments do not reveal a shred of evidence that supports tetany/asphyxiation, a broken or ruptured heart, or divine intervention as the cause of Jesus's death (charts I, III, V, VI-A; figures V, VI; chapters 4, 5, 9, 12).

Third, the sovereign Lord is a God of specifics—detail, order, and accuracy. For example, recall the exact details and orderly instructions the Lord revealed to Moses concerning the specific materials and the precise measurements for the construction of His tabernacle—the furniture, curtain rods and hooks, walls, and columns (Exodus 25–27, 36–38).

The sovereign Lord also gave detailed instructions for the exact species and specific number of animals to be sacrificed as well as the precise instructions for when, where, and how to sprinkle the sacrificial blood (Leviticus 4:1–2, 6:17–23, 23:1–44). Almighty God recorded the genealogies of each Hebrew family and tribe in perfect order (1 Chronicles 1:1–42). During the Sermon on the Mount, Jesus appealed for accuracy and detail with respect to the fulfillment of prophetic scripture— "Not one jot or one tittle will pass from the law till all is fulfilled" (Matthew 5:17–18 NKJV).

Since God's Word reveals the details, order, and accuracy with respect to His holy temple and the Levitical sacrificial system, we should avoid error and seek to grow in the grace and knowledge of how Jesus Christ suffered and died (2 Peter 3:17–18).

The gospel is "the *power* of God for the salvation of everyone who believes" (Romans 1:16). Only almighty God possesses the power and wisdom to reverse the fallen nature of humanity (2 Peter 1:4), bestow freedom from sin and death (Romans 8:2), merit eternal redemption (Hebrews 9:12), and grant new resurrection life (Colossians 2:12).

Jesus boldly announced the cause of His impending death:

"This is My body which is broken for you" (1 Corinthians 11:24 NKJV). There is power in the broken body and torn flesh of Christ caused by massive water losses and secondary cellular dehydration, dysfunction, and death (1 Corinthians 10:16; John 6:53–56; Hebrews 10:5, 10, 20; charts I, V, XI).

Jesus proclaimed, "This is My blood of the new covenant which is shed for many for the remission of sins" (Matthew 26:28 NKJV). There is power in the shed blood of Christ that grants infinite mercy (Titus 3:5), sanctifying grace (Romans 6:22), and a share of His divine nature (2 Peter 1:4). The power of the blood of Jesus Christ is present in the Lord's Supper/Eucharist and our prayers that invoke the Lord's protection, deliverance, healing, and sanctifying grace. Moreover, "The saints have conquered Satan by the [power of the] blood of the Lamb and by the [power of the] words of their testimony" (Ephesians 5:26; 1 John 4:4, 5:6–8; Revelation 12:11, 21:6, 22:17).

For the glory of the Lord, the gospel of truth and power blesses us with the marvelous exchanges[9] empowered by the incarnate Son's shed blood and broken body.

1. The Son who was divine assumed our fallen human flesh and blood so we might share in the divine nature (2 Peter 1:4).
2. The Son who was rich became poor so we might become wealthy (2 Corinthians 8:9).
3. The Son who was without sin became sin so we might become the righteousness of God (2 Corinthians 5:21).
4. The Son who was without the curse became the curse so we might be liberated, healed, and redeemed (Romans 6:18; Galatians 3:13; 1 Peter 2:24).

5. The Son who was the light of the world became the hour of darkness so our light might shine before others from the city set on a hill, reveal our good deeds, and glorify our heavenly Father (Matthew 5:14–16; Luke 22:53; Hebrews 11:10, 14, 13:14).

REFERENCES

1. Barbet, P. 1950. *A Doctor at Calvary.* Indre, France: Dillion & Cie.
2. Hahn, S. and C. Mitch, editors. 2010. *The Ignatius Catholic Study Bible* (RSV). San Francisco: Ignatius Press.
3. MacArthur, J. 1997. *The MacArthur Study Bible* (NKJV). Nashville: Thomas Nelson.
4. Beers, R. A., editor. 2007. *Life Application Study Bible* (NLT). Carol Stream, IL: Tyndale House.
5. Edwards, W. D., W. J. Gabel, and F. E. Hosmer. "On the Physical Death of Jesus Christ." *Journal of the American Medical Association* 1986, 255:1455–63.
6. Renner, R. 2008. *Paid in Full.* Tulsa, OK: Teach All Nations.
7. O'Reilly, B. and M. Dugard. 2013. *Killing Jesus.* New York: Henry Holt.
8. Batterson, M. 2011. *The Circle Maker.* Grand Rapids, MI: Zondervan.
9. Marmion, C. 2005. *Christ, The Life of the Soul.* Bethesda, MD: Zaccheus Press.

Part I

Basic Science

Chapter 1

The Sacred Scriptures

The sacred scriptures are the "light of my path," the primary resource in my search for the truth, light, and power to solve the mystery of how Jesus died (Psalm 119:105; Romans 1:16; John 17:17). The sovereign Lord wrote a rapturous and loving letter to His wayward creation about His beloved Son's incarnation, passion, and sacrificial death in simple words of love, hope, beauty, and life.

The sacred scriptures (Gr. *hagios* + *graphē*, "holy words") along with modern medical science are the synergistic cornerstones that solve the mysterious death of Jesus Christ. The synergism of scripture and science reveal precisely why the blood and water are such vital biblical concepts (charts I, V; figures I-A, I-B, I-C; chapter 7).

By His powerful word, God effortlessly created the atom, the fundamental unit of matter; the universe, the whole of all things held together by Himself; and the cell, the fundamental unit of life (Genesis 1:1–3; Psalm 33:6–9; Hebrews 1:3, 11:3; figure II; chapter 2).

Through the wisdom of Solomon, the Lord God revealed His good purpose and perfect will: "Fear God and keep His commands, for this is man's all" (Ecclesiastes 12:13). The sacred scriptures are living in that they can penetrate and judge the human heart and soul

(Hebrews 4:12). They are inerrant, inspired, and useful for teaching, correcting, and training in righteousness (2 Timothy 3:16).

The glorious fulfillments and perfections of the prophetic scriptures reveal the Lord's sovereignty, power, and wisdom. His prophets searched and spoke about the saving work of the Messiah by the use of persons (the Suffering Servant, the prophet Jeremiah, and the Pierced One), events (the Levitical animal sacrifices, the liquid offerings, the Passover feast, and the Day of Atonement), and things (the temple, altars, and mercy seat; 1 Peter 1:10–12; chart IX). The sovereign Lord, our Great Physician, is glorified on earth and in heaven by the perfect incarnation, sacrificial death, and passion of the Son including the fulfillment of prophetic scripture that preserved the sacred unity of the Bible (Matthew 5:17–18; Luke 18:31–33, 24:25–27, 44–45; John 5:39, 46–47, 19:24, 28, 36–37; Romans 11:36; 1 Peter 1:10–12).

The scriptures reveal that "the life of the flesh is in the blood, and I have given it to you upon the altar to make atonement for your souls" (Leviticus 17:11–14 NKJV; Deuteronomy 12:23); further, they teach that "without the shedding of blood there is no forgiveness of sin" (Hebrews 9:22). For the survival of humanity, the sovereign Lord created blood as an incomparable tissue that continuously flows through the fifty thousand miles of the circulatory system. The wondrous bloodstream transports and delivers O_2 and nutrients for energy, defends against microorganisms, and arrests hemorrhage. The shed blood of Jesus Christ is an absolute requirement for the forgiveness of sins (Matthew 26:28; Hebrews 9:12–14, 22, 13:12; 1 Peter 1:18–19; figure I-A).

The sovereign Lord is the source of living water that is transcendent throughout scripture (Jeremiah 2:13).

1. Fountains of living water symbolize the Holy Spirit, eternal life, purification, and revival (Psalm 36:9; Zechariah 13:1, 14:8).
2. Wells of life-giving water represent nourishment, new life, and marriage (Genesis 24:11; Exodus 2:15–19).
3. Springs of crystal-clear water represent God's provisional gifts and His favor (Leviticus 11:36).
4. Streams and rivers symbolize God's grace, new life, wisdom, and prosperity (Psalm 1:2–3, 42:1–2; Jeremiah 17:7–8).
5. Rain and showers represent the Lord's provisional blessings and His Word, which never returns void (Isaiah 55:10–11).
6. Chaotic waters symbolize the omnipotence and sovereignty of almighty God including the purifying waters of the flood (Genesis 7:6–23; 1 Peter 3:20–21) and the lifesaving waters of the Red Sea (Exodus 14:10–31, 15:3–14).

These Old Testament examples of living water are fulfilled and perfected in the New Testament, for example,

1. the Holy Spirit (John 7:37–39, 19:34; Revelation 7:17, 22:17),
2. the new birth (John 3:5),
3. the washing of the church by the Word (Ephesians 5:26; Titus 3:5),
4. eternal life (John 4:10, 14; Revelation 7:17, 22:1–2), and
5. Christian water baptism (Matthew 28:19; Acts 8:36–39; Romans 6:3; chapter 7).

The incarnate Son came into the world "like his brothers in every way except sin" (Hebrews 2:14, 17, 4:15). He was the anticipated "Redeemer" and "the Lamb of God who takes away the sins of the world" (Genesis 3:15; Job 19:25; Isaiah 9:5–6, 53:7, 10–12; John

1:29; Hebrews 11:24–27; 1 Peter 1:19). He has graciously merited humankind with the infinite forgiveness of sin and eternal access to the Father by a new and living way by His shed blood and broken body (Matthew 26:26–28; Hebrews 4:16, 9:11–15, 10:5, 19–20).

Jesus spoke with two of His disciples on the road to Emmaus after His passion and resurrection: "Was it not necessary that the Messiah should suffer these things and then enter into His glory?" (Luke 24:26–27). Later in Jerusalem, He said, "Everything written about me in the law of Moses and in the prophets and psalms must be fulfilled" (Luke 24:44–46; chart IX). The prophets of old were empowered by the Spirit of Christ, who testified to the "sufferings destined for Christ and the glories to follow" (1 Peter 1:10–12).

It is not unreasonable to suppose Jesus made known the following notable prophetic scriptures to His disciples (chart IX; chapters 7, 10, 12).

1. The protoevangelion (Genesis 3:15).
2. The blood of all creatures is "sacred" (Genesis 9:4–6).
3. Blood is "the life of the flesh" and for "atonement on the altar" (Leviticus 17:11).
4. The Old Testament blood covenants between God and Noah (Genesis 8:20–9:17), God and Abraham (Genesis 12:1–3, 15:6–21), and God and Moses (Exodus 24:3–8) were cut and ratified by the blood of sacrificial animals (chapter 8).
5. The blood of "unblemished Passover lambs" redeemed and delivered Israel from Egyptian slavery (Exodus 12:5–7, 23–27, 46).
6. The lifesaving waters of the Red Sea protected and delivered the people of God (Exodus 14:23–31).

7. The blood sacrifices on the Day of Atonement covered the sins of the Israelites and restored their friendship with God (Leviticus 16:11–19).
8. The Suffering Servant was "afflicted by God" with mental sufferings that included anguish, torture, stress, spitting, and shame, and physical injuries consisting of scourging, battery, and piercings (Isaiah 50:6, 52:14, 53:4–8, 10–12).
9. The "Abandoned/Righteous One" was tortured, taunted, and pierced and suffered severe dehydration (Psalm 22:6–16 NKJV).
10. The "Pierced One" will be looked upon and mourned and "a fountain of living water shall be open to the House of David and the inhabitants of Jerusalem to purify from sin and uncleanness" (Zechariah 12:10, 13:1, 14:8).

My analysis of the prophetic scriptures suggests impressive evidence for mental afflictions and physical trauma during the passion (chart IX, see 2, 10, 11, 12, 15, 16, 19). The psychological stressors included fear, terror, anguish, threats, humiliation, powerlessness, and abandonment. The shameless attacks of "spitting in the face" and "pulling the beard" were considered to be the most contemptuous behavior in the Hebrew culture (Isaiah 50:6 NIV).

The "melting of the heart" indicates either the severity of the emotional responses to fright, horror, and terror, or the presence of acute cardiac failure, or both (Psalm 22:14 NKJV; charts IV-A, IV-B, VIII-B; figure III; chapters 3, 4, 5).

The descriptions of the physical trauma involved in the Old Testament typology are consistent with Jesus's mortal wounds (chart VI-A; glossary). For example, the Suffering Servant was "marred beyond recognition" (Isaiah 52:14); there were also numerous piercings, multiple wounds (stripes) secondary to scourging, and a "surrender to death" (Isaiah 53:4–5 NLT). The psalmist's "Abandoned/Righteous One" was described as "dried up like sunbaked clay" indicating life-threatening dehydration (Psalm 22:15 NLT).

The sovereign Lord foreordained and directed every step of the Son's incarnation through His last breath on Calvary (Acts 2:23; 2 Timothy 1:9; 1 Peter 1:20; chapter 13). Each drop of blood and water was sovereignly determined and coordinated to fulfill His good purpose and perfect will. His set plan was to glorify Himself by His gracious redemption of humanity, His fulfillment and perfection of the prophetic scriptures, and His unfathomable wisdom and power in the creation of modern medical science and the amazing transcendency of blood and water.

The Old Testament prophetic scriptures are fulfilled by the New Testament; they preserve the sacred unity of the Bible and provide evidence that solves the mystery of how Jesus died (Matthew 5:17–18; Mark 14:49; Luke 18:31–33, 24:25–27, 44; John 19:24, 28, 36–37; chart IX; prologue; chapters 7, 9, 10, 12).

The following New Testament fulfillments and perfections also underscore why the blood and water are such important transcendent biblical concepts (chart X; figures I-A, I-B, I-C; chapter 13).

- The foot washing exemplifies the cleansing of sin by living water and the humiliation, servanthood, and self-sacrificial love of Jesus Christ in His approaching sacrificial death (Mark 10:43–45; John 1:29, 3:5, 4:10, 14, 7:37–39, 12:24, 13:12–17; Philippians 2:6–8; chart IX, see 19, 20).
- The Lord's Supper/Eucharist is the memorial meal of the new blood covenant of grace: Jesus announced the cause of His sacrificial death by shed blood, broken body, and torn flesh

(Matthew 26:26–28; John 6:53–56; Hebrews 10:5, 10, 20, 22; chart IX, see 7).

- The acute stress reaction (ICD-10) in the Garden of Gethsemane was a life-threatening psychopathological affliction complicated by "bloody sweat" (blood and water loss) and adrenal fatigue ($\downarrow$cortisol; Mark 14:33–36; Luke 22:43–44; chart IX, see 9, 11, 12, 15, 16).
- The Roman trial consisted of fatal scourging, defenseless battery, and piercings by thorns that caused multiple wounds, severe blood and water loss, and decompensated multifactorial shock (John 19:1–5). Pilate "washed his hands of the blood of Jesus," saying, "I am innocent of this man's blood." But the indignant and outraged Jews stood their ground with the following scandalous proclamation, "His blood be on us and our children" (Matthew 27:24–25; John 18:38, 19:12, 19; chart IX, see 9, 10, 14, 16).
- Jesus sustained the balance of mental afflictions including fear, sorrow unto death, anguish (Mark 14:33–36), and physical trauma of multiple wounds, rapid blood and water loss, and severe multifactorial shock. He passed beyond the *golden hour*—the first vital hour following the mortal trauma in the Roman court without receiving treatment. He arrived on Calvary in critical condition (Matthew 27:26-32; John 19:1-5; chart IX, see 2, 3, 4, 12, 15, 20, 21; glossary).
- The centurion's postmortem blow of the lance resulted in the immediate flow of blood and water that symbolized the following: (1) the certain death of Jesus caused by rapid and massive losses of blood and water; (2) the gracious gifts for the church flowed from the Savior's open heart down the slopes of Mount Calvary and through the streets of Jerusalem to

the ends of the earth (John 19:33–34; Acts 1:8); and (3) the fulfillment of prophetic scripture (John 19:35–37; chart IX, see 8, 17, 19).

The currently popular theories for the death of Jesus include the tetany/asphyxiation theory, the broken/ruptured heart theory, and the divine intervention theory (figure V; chapter 9). These inaccurate, untenable, and indefensible medical conditions must be repudiated and discredited since they do not fulfill the prophetic scriptures (chart IX) and do not satisfy the demands of modern medical science (charts I, III, V, VI-A, IX; figures VI, VII; chapters 4, 5, 12).

By His "set plan and foreknowledge," the sovereign Lord directed each step of the passion—from Gethsemane to Calvary—leaving nothing to happenstance (Acts 2:23; chapter 13). The Author of the sacred scripture, the Creator of modern medical science, and the Great Physician and Surgeon revealed that the preliminary traumas and sufferings caused the rapid demise of Jesus Christ (charts III, V, XI; chapter 12). The glorious fulfillments and perfections of the prophetic scriptures confirm the sacred unity of God's Word "for the praise of His glory" (Matthew 5:17–18; Luke 18:31–33, 24, 25–27, 44; Ephesians 1:10–12; Romans 11:33–36 NKJV; 1 Peter 1:10–12).

REFERENCES

1. Harrison, R. K., editor. 1988. *Unger's Bible Dictionary.* Chicago: Moody Publishers.
2. Youngblood, R. F., editor. 1995. *Nelson's New Illustrated Bible Dictionary.* Nashville: Thomas Nelson.
3. Ferguson, E., editor. 1999. *Encyclopedia of Early Christianity.* New York: Routledge, Taylor and Francis.
4. Stuhlmueller, C., editor. 1996. *The Collegeville Pastoral Dictionary of Biblical Theology.* Collegeville, MN: Liturgical Press.
5. Ferguson, S. B. and D.F. Wright, editors. 1998. *New Dictionary of Theology.* Downers Grove, IL: Intervarsity Press.

Chapter 2

The Human Cell

The cell is the fundamental unit of life. The typical human cell[1-4] (Lat. *cella*, "compartment"; Gr. *cyto*, "hollow vessel") consists of three parts (figure II).

1. the cell membrane or the envelope, which contains the cellular contents and controls the functions of entry and exit
2. the cytoplasm that consists of aqueous gel (around 70 percent water) and subcellular organelles that produce energy (ATP), synthesize protein (enzymes), transport compounds, and perform other vital functions
3. the nucleus, which contains the twenty-three pairs of the chromosomes consisting of DNA (the genetic code) and the messenger RNA.

The importance of the human cell in this scientific and scriptural investigation cannot be overstated since the incarnate Son was "like His brothers in every way except sin" (John 1:14; 1 Timothy 3:16; Hebrews 2:14, 17, 4:15). The human body of Christ—identical to yours and mine—consisted of flesh and blood with an estimated one hundred trillion cells organized into multiple organ systems, for example the cardiovascular or circulatory system, the respiratory system, the neuroendocrine system, and the musculoskeletal system (figures I-A, I-B, I-C, VII).

The mental afflictions and physical trauma that Jesus sustained caused severe *cellular injuries* involving multiple organs.[3–5] For example, acute multifactorial shock resulted in secondary cellular dehydration, hypoxia ($\downarrow O_2$), acidosis ($\downarrow pH$), and ultimately irreversible cellular and microvascular injuries (charts V, XI; figures II, VI, VII; glossary). The human cellular responses of Jesus Christ secondary to His mental afflictions and physical wounds, blood and water losses, and severe shock were similar to those of His brothers and sisters (Hebrews 2:14, 17).

Human life consists of vital functions that distinguish it from death—organization, movement, growth and repair, production of energy, excretion, adaptation, and reproduction (figure II; chapter 7). Perhaps the best method to define cellular life is by the attributes that permit it to exist.

1. the production of cellular energy stored in chemical bonds (ATP)
2. cellular reproduction by chromosomal replication and cellular division
3. growth and repair by the synthesis of proteins
4. communication with other cells known as crosstalk
5. cellular movement to avoid danger and locate nutrients
6. absorption of O_2, H_2O, glucose, and other essential nutrients
7. excretion of toxic cellular waste products, for example CO_2, BUN, and lactic acid (chart XII)

8. specialized functions such as contraction (muscle cells), inflammation (WBCs), and transport and delivery of O_2 (RBCs).

The crucial discovery of the microscope[6] by Robert Hooke (1635–1703) made it possible to identify the first cells that were called "little boxes." Each box represented an amazing living cell—the fundamental unit of life. By the twentieth century, the study of cytology was revolutionized by the electron microscope, which has produced the cutting-edge research of the cellular organelles (figure II), molecular biology, and genomics.

The incredulous functions that make cellular life possible (above) are performed by the subcellular cytoplasmic organelles or the "cellular engines" outlined in the following (chart XI; figure II).

1. The mitochondria (power plants) produce cellular energy (ATP) by the oxidation of CHO and fat.
2. The ribosomes (protein factories) synthesize enzymes for chemical reactions.
3. The endoplasmic reticulum (traffic control) directs the absorption of nutrients and the excretion of waste.
4. The lysosomes (warehouses) store powerful enzymes that destroy intracellular debris; cellular injuries caused by shock-trauma and dehydration result in the abnormal release of these destructive lysosomal enzymes capable of digesting the cell (autodigestion).

Over the course of the passion, the human cells of Jesus Christ were the site and source of His injuries, pain, dysfunction, and death.

Through the power of His supernatural words, the sovereign Lord effortlessly created the universe out of nothing (Genesis 1:1–3; Psalm

33:6, 9; Hebrews 11:3). Adam's body contained more than one hundred trillion cells and about 70 percent water and 30 percent clay—protein, carbohydrate, fat, minerals, vitamins, and other complex compounds. The Lord God "blew the breath of life into Adam's nostrils and man became a living being" (Genesis 2:7).

The creation of blood was exalted by God as "sacred" and "the seat and center of life." In addition, He revealed that "the life of the flesh is in the blood, given to make atonement upon the altar for your souls. It is blood that sustains [life]" (Leviticus 17:11–14 NKJV). Furthermore, "without shedding of blood there is no remission [of sin]" (Hebrews 9:22 NKJV).

To thoroughly identify with humanity, the Son of God assumed fallen human flesh complete with one hundred trillion cells, fifty thousand miles of blood vessels, and human blood (the life of the flesh); "In all things He had to be made like His brethren, that He might be a merciful and faithful High Priest" (Philippians 2:6–8 NKJV; Hebrews 2:14, 17 NKJV).

References

1. Gray, H. 2010. *Gray's Anatomy*. New York: Barnes and Noble.
2. Patton, K. T. and G. A. Thibodeau. 2010. *Anatomy and Physiology*. St. Louis: Mosby, Elsevier.
3. McCance, K. L. and S. E. Huether, editors. 2010. *Pathophysiology*. Maryland Heights, MO: Mosby, Elsevier.
4. Spence, A. P. 1990. *Basic Human Anatomy*. Redwood City, CA: Benjamin/Cummings.
5. Kumar, V., A. K. Abbas, and J. C. Aster. 2013. *Robbins Basic Pathology*. Philadelphia: Elsevier, Saunders.
6. Bynum, W. and H. Bynum, editors. 2011. *Great Discoveries in Medicine*. New York: Thames and Hudson.

Chapter 3

Homeostasis

In the nineteenth century, Claude Bernard[1] defined homeostasis (Gr. *homo + stasis*, "balance," "steady state," "equilibrium") as the "constancy of the body's internal environment that provides for a free and independent life by a variety of chemical compounds (hormones) that balance the system." Homeostasis is the involuntary capacity to regulate, adapt, and prepare the human body to restore and maintain the steady state and equilibrium of the internal environment. Without homeostasis, the human race could not survive. In the twenty-first century, physicians and surgeons have a thorough understanding of homeostasis.[2–6]

The human brain is watchful to a fault: it carefully monitors, mediates, and responds to numerous stressors, each of which is capable of interrupting the steady state of the body (chart IV-A; figure III). The internal stressors include a variety of afflictions such as fear, sorrow, anxiety, hypotension ($\downarrow$BP), dehydration, and abnormal laboratory values, for example, anemia ($\downarrow$Hct), hypoglycemia ($\downarrow$BG), hypoxia ($\downarrow O_2$) and acidosis ($\downarrow$pH; glossary). External stressors include danger, auto crashes, assault, serious falls, and severe hemorrhage.

To restore homeostasis, the limbic brain and the autonomic

neuroendocrine system operate by the activation of two systems: first, the circulatory system delivers hormones via the bloodstream, and second, the peripheral nervous system delivers sympathetic and parasympathetic nerve stimulation (charts IV-B, V; figure III; glossary).

In the twentieth century, Hans Selye[5-7] presented the general adaptation syndrome; his remarkable research established the compensatory responses by the limbic and neuroendocrine systems (chart IV-A). The following examples explain why homeostasis is essential for human survival (glossary).

- The homeostasis of blood glucose[7] (BG): BG is the universal fuel for the production of energy (ATP) that requires continual monitoring to maintain normal blood levels, 75–110 mg/dL (chart XII). An elevated BG level is corrected by the direct stimulation of the pancreas, which releases the hormone insulin into the bloodstream, which in turn activates the cellular uptake of glucose; as the BG level returns toward normal, the release of insulin decreases. Homeostasis is a complex, involuntary, and dynamic process that operates continuously maintaining the equilibrium of the internal environment.
- The homeostasis of vigorous physical exercise:[8] climbing stairs, strength training, and cycling create physical overloads of the muscles, lungs, and heart. In this example, there is an increased demand for O_2 and blood glucose for the production of energy and the increased excretion of two toxic by-products—CO_2 and lactic acid.

    The compensatory responses of the limbic brain and the autonomic neuroendocrine system activate the respiratory system, which increases the respiratory rate and ventilatory volume ($\downarrow CO_2$ and $\uparrow pH$) and the circulatory system, which elevates blood pressure ($\uparrow BP$), heart rate ($\uparrow HR/P$), and cardiac output ($\uparrow CO$). These homeostatic responses—the general adaptation syndrome—rapidly restore the body toward its normal steady state permitting the exercise to continue (chart IV-A).

Upon entering the Garden of Gethsemane, Jesus suffered a sudden, devastating attack of fear, stress, and sorrow—a life-threatening acute stress reaction (ICD-10) that resulted from His impending sacrificial death for the sins of the world and His unimaginable separation from the Father (Mark 14:33–36; Luke 22:43–44; chart IV-B; chapter 4).

Twelve hours later in the Roman court, Jesus suffered major trauma resulting in multiple wounds (chart VI–A), severe losses of blood and water (chart I), and acute multifactorial shock (chart V). These mortal mental and physical episodes overwhelmed His homeostatic systems prior to Mount Calvary (chart III; figures III, VI, VII; chapters 4, 5, 12, 13).

His compensatory mechanisms failed to restore homeostasis, and He developed decompensated multifactorial shock for three fundamental reasons (chart V; chapters 4, 5).

1. the multiple wounds and the rapid and massive blood and water losses (charts I, II-B, VI-A; chapter 9)
2. the absence of emergency resuscitation during the golden hour (charts V, XI, XII; figure IV; glossary)
3. the onset of adrenal fatigue following the episode in Gethsemane—the decreased blood levels of cortisol resulting in the persistence of severe hypotension and hypoperfusion (chart XII; figures VI, VII; chapter 5; glossary)

In conclusion, homeostasis is an involuntary, dynamic mechanism that restores the balance and equilibrium of the internal environment. This is accomplished by the responses of the limbic brain and autonomic neuroendocrine system to various internal stressors (fear, terror, and conflict) and external stressors (scourging, pain, and shock). The preliminary traumas and sufferings sustained by Jesus *prior* to His crucifixion overpowered His homeostatic mechanisms and resulted in His rapid demise (Mark 15:44; John 19:33; charts I, III, IV-B, V; figure VI; chapter 12).

REFERENCES

1. Bynum, W. and H. Bynum, editors. 2011. *Great Discoveries in Medicine.* New York: Thames and Hudson.
2. Townsend, C. M., R. D. Beauchamp, B. M. Evers, and K. L. Mattoc. 2012. *Sabiston Textbook of Surgery.* Philadelphia: Elsevier, Saunders.
3. Eckman, M., editor. 2011. *Professional Guide to Pathophysiology.* Ambler, PA: Lippincott Williams & Wilkins.
4. Lewis, T., F. Amini, and R. Lannon. 2001. *A General Theory of Love.* New York: Random House.
5. Howard, P. J. 2006. *The Owner's Manual for the Brain.* Austin: Bard Press.
6. Sadock, B. J. and V. A. Sadock. 2007. *Synopsis of Psychiatry.* Philadelphia: Lippincott Williams & Wilkins.
7. McCance, K. L. and S. E. Huether, editors. 2010. *Pathophysiology.* Maryland Heights, MO: Mosby, Elsevier.
8. Fox, E. E., R. W. Bowers, and M. L. Foss. 1993. *The Physiological Basis for Exercise and Sport.* Madison, WI: Brown and Benchmark.

CHAPTER 4

PSYCHOPATHOLOGY

Emotional disorders have been present in society since the beginning of time; not a single human being has immunity from psychopathological behavior (Gr. *psycho* + *pathos* + *logos*, "the study of mental disorders and abnormal behavior").

After their original sin in Eden, Adam and Eve were overcome with fear, guilt, and shame and "hid themselves from the presence of the Lord God" (Genesis 3:7–10 NKJV). Out of envy, contempt, and hatred, Cain chose to murder Abel (Genesis 4:7–10). Overwrought with frustration and anger, Moses disobeyed God when he angrily "struck the Rock that flowed with spiritual and lifesaving water" and precluded his entering the Holy Land (Numbers 20:10–12; 2 Corinthians 10:4–5). Pontius Pilate recognized that the chief priests "handed Jesus over out of envy"; but for political expediency and an utter fear of failure, he determined to execute an innocent man (Mark 15:10; John 19:6–8, 15–16).

To correctly evaluate the mental afflictions of Jesus Christ, we must appreciate the human nature of the incarnate Son—"He had to become like His brothers in every way" but "without sin" (Hebrews 2:17, 4:15). Jesus's humanity consisted of a human soul—the essence of His human life; a human mind—His intellectual powers, free will, memory, and language skills; and a human psyche—His emotional responses to fear, agony, pain, sorrow, and conflict by His limbic brain and autonomic neuroendocrine system (charts IV-A, IV-B; figure III; glossary). Moreover, Jesus's human nature permitted Him to thoroughly identify with each of us during His incarnation, passion, and sacrificial death for our salvation.

The sacred scriptures reinforce the human emotions possessed by Jesus Christ; in particular, He "prayed with loud cries and tears" (Hebrews 5:7). On certain occasions, Jesus became deeply troubled, distressed, and perturbed (Gr. *embrimaomai*, "deep groaning and anger"; Luke 12:50; John 11:33, 38, 12:27, 13:21). Upon His arrival at Gethsemane, Jesus abruptly became "troubled and distressed" saying, "My soul is sorrowful even to death" (Mark 14:33–34).

In my judgment, the incarnation—the unity of divinity and humanity in Jesus Christ—was the first step of the passion. The incarnate Son "emptied Himself" (Gr. *kenosis*) of the prerogatives of His divine glory and assumed fallen flesh and blood (Philippians 2:6–8; Hebrews 2:14, 17). Jesus totally identified Himself with sinful and evil humankind, which was helplessly and hopelessly overburdened, consumed, and exhausted with the emotional struggles of daily life, for example pride, sloth, covetousness, murder, guilt, rape, shame, envy, lust, greed, gossip, anxiety, false testimony, anger, conflict, and fear (Proverbs 6:16–19; Romans 1:18–32).

After my analysis of the sacrificial lives of Abel, Job, the Pierced One, the Abandoned/Righteous One, the Suffering Servant, Jonah, and Jeremiah, I developed a greater appreciation for the sovereign Lord's predetermined plan—the future *Redeemer* would suffer and die from both *mental* afflictions and *physical* traumas (Job 19:25; Isaiah 44:6; 53:4–6; Acts 2:23 NKJV, 11:24–27; chart IX, see 3, 11,

12, 15, 16, 18, 19). The incarnate Son was in perfect solidarity with each member of the human race: By His "stripes"—the wounds of His spirit, mind, and body—"we were healed" (Isaiah 53:5; 1 Peter 2:24).

The Jewish religious establishment exerted deep-seated hostility and strong opposition that significantly influenced the life and times of Jesus Christ—His childhood, three years of ministry, and passion. Although disregarded and seriously underestimated by previous authors and scripture scholars, the psychopathological stressors and struggles Jesus Christ included overwhelming emotional episodes of fear, conflict, sorrow, anguish, abandonment, and humiliation that influenced His rapid demise (charts IV-A, IV-B, V; figure VI).

According to scripture, the childhood of Jesus consisted of emotional, life-changing events.

1. the controversial pregnancy of the Virgin Mary—the question of illegitimacy (Matthew 1:18-23; John 8:41)
2. the rejection in Bethlehem—a difficult Nativity (Luke 2:4–7)
3. the strange gift of myrrh—death and burial (Matthew 2:10–11)
4. Simeon's prophetic words of contradiction—conflict, tragedy, and death (Luke 2:33–35)
5. the attempted "assassination" by King Herod—stress, torment, and fright (Matthew 2:16–18)
6. being a fugitive in Egypt—alienated in a foreign culture obsessed by the worship of idols (Matthew 2:13–15)
7. being found in the temple—consumed by the will of the Father and His future passion and sacrificial death (Luke 2:43–50)

During His ministry, the Jewish religious establishment—Pharisees, scribes, chief priests, and temple police—endeavored to entrap, arrest, and murder Jesus (Mark 3:6, 11:17–18, 12:13–17, 14:1–2). On one occasion in Nazareth, an enraged mob attempted to kill Him by "hurling him down a steep cliff" (Luke 4:28–29). There were other heated disputes and violent conflicts during which the envious and enraged Jews attempted to stone Jesus (John 5:17–18, 8:59, 10:31, 39).

In my analysis, Jesus satisfies the twenty-first century diagnostic criteria[5] for post-traumatic stress disorder based upon the repetitive nature and severity of the mental afflictions and violent struggles He had encountered. The scriptures point out several episodes during which He became "agitated, distressed, and perturbed" (Luke 12:50; John 11:8, 33, 38, 12:27, 13:21). The crescendo of these psychopathological episodes reached a life-threatening climax in the Garden of Gethsemane with the explosive onset of the acute stress reaction or "fight-or-flight syndrome"—His greatest conflict, agony, decision (chart IV-B; glossary).

This event in Gethsemane was a serious medical emergency that has been underestimated and incorrectly diagnosed. For example, Edwards[1] described "chills during the night;" O'Reilly[2] said that "death-row inmates frequently experienced hematidrosis"; and Barbet[3] wrote, "The mental sufferings were not important factors in the rapid demise of Jesus." On the other hand, Zugibe[4] correctly offered a different point of view: "The presence of *hematidrosis* reflected the severity of Jesus' mental sufferings" (Mark 14:33–36; Luke 22:44; chart IV-B).

Patients with emotional and behavioral disorders have historically been labeled as mad or crazy, placed in asylums, and not infrequently chained to their beds. However, during the twentieth and twenty-first centuries, mental health professionals have taken positive steps to reverse these unfortunate attitudes and conditions as follows.

1. the publications of diagnostic classifications[5] of psychiatric diseases, *The International Classification of Disease (ICD-10)* and in the United States, *The Diagnostic and Statistical Manual of Mental Disorders* (DSM-IV-TR)
2. neuroscientists' reports that certain psychopathological conditions are caused by deficiencies of specific neurotransmitters[6,7] that communicate between neurons, for example, dopamine, serotonin, and norepinephrine
3. neuroimaging studies of the brain that have correlated the neuroanatomy (structure) with the neurophysiology (function; figure III)
4. Sigmund Freud's theory of psychoanalysis[5]
5. advancements in psychotherapy and psychopharmacology[5]

Two renowned scientists influenced my psychopathological investigation of Jesus Christ. Walter Cannon[5] (1875–1945) suggested that "stress is a disturbance of homeostasis" resulting from severe physical trauma and mental distress that stimulate an autonomic neuroendocrine response. Cannon identified this condition as the fight-or-flight syndrome—an acute stress reaction that prepares and adapts the body for survival.

However, if and when these stressors are extreme—as in the case of Jesus Christ—they are rarely complicated by serious secondary psychosomatic (mind-body) diseases (chart IV-B).

Hans Selye[7,8] (1907–1982) developed the model for human responses to stress identified as the general adaptation syndrome—the autonomic neuroendocrine mechanism that prepares and adapts human beings for survival (homeostasis; charts IV-A; chapter 3; glossary).

The brain is the preeminent and most complex human organ.[5–9]

Its hardware consists of an estimated two hundred billion neurons and supportive glial cells, while the human mind and psyche serve as the brain's software. The axons are the extensions or "electrical wires" of the neurons that communicate nerve impulses to other neurons and structures throughout the body.

The cortical brain is the cognitive (Lat. *cognito*, "to know") and thinking brain; it consists of highly developed cerebral hemispheres that provide knowledge, thought, and judgment (figure III). The cortical brain also provides oversight for the involuntary responses of the limbic and neuroendocrine systems; however, in my analysis, the psychological stressors of fear, conflict, terror, and sorrow present in Gethsemane were of such magnitude that the cortical brain of Jesus was unable to perform its oversight function and restrain the life-threatening reaction He suffered. Such episodes are identified as "white outs" since there is no memory of the event.

The limbic brain—the emotional brain and biblical heart—is located on the inferior surface of the cortical brain (figure III). Neuroscientists describe this system as individual centers of neurons that involuntarily prepare and adapt the human body for a variety of incoming abnormal signals or stressors—fear, conflict, pain, danger, dehydration, blood loss, shock, hypotension, and hypoxia (charts IV-A, IV-B, V).

Modern imaging studies have identified specific neuron centers of the limbic brain. The amygdala—the best understood and most dominant—is activated by fear and sorrow. In addition, the limbic brain includes the hippocampus (memory of important relationships and events), the thalamus (relay station), and the hypothalamus which makes the vital connection between the brain and the H-P-A axis and the SNS and PNS (charts IV-A, IV-B, V; figure III; glossary).

The courageous American combat soldier has unknowingly been

a participant in the investigation of post-traumatic stress disorder. Each American war has resulted in thousands of veterans suffering complex clinical manifestations of serious mental disorders. After the Civil War (1861–1865), numerous soldiers complained of heart palpitations, chest pain, shortness of breath, and sleep disturbances. The psychiatric diagnosis was cardiac neurosis.

During World War I (1914–1918), similar clinical manifestations were observed, but physicians identified this condition as shell shock, a brain injury caused by the forces of exploding artillery shells.

The veterans of World War II (1941–1945) and the survivors of prison camps suffered from fatigue, loss of concentration, headaches, and repetitive episodes of anxiety and sweating, insomnia, and heart palpitations; their diagnoses included both battle fatigue and combat neurosis.

Soldiers returning from Vietnam (1968–1972), Iraq (1991 and 2003–2010), and Afghanistan (2001–2017) complained of similar behavioral problems.

This mysterious and unique condition has finally been classified[5,6] as the post-traumatic stress disorder—a psychopathological condition not limited to wars, but resulting from all types of violence, terror, and abuse and consisting of the following clinical manifestations.

1. exposure to a terrifying or life-threatening event or events resulting in distress (found in almost anyone)
2. recurrent flashbacks of the stressful and violent event
3. avoidance of any circumstance resembling the original event
4. recollection of the event that may result in sleep disturbances, poor concentration, or rarely, the onset of a fight-or-flight syndrome (charts IV-A, IV-B).

Over the course of His ministry, Jesus was persecuted, insulted, victimized, slandered, berated, and almost killed by the Jewish religious establishment. It is my medical judgment that over the course of His stressful, conflicted, and violent ministry, Jesus Christ suffered post-traumatic stress disorder (ICD-10)—a relevant psychopathological condition that predisposed the life-threatening acute stress reaction in Gethsemane complicated by hematidrosis (blood and water losses) and adrenal fatigue (↓cortisol levels) which contributed to His rapid demise (Mark 14:33–36, 15:44; Luke 22:44; John 19:33–34; charts IV-B, V; figures VI, VII; chapter 12; glossary).

The hour of Jesus had arrived! But would the incarnate Son of God make His glorious exodus and "pass from this world returning to the heavenly Father"? (Luke 9:31; John 12:24, 27, 13:1, 3, 17:1; Chapter 11). Would He trust the Father's perfect will, drink His "cup of fury," and undergo transformation into the sin of the world? The curse? The son of Satan? The hour of darkness? Would the incarnate Son suffer the unthinkable separation from the Father and the inconceivable sacrificial death for the sins of the world?

In the Garden of Gethsemane, Jesus was abruptly and violently afflicted by extreme fright, sorrow unto death, and severe conflict—an acute stress reaction that created a bona fide, life-threatening medical emergency. He was "deeply troubled and distressed" falling helplessly across the stone of agony saying, "Father, take this cup away from me." "He agonized and prayed with such zeal that *His sweat became like great drops of blood* falling down to the ground." This dramatic, psychopathological episode was the incarnate Son's greatest conflict, agony, and decision (Mark 14:33–36; Luke 22:44 NKJV; charts I, IV-B; figure VI).

The psychopathology of the acute stress reaction (ICD-10) originated from the life-threatening stressors in Jesus's limbic brain—unrestrained fear, anguish, conflict, and grief. His amygdala, hippocampus, and thalamus unleashed a violent, uncontrolled reaction that overpowered the peripheral nervous system—the SNS squeezed the arteries, and the PNS simultaneously relaxed the arteries, and the endocrine system—the H-P-A axis—released massive, life-threatening levels of stress hormones[6] into the bloodstream (charts IV-A, IV-B; figure III).

For two hours, Jesus struggled to survive the following temporary conditions: severe hypertension (BP >220/140), tachycardia (HR/P >180), tachypnea (RR >40), fever, headache, nausea and vomiting, excessive sweat (hyperhidrosis), and bloody sweat (hematidrosis; glossary).

Jesus sustained two serious psychosomatic (mind-body) complications that would shorten His survival time on the cross (chart III). First, hematidrosis[4, 10, 11] caused significant blood and water losses secondary to the lethal levels of the stress hormones[6] (chart I). The mechanism of this phenomenon consisted of simultaneous vasoconstriction and vasodilation of small cutaneous arterioles causing the escape of red blood cells across the thin-walled arterioles (diapedesis) and the extraordinary rupture of the small arterioles into the sweat glands and ducts (hematidrosis) and the skin (ecchymosis; chart VI-A; glossary).

The second complication resulted from the excessive stimulation of the pituitary gland by the hypothalamus: The elevated levels of ACTH were so extreme that they exhausted the adrenal glands (H-P-A axis) which prevented the production and release of cortisol—the preeminent hormone required for the compensation of hypotension and hypoperfusion present during shock (charts IV-B, V, VII-A, XII; figures III, VI, VII; chapters 3, 5; glossary).

Jesus's titanic struggle in Gethsemane caused His stress hormones—epi, nepi, and cortisol—to be elevated as much as forty times[6] their normal values (chart XII; glossary). Make no mistake about the episode in the Garden of Gethsemane—it was a full-blown psychiatric and medical emergency! The acute stress reaction accelerated the death of Jesus by blood and water losses and the fatigue of His adrenal glands with inadequate blood levels of cortisol (charts I, V, XII).

Jesus's mental afflictions did not end in Gethsemane. He had to face rowdy and hateful Passover crowds, the contempt of the chief priests and temple police, and the off-loading of the Roman legionnaires who mocked and taunted him, spat in His face, and pulled His beard.

In addition, Jesus suffered from illegal trials, defenseless facial buffeting, the cynical king's game, and several humiliating falls on the Via Dolorosa. His deepest psychological wounds were humiliation, abandonment, and powerlessness. Truly, the sacrificial death of the incarnate Son is the most powerful revelation of the Father's love for us[12] (John 3:16; Romans 8:32; 1 John 4:9–10).

The psychopathology of Gethsemane has been seriously underestimated with respect to how Jesus died; His acute stress reaction greatly surpasses a routine anxiety reaction[3] and chills during the night.[1] Jesus suffered an unprecedented psychiatric emergency that resulted in a mortally *wounded* state. This predetermined plan by the sovereign Lord arouses several thought-provoking thoughts.

1. The balance between Jesus's mental afflictions and physical injuries influenced His rapid demise.
2. The complication of hematidrosis revealed the severity of His acute stress reaction.
3. The bloody sweat of Gethsemane reflected the transcendency of blood and water during the passion.

4. The cup of God's wrath represented the totality of humankind's sin, corruption, and unbelief—the object of God's fury was not the incarnate Son.
5. Our salvation is merited by the mental, physical, and spiritual sufferings of the incarnate Son.
6. Three gardens participated in the redemption of humanity: Eden (sin), Gethsemane (death), and resurrection (life).
7. During a personal crisis, Gethsemane teaches us the importance of daily prayer, watchfulness, and meditation in the presence of the Lord Jesus (Mark 14:37–38).
8. As a human being, Jesus Christ was in solidarity with you and me; as our Great High Priest, He willingly offered Himself as the sacrificial Lamb of God.
9. The greatest decision made by Jesus in Gethsemane stands as the *epic moment* of His passion and sacrificial death.

REFERENCES

1. Edwards, W. D., W. J. Gabel, and F. E. Hosmer. "On the Physical Death of Jesus Christ." *Journal of the American Medical Association* 1986, 255:1455–63.
2. O'Reilly, B. and M. Dugard. 2013. *Killing Jesus*. New York: Henry Holt.
3. Barbet, P. 1950. *A Doctor at Calvary*. Indre, France: Dillon & Cie.
4. Zugibe, T. Z. 2005. *The Crucifixion of Jesus*. New York: M. Evans.
5. Sadock, B. J. and V. A. Sadock. 2007. *Synopsis of Psychiatry*. Philadelphia: Lippincott, Williams & Wilkins.
6. Howard, B. J. 2006. *The Owner's Manual for the Brain*. Austin: Bard Press.
7. Patton, K. T. and G. A. Thibodeau. 2010. *Anatomy and Physiology*. St. Louis: Mosby, Elsevier.
8. McCance, K. L. and S. E. Huether, editors. 2010. *Pathophysiology*. Maryland Heights, MO: Mosby, Elsevier.
9. Blumenfeld, H. 2002. *Neuroanatomy through Clinical Cases*. Sunderland, MA: Sinauer.
10. Scott, C. T. "A Case of Haematidrosis." *British Medical Journal* 1918; 1:532–33.
11. Holoubek, J. E. and A. B. Holoubek. "Blood, Sweat and Fear, A Classification of Hematidrosis." *Journal of Medicine* 1996; 27:115–33.
12. Balthasar, H. U. 1981. *Mysterium Paschale* (The Mystery of Easter). San Francisco: Ignatius Press.

Chapter 5

Pathophysiology

Pathophysiology is the study of disease and trauma that contrasts the normal structure and function of cells, tissues, and organs with the abnormal. As the heart and soul of the clinical medical sciences, pathophysiology (Gr: *patho* + *physio* + logo: "the study of disordered physiology") answers the most fundamental questions that physicians and surgeons search to answer: Why? What? When? How?

Over the course of this groundbreaking investigation, I made the following inquiries concerning Jesus's pathophysiology to determine exactly how He died.

1. Could this mystery be solved by the Old Testament prophetic scriptures?
2. Does Jesus Christ solve the mystery by His words and works?
3. What caused the life-threatening medical emergency in the Garden of Gethsemane? Did this episode influence His rapid death on the cross?
4. What is the pathophysiology and significance of bloody sweat?

5. Is it possible to estimate the number, types, and locations of the wounds He sustained two thousand years ago? The loss of blood and water?
6. What was the pathophysiology of the savage Roman scourging? How many lashes? Was it a fatal event?
7. What is the shock syndrome? Did Jesus suffer from multifactorial shock? How does shock cause death?
8. Why did Jesus survive for only three hours on the cross yet other victims reportedly survived for several days?
9. How did Jesus die?
10. What is tetany/asphyxiation? If Jesus Christ died by suffocation on the cross, does that fulfill the Old Testament prophetic scriptures? Is death by suffocation consistent with the words of Jesus, "My shed blood" and "My broken body" (Matthew 26:26–28; John 6:53–56; 1 Corinthians 11:23–26; chart I)?
11. Do the highly favored, much endowed, and unchallenged causes for the death of Jesus—tetany/asphyxiation; broken/ruptured heart, and divine intervention—satisfy the scrutiny of the modern medical, psychiatric, and surgical sciences (figure V)?

By steadfastly searching for the correct answers to these questions, I have solved the untold story of how Jesus died—a mystery that no one else has comprehensively understood and solved. The incarnate Son "was delivered up by the set plan and foreknowledge" of the *sovereign* Lord, our Great Physician who perfectly and eternally coordinated the following components of the passion (Acts 2:23).

1. a specific collection of Old Testament prophetic scriptures fulfilled by the passion and sacrificial death of Jesus Christ (chart IX)
2. the theological effects of the Christ event, for example redemption, reconciliation, justification, and access to God
3. the transcendent participation of blood and water in the passion and throughout scripture
4. the pathophysiology of modern medical science—emergency and critical care medicine, psychiatry, surgery, and traumatology (charts I, IV-B, V, VI-A; figures VI, VII; chapters 4, 9, 12)

The mystery of how Jesus died is solved by the synthesis of scripture and science!

Although Morgagni and Hunter[1] presented a system of post-traumatic pathological specimens many centuries ago, the mysterious pathophysiology of shock-trauma has only recently been thoroughly unlocked and successfully treated. The primary credit for these advancements belongs to American combat soldiers and front-line surgeons.[2-4]

In the twenty-first century, the trauma surgeon examines the injured patient, evaluates the laboratory and imaging studies, and determines the pathophysiology in light of the following.

1. the etiology—the cause of each injury
2. the pathogenesis—the progression of the abnormal conditions involving the injured cells, tissues, and organs
3. the clinical manifestations—the symptoms (subjective) and signs (objective)
4. the clinical course—the observed positive or negative progress

5. the prognosis—the expected outcome of the injury or disease
6. the condition—the current medical status such as "good," "fair," "serious," or "critical" (glossary).

My initial assessment of Jesus Christ consisted of a thorough history, physical examination, and clinical assessment as follows

- chief complaint (subjective)— "What is your problem?"
- history of the present illness (subjective)— "Tell me your story."
- past medical history (subjective)— "Tell me about your prior illnesses, operations, medications, habits, and allergies."
- review of systems (subjective)— "Do you have current complaints regarding your heart, lungs, kidneys, and so on?"
- vital signs (objective)—blood pressure (BP), heart rate/pulse (HR/P), respiratory rate (RR), temperature (T), height (Ht), and weight (Wt)
- physical examination (objective)—head, eyes, ears, nose, throat, neck, chest, heart, lungs, abdomen, extremities, spinal exam, neurological exam, and psychological exam
- laboratory—blood cell counts, chemistries, arterial blood gases, urine exam, cultures, EKG, radiology, and imaging (chart XII; glossary).

As Jesus passed beyond the golden hour on the Via Dolorosa, I performed the following clinical assessment.

Friday 11:45 a.m. (figure IV; station 15, chapter 13). Jesus presents as a thirty-three-year-old Hebrew male in acute distress secondary to severe physical injuries and mental afflictions. My historical information consists of the preliminary events of Gethsemane and the Jewish and Roman trials that caused the life-threatening acute stress reaction and the multiple wounds (chart VI-A), rapid losses of blood and water (charts I, II-B), and severe multifactorial shock (charts V, VII-A, VII-D, XI; chapters 12, 13).

Jesus is confused. His vital signs are unstable; His blood pressure is below normal (<90/60); His pulse rate is rapid and thready (>160); His respirations are rapid and distressed (>30). I observe multiple hemorrhagic puncture wounds across the scalp; His face is bloodstained and swollen, including a partially dislocated nasal cartilage. There are repetitive, parallel lacerations or patterned injuries across His arms, back, chest, abdomen, hips, and legs that include partial-thickness mechanical burns secondary to the leather straps of Roman scourging, and abrasions, contusions, and hematomas consistent with the attached lead dumbbells (chart VI-A; figures VIII-A, VIII-B).

Clumps of purplish blood clots are entangled in His beard and ponytail. Streamlets of bright, scarlet-red blood are scattered across His chest, abdomen, back, and His upper and lower extremities (figures VIII-A, VIII-B).

My examination of the chest reveals lung congestion and distant heart sounds. The abdomen is distended, tense, and silent. His gait is unsteady secondary to shock-trauma, losses of blood and water, unstable vital signs, a mild post-concussion state, and the heavy crossbar (100 to 150 lbs.) resting on His upper back and tied to His outstretched arms.

In summation, Jesus Christ presents as an unstable Hebrew male in serious condition secondary to an acute stress reaction, blunt-force trauma, and severe shock.

- rapid blood and water losses
- acute dehydration

- acute multifactorial shock syndrome (traumatic, hemorrhagic, and hypovolemic)
- contusions of the chest wall and lungs, but consider the presence of bilateral plural (lungs) and pericardial (heart) effusions
- a paralytic ileus, but also consider the presence of intra-abdominal injuries and "hidden" bleeding
- a mild concussion (DAI; charts I, V; chapters 10, 12, 13)

The emergency medical treatment on the Via Dolorosa consists of twenty-first century extraction and resuscitation[2-5] within the golden hour.

- the immediate arrest of arterial bleeding and the immediate establishment of an airway (endotracheal intubation and ventilation with O_2 therapy)
- the rapid infusion of crystalloid solutions (salt and water) and blood components (packed red blood cells, fresh frozen plasma, and platelets; chart VII-B)
- the insertion of a nasogastric suction tube to remove fluid from the stomach and small intestine
- complete blood workup (chart XII)
- an emergency ultrasound study of the chest and abdomen; if the diagnosis of a pericardial effusion is confirmed, proceed with an emergency needle aspiration of the pericardial sac, or if necessary, an open thoracotomy for the decompression of the heart and prevention of acute cardiac tamponade and cardiac failure (chart VIII-B; glossary)

The US military aggressively treats its injured soldiers[1-6] with the finest medical care available; in doing so, it has made tremendous discoveries and advancements in shock-trauma, for example, frontline surgery, emergency resuscitation, the golden hour, mobile blood banks, the pathophysiology and treatment of shock, and the psychopathology and treatment of post-traumatic stress disorder.

Although the fatal mental and physical wounds of Jesus Christ occurred two thousand years ago, His psychopathology and pathophysiology are easily correlated with modern medical and surgical sciences.

Yet despite the impressive scientific research and advancements in emergency medicine, traumatology, and surgery, present-day morbidity and mortality rates for trauma patients have reached epidemic levels in the United States. Shock-trauma has become a leading cause of death following heart disease, stroke, and cancer.[7] Recent studies confirm that severe blood loss and acute hemorrhagic shock cause 60 to 70 percent of the deaths in trauma patients[2-6] (figure IV). As a typical example, Abel was murdered several thousand years ago by blunt-force trauma, severe losses of blood and water, and hemorrhagic shock (Genesis 4:3-11; chart IX, see 3).

Modern surgical research has concluded that 30 percent or more of the mortalities due to shock-trauma occur because of treatment delay beyond the golden hour[2-4] (figure IV). The afflictions and traumas suffered by Jesus Christ are comparable to the modern-day patient with severe shock-trauma who failed to receive emergency treatment during the critical golden hour.

The golden hour on that Good Friday was between 10:45 and 11:45 a.m. Jesus survived only three hours on the cross (chart III). The primary cause of death was decompensated multifactorial shock secondary to shed blood (blood loss → acute hemorrhagic shock → death) and a broken body and torn flesh (water loss → severe dehydration → death).

I identified the following eight pathophysiological conditions that resulted in Jesus's death. Each diagnosis was the result of the preliminary traumas and sufferings *prior* to Roman crucifixion (chart III; chapter 12). The sovereign Lord and Great Physician determined and coordinated the mental sufferings and physical traumas that fulfill and perfect the prophetic scriptures and satisfy modern medical science[2-4] (Acts 2:23; 1 Peter 1:20; chart IX).

1. The **acute stress reaction** (ICD-10) was His greatest conflict, agony, and decision (chart IV-B; chapter 4). Inside the gate of Gethsemane, Jesus was overcome by extreme fear, sorrow, and stress that triggered an acute psychopathological conflict by His limbic brain and autonomic neuroendocrine system (figure III). Would the incarnate Son drink the cup of God's fury and endure the unimaginable separation from the Father? Would He suffer the sacrificial death for the sins of the world? This life-threatening mental disorder was complicated by hyperhidrosis (excessive sweat), hematidrosis (bloody sweat), and adrenal fatigue ($\downarrow$cortisol) secondary to the unprecedented levels of stress hormones, which were twenty to forty times above normal.[8]

Dr. Luke—a recognized Greek physician, artist, and evangelist—was inspired by the Spirit of God two thousand years ago to describe *hematidrosis*—a rare and potentially fatal medical complication. In addition, this episode revealed a second impressive revelation: our sovereign Lord and Great Physician was emphasizing the transcendency of blood ("my shed blood") and water ("my broken body") in the mystery of how Jesus died (Luke 22:44; John 7:37–39, 19:34;1 John 1:7, 5:6–8; Revelation 1:5, 5:9, 7:14, 17, 12:11, 19;13, 22:1, 17).

2. There were an estimated **255 wounds** and **4.5 percent mechanical skin burns** that resulted in the following (chart VI-A, VI-B; figures

VIII-A, VIII-B): blood loss, an estimated 4.25 U or 42.5 percent of the blood volume consistent with class IV hemorrhagic shock—a *fatal* condition in the absence of emergency resuscitation (charts I, V, VII-B, XII, figure IV), and water loss, an estimated 8.0 L or 17.6 lbs. consistent with severe dehydration—a *fatal* condition without fluid replacement and intensive care (charts I, II-B, V).

3. **Multifactorial shock syndrome**[2-6] included traumatic, hemorrhagic, hypovolemic, cardiac, and adrenal shock (charts I, V, VII-A, VII-B, VII-C, VII-D, XI, XII; figures IV, VI; glossary).

Severe blunt-force trauma during the Roman trials—excessive scourging and defenseless battery—caused rapid blood and water losses (above) with the onset of hypotension ($\downarrow$BP), hypoperfusion ($\downarrow$BF), hypoxia ($\downarrow O_2$), lactic acidosis ($\downarrow$pH), and decreased energy production ($\downarrow$ATP). The pathophysiology of shock is the failure of the circulatory system—the heart, blood vessels, and blood—to adequately perfuse the tissues and deliver sufficient amounts of O_2 and nutrients essential for cellular life (glossary).

In the absence of resuscitation, Jesus developed decompensated shock with irreversible cellular and microvascular injuries, third-space fluid loss, and multiple organ dysfunction that resulted in His rapid demise (Mark 15:44; John 19:33; chart V, XI; figures IV, VII; glossary).

4. **Acute respiratory failure** secondary to scourging and battery resulted in contusions, abrasions, lacerations, and hematomas of the chest wall and lungs (charts VI-A, VIII-A; figures VIII-A, VIII-B). Jesus developed the rapid onset of pulmonary contusion, also known as acute respiratory distress syndrome (ARDS); both conditions are frequently observed in shock-trauma and characterized by alveolar-capillary membrane injury and inflammation (glossary).

Furthermore, congestion of the alveolar air sacs resulted from hemorrhage (blood) and edema (water) obstructing the vital exchange of O_2 and CO_2.[2-6] While on the Via Dolorosa, Jesus suffered from sharp pleuritic chest pains, dyspnea, and hypoxia (↓PaO_2; chart XII; glossary). Acute respiratory failure ensued on Calvary with hypercapnia (↑$PaCO_2$) and respiratory acidosis (↓pH; charts VIII-A, XII; figure VI).

The brutal Roman flogging also caused bilateral plural effusions secondary to the inflammatory weeping of serous fluid into the pleural sacs, an estimate of 2.0 L of water loss (charts II-B, VI-B; figures VI, VII). Roman scourging occasionally caused the fracture of one or more ribs with a pneumothorax (collapsed lung); however, Jesus did not sustain a fracture since the prophetic scriptures must be fulfilled. Passover lambs and Levitical sacrificial animals were described by scripture as unblemished and emphasized no broken bones (Exodus 12:5, 46; Leviticus 1:3; Deuteronomy 17:1; Psalm 34:21; John 19:36; 1 Peter 1:19; chart IX, see 6, 20).

5. **Acute cardiac failure** was caused by acute pericardial effusion complicated by cardiac tamponade.[2,5,6,17] As Jesus struggled on the Via Dolorosa, His pericardial sac was filling with serous fluid, an estimated 250–300 mL (normal: 10–20 mL). The severe scourging just minutes earlier caused the inflammatory weeping by the pericardial membrane with the formation of an acute pericardial effusion and the compression of the sacred heart of Jesus Christ. This pathophysiology first precluded the return of venous blood to the right atrium and then restricted the pumping of freshly oxygenated blood to the body by the left ventricle (chart VIII-B; figures VI, VII, X; glossary).

The fourth gospel uniquely provides additional testimony for the diagnosis of a pericardial effusion. The postmortem blow of the lance produced distinct flows of blood (from the right atrium and right ventricle) and water (serous fluid from the pericardial effusion; John 19:34;1 John 5:6–8; figures VIII-A, VIII-B, X). In my analysis, a pericardial effusion is the one condition in this anatomical region capable of causing this remarkable phenomenon (glossary).

6. **Paralytic ileus** is a functional or non-mechanical intestinal obstruction that results from the combination of scourging (abdominal wraparound lashes), battery (rods and fists), severe shock, and electrolyte imbalances. This abdominal condition—markedly common in patients following shock-trauma—resulted in loops of dilated intestine containing large amounts of fluid and air.

On the Via Dolorosa, Jesus suffered from abdominal swelling, nausea and vomiting, possible lung aspiration, and third-space fluid loss estimated to be 750 mL (chart II-B; figure VII; glossary).

7. A mild **concussion** or diffuse axonal injury[6] was caused by an estimated thirty to forty defenseless blows to the head. In my judgment, Jesus sustained a mild concussion of His brain consisting of inflammation and swelling of the axons—the long projections (wires) that communicate between neurons. Jesus suffered from amnesia, confusion, headache, dizziness, ringing in the ears, double vision, and an unsteady gait.

8. **Multiple organ dysfunction syndrome** (MODS)[2,5,6,9] resulted secondary to the major losses of blood and water and the rapid onset of decompensated multifactorial shock complicated by the lethal triad of acidosis, hypothermia, and coagulopathy (charts I, V, VII-A, VII-D; figures VI, VII; glossary). The collapse of Jesus's cardiovascular system caused hypoperfusion and irreversible cellular and microvascular injuries in multiple organs—heart, brain, lungs,

Blood and Water

liver, and kidneys (chart XI). Despite the advancements of modern medicine and surgery, the mortality rate[6] for MODS with the involvement of two or more organs remains greater than 70 percent (glossary).

Over the course of this investigation, I have encountered several challenging issues pertaining to Roman crucifixion. For example, does Roman crucifixion cause death? If so, what is the pathophysiological mechanism of death? Why were there such large differences for the survival times of the victims of crucifixion (chart III)? Jesus Christ's estimated survival time was about three hours. Those slaves and traitors undergoing routine Roman crucifixions survived an estimated eight to ten hours. Yet, many Jewish prisoners crucified during the Jewish-Roman War[10–14] (AD 70) survived for as long as five to nine days.

The answer to this critical question is contingent upon the following important principle: *the survival time on a Roman cross was inversely proportional to the severity of the preliminary traumas and sufferings* (chart III; chapter 12). The rapid death of Jesus Christ—three hours on the cross—was *not* related to Roman crucifixion, but rather to the severity of His preliminary agonies. His life-threatening mental afflictions in Gethsemane and fatal scourging, battery, and piercings in the Roman court resulted in the rapid losses of blood and water, the accelerated onset of decompensated multifactorial shock along with the lethal triad, and multiple organ dysfunction syndrome (charts V, VII-D; figure VII). In sharp contrast to Jesus Christ, the Jewish prisoners of the Jewish-Roman War were captured, crucified (absent PTS), and abandoned—many survived for several days. Several investigators[10–14] have reported that "some of the victims lingered for 5 to 9 days on their crosses."

In conclusion, Roman crucifixion did not cause death by tetany/asphyxiation or a broken or ruptured heart (chapter 9; glossary). Jesus Christ sustained severe preliminary agonies prior to His crucifixion that resulted in rapid death secondary to shed blood (blood loss → acute hemorrhagic shock → death) and a broken body (water loss → severe dehydration → death). He died on a Roman cross, but crucifixion was not the mechanism for His death (charts I, III, V, XI, XII; figures IV, VI, VII; chapters 9, 10, 12, 13).

In the absence of the PTS and crucifracture, many victims of Roman crucifixion survived for several days.[10-14] They suffered and died from a variety of serious medical conditions. The following discussion contrasts these *chronic* deaths versus the acute death of Jesus Christ secondary to the PTS (chart III; chapter 12; glossary).

- Severe dehydration ranks first as the most common cause of death for the victims of crucifixion who survived for several days. Large fluid losses[15-17] and nothing by mouth are complicated by serious medical conditions such as hypovolemic shock, acute kidney failure, and electrolyte imbalances (chart II-A; glossary). The isolation on a Roman cross for forty-eight hours resulted in an estimated negative water balance of as much as 4.5 L and 9 lbs.

Exposure to the elements—wind, temperature, dust, insects, microorganisms, and carnivorous birds and animals—resulted in additional losses. After three to four days without fluids, the clinical manifestations include extreme thirst, muscle fatigue, mental confusion, and decreased urine output. After seven to nine days, the following medical conditions can ensue

1. airway obstruction secondary to dried secretions, vomitus, and a swollen tongue,
2. acute bronchitis and pneumonia,
3. severe hypovolemic shock,
4. acute kidney failure,
5. electrolyte imbalances resulting in severe muscle weakness, seizures, and cardiac arrhythmias,
6. cellular dysfunction and decreased energy production ($\downarrow$ATP) in multiple organs
7. septicemia, and
8. coma.

When a patient has nothing by mouth (NPO), death generally results within nine to eleven days depending on age and medical status (chart III).

- Electrolyte abnormalities are frequent complications during severe dehydration, hypovolemic shock, and acute kidney failure. An elevated sodium (Na^+) level (hypernatremia) causes serious sequelae of the brain including confusion, slurred speech, convulsions, coma, and death (chart XII). An elevated potassium (K^+) level (hyperkalemia) causes muscle cramps, cardiac arrhythmias, and cardiac arrest (chart XII).
- Acute kidney failure complicates severe dehydration and hypovolemic shock with secondary hypotension ($\downarrow$BP) and hypoperfusion ($\downarrow$BF) of the kidneys; the results include a diminished urine output, electrolyte abnormalities (above), and depressed clearance of BUN and creatinine—toxic compounds normally excreted by the kidneys (chart XII; glossary).

- Heat-related illnesses or hyperthermia[6, 15–17] consist of dehydration, increased body temperature, and loss of body weight during exposure to elevated environmental temperatures and strenuous physical activity. The mildest form of hyperthermia is muscle cramping—a body temperature ≥102°F (39°C). Heat exhaustion consists of a temperature ≥104°F (40°C) plus the loss of 3 to 5 percent of total body water, profuse sweating, hypotension (↓BP), tachycardia (↑HR/P), tachypnea (↑RR), weakness, nausea, and vomiting. In the absence of treatment, the onset of a fatal heat stroke will cause decompensated shock, multiple organ dysfunction syndrome, coma, and death.
- Subsequent to several days on a Roman cross, the early stages of starvation result in malnutrition and catabolism—a negative calorie balance and negative nitrogen balance (glossary). Such conditions depress the immune system and increase the likelihood of serious bacterial infections such as pneumonia (lungs) and septicemia (bloodstream).

Deaths secondary to starvation generally result after forty to sixty days (depending on age and medical status) most commonly due to infection and anemia (decreased Hct and Hb with a diminished oxygen-carrying capacity; glossary).

- The risk factors for deep-vein thrombosis (DVT) and pulmonary embolism (PE)[5, 18] are significantly increased during crucifixion due to the following predisposing factors.

1. prolonged immobilization
2. venous stasis of the femoral veins (thigh) and popliteal veins (calf)

3. a hypercoaguable state—the increased risk for blood clots secondary to trauma, stress, venous stasis, and dehydration. DVT is characterized by localized calf pain, tenderness, and swelling and systemic fever. A PE occurs when a piece of the venous thrombus (blood clot) breaks free and travels in the circulatory system to the heart and lungs resulting in the obstruction of normal pulmonary blood flow, hypoxia ($PaO_2\downarrow$), and respiratory distress ($\uparrow RR$). If the circulation to the lungs is obstructed by greater than 50 percent, sudden death will ensue secondary to a cardiac arrest.

REFERENCES

1. Bynum, W. and H. Bynum, editors. 2011. *Great Discoveries in Medicine.* New York: Thames and Hudson.
2. Mulholland, M. W., K. D. Lillemoe, J. M. Doherty, R. V. Maier, D. M. Simeone, and G. R. Upchurch. 2011. *Greenfield's Surgery.* Philadelphia: Lippincott Williams & Wilkins.
3. Townsend, C. M., R. D. Beauchamp, B. M. Evers, and K. L. Mattox. 2012. *Sabiston Textbook of Surgery.* Philadelphia: Elsevier, Saunders.
4. Martin, M. and A. Beckley, editors. 2008. *Front Line Surgery.* New York: Springer.
5. Kumar, V., A. K. Abbas, and J. C. Aster. 2013. *Robbins Basic Pathology.* Philadelphia: Elsevier, Saunders.
6. McCance, K. L. and S. E. Huether, editors. 2010. *Pathophysiology.* Maryland Heights, MO: Mosby, Elsevier.
7. Jin, J. "Death in the United States: Changes from 1969–2013." *Journal of the American Medical Association* 2016, 315(3): 318.
8. Howard, B. J. 2006. *The Owner's Manual for the Brain.* Austin: Bard Press.
9. Tilney, N. I., G. I. Bailey, and A. P. Morgan. "Sequential system failure after rupture of abdominal aneurysm: an unsolved problem in postoperative care." *Annals of Surgery* 1973. 178(2): 117–22.
10. Harrison, R. K., editor. 1988. *Unger's Bible Dictionary.* Chicago: Moody Publishers.
11. Finegan, J. 1946. *Light from the Ancient Past.* Princeton: Princeton University Press.
12. Hengel, M. 1977. *Crucifixion in the Ancient World and the Folly of the Message of the Cross.* Philadelphia: Fortress Press.

13 Josephus, B. J. *Jewish Antiquities and the Jewish War.* Whiston, W. (Translation). 1960. Kregel Publishing. Williamson, G. A. (Translation). 1959. New York: Penguin.

14 Brown, R. E. 1994. *The Death of the Messiah* (Volume II). New Haven: Yale University Press (page 1177, footnote 88).

15 Thompson, J. and M. Manore. 2005. *Nutrition: An Applied Approach.* San Francisco: Benjamin Cummings.

16 Fox, E. L., R. W. Bowers, and M. L. Foss. 1993. *The Physiological Basis for Exercise and Sport.* Madison, WI: Brown and Benchmark.

17 Patton, K. T. and G. A. Thibodeau. 2010. *Anatomy and Physiology.* St. Louis: Mosby, Elsevier.

18 Thompson, A. E. "Deep Vein Thrombosis." *Journal of the American Medical Association* 2015, 313 (20): 2090.

Chapter 6

The Shroud of Turin

Joseph of Arimathea and Nicodemus—active members of the powerful Jewish Sanhedrin and secret disciples of Jesus Christ—depositioned and carried the Roman crossbar and the nailed corpse of Jesus Christ to the stone of anointing in the Garden of Resurrection. The wrist nails were extracted, and the body was wrapped in a large burial cloth[1-4] (Gr. *sindone*, "a linen cloth wrapped vertically for burial"; Matthew 27:59; Mark 15:46; Luke 23:53; figures VIII-A, VIII-B; glossary).

Prior to entombment, "They bound the body of Jesus in strips of linen" (Gr. *othonion*, "narrow strips of linen wrapped horizontally for burial"; John 19:40 NKJV).

On the first day of the week, the disciple Jesus loved entered the garden tomb and observed the burial clothes: "He saw and believed" (John 20:7–8). This astounding confession—the resurrection of Jesus Christ—has profoundly shaped the course of religious and world history. But precisely what did the beloved disciple observe inside the virgin sepulcher? Was it possible he saw the actual blood markings and body image of Jesus miraculously encoded on the shroud? Were the grave clothes shaped like an empty cocoon?

In spite of these unknowns, the absence of His body initiated a sensational mystery that influenced the Christian and scientific worlds. The mysterious shroud that at one time had contained the body of the incarnate Son of God was on the threshold of becoming an international phenomenon—the preeminent sacred relic as well as a scientific enigma (figures VIII-A, VIII-B).

The shroud of Turin (the city in northern Italy where the shroud has been displayed since the sixteenth century) is a linen burial cloth originating from the region of Judea. It is fourteen feet, three inches in length and three feet, seven inches in width. It has been scrupulously investigated for its authenticity by the world's leading physicians and scientists.[1-6]

The historical movements of the shroud including numerous exhibits, miraculous healings, and personal testimonies have been meticulously investigated throughout Asia and Europe. More specifically, the shroud's travels were traced from Jerusalem (AD 30) to Asia (about AD 50 to 400), to Constantinople (about AD 500 to 1000), to several locations in France, and finally to Turin (1535 to the present).

Researchers have examined the shroud for the presence of pollen, dust, chemicals, hair, blood, and plasma plus additional investigations with the electron microscope, photography, computer technology, and carbon dating.[1-3]

A chance photograph[1] of the shroud in 1898 sent shock waves around the globe. Church authorities, scientific leaders, medical specialists, and archaeologists were immediately invigorated to seek the truth. From an ordinary burial cloth containing a few scattered, red-brown markings, the shroud of Turin had been mysteriously transformed into a stunning portrait of a severely beaten, pierced, and crucified Hebrew male. Was this a photographic negative of

Jesus Christ including His body image and blood markings? The wondrous shroud was in great demand; it gained worldwide scientific and religious notoriety at a level not previously seen in the annals of sacred relics.

Unique among burial garments, the shroud of Turin reveals the following.

1. Its very existence is supernatural! Furthermore, it contains no evidence of corruption or decomposition.
2. The photographic negatives of the shroud consist of frontal and dorsal images of a Hebrew male (figures VIII-A, VIII-B).
3. The visibility of the body image improves as the distance increases.
4. Computer technology transforms the shroud from a two-dimensional cloth into a three-dimensional image.
5. The shroud contains numerous blood markings consisting of scientifically proven human blood cells and plasma and an anatomically correct body image of a Hebrew male who measured an estimated five feet, ten inches tall and weighed 170 pounds.
6. There is no evidence of paint, dye, pigment, ink, bacteria, or electrical markings making a forgery unlikely.

The shroud of Turin contains two inexplicable scientific challenges that continue to be investigated.

- What is the body image? The silhouette of a Hebrew male with normal proportions, lengths, and ratios reveals multiple soft-tissue wounds and deformities of the face, torso, and extremities consistent with severe scourging, battery, and Roman crucifixion. A select group of medical and scientific experts[3,4] currently believe that the body image was miraculously encoded on the shroud during a resurrection event that included heat, light, and particular radiation (figures VIII-A, VIII-B; glossary).

- What are the blood markings? These extraordinary markings reveal the presence of exquisite microscopic human blood clots[1–5] surrounded by halos of authentic human serum. The blood markings demonstrate normal blood-flow patterns compatible with scourging, battery, and piercings by thorns, nails, and a Roman lance (figures VIII-A, VIII-B).

The man in the shroud has blood clots scattered over His entire body including His ponytail and beard. Multiple puncture wounds are observed over the scalp. There are unique patterned injuries of parallel stripes secondary to scourging wounds across His arms, back, chest, abdomen, hips, and legs (figures VIII-A, VIII-B). There are numerous swollen areas over the chest and back consistent with contusions and hematomas of the skin, subcutaneous tissue, and muscle tissue (chart VI-A). Despite the magnitude of the trauma, there is the striking absence of broken bones (Exodus 12:46; John 19:36).

In my analysis, I have identified an estimated 255 wounds of which about 80 percent were the result of blunt-force trauma caused by scourging, battery, and falls (chart VI-A; figures VIII-A, VIII-B). The remainder consist of sharp-force trauma secondary to piercings by thorns, nails, and a Roman lance (figures IX, X). The partial-thickness skin damage and mechanical burns resulted from scourging, an estimated 4.5 percent of the total body surface area (TBSA; chart VI-A; chapter 9).

The shroud of Turin is a remarkable portrait of the passion of

Jesus Christ, an invaluable asset during my estimates of the wounds and the blood and water losses (charts I, VI-A). The lethal scourging wounds are extensive and deserve special emphasis: they are best characterized as multiple parallel blood markings and skin damage known as *patterned injuries* inflicted by leather straps with attached lead dumbbells that included contusions, hematomas, lacerations, and partial-thickness mechanical burns (figure VIII-B).

Through my extensive analysis, I believe that the shroud is consistent with the following.

1. the sovereignty and choreography by our Lord and Great Physician concerning the passion and sacrificial death of Jesus Christ (Acts 2:23)
2. the fulfillment and perfection of the Old Testament prophetic scriptures (Luke 24:44; chart IX; chapter 1)
3. the passion narratives of the New Testament along with the theological results of the Christ event, for example redemption by His blood and the access to God by His blood (Hebrews 9:12, 10:19-20)
4. modern medical and surgical sciences (charts I, V, VI-A, XII; figures I-A, I-B, I-C, IV, VI, VII, IX, X; chapters 5, 10, 12, 13)
5. the transcendency of blood and water (the presence of human blood and serum on the shroud)

In 1978, the Shroud of Turin Research Project (STURP) was assembled to unlock the scientific mysteries of the shroud. This unique endeavor attracted the world's most prominent physicians, scientists, archaeologists, molecular biologists, physicists, biochemists, pathologists, microbiologists, computer scientists, and space technologists.

The primary assignment of the STURP was to authenticate the shroud as the burial cloth of Jesus Christ by solving the mysterious secrets of the blood markings and the body image.[2-7]

The research and publications from the STURP have assisted me in solving the mystery of how Jesus died (figures VIII-A, VIII-B).

- There is conclusive scientific evidence that the shroud had contained a dead human body (corpse); however, it is a scientific aberration for the body image and blood markings of a corpse to be present on the burial garments two thousand years later.
- Computer science revealed that the two-dimensional shroud contains a three-dimensional image indicating that the dematerialized body either passed through the cloth or the cloth collapsed through the body.[3,4]
- The blood markings contain the AB blood group (common among Hebrews) as well as human hemoglobin, iron (Fe^{++}), plasma, albumin, immunoglobulins, and DNA. There is no laboratory evidence for the presence of paint, dye, ink, or pigment indicating that a forgery is unlikely.[2-6]
- Each blood marking is surrounded by a microscopic halo of human serum[2,3] containing immunoglobulins (antibodies produced by WBCs) and bilirubin (a by-product of hemoglobin metabolism). The shroud of Turin miraculously contains the shed blood and the living water of Jesus Christ!
- Numerous research projects[1-3] failed to duplicate the exact body image present on the shroud; however, the straw color of the linen fibers closely resembles the combination of oxidation (chemical breakdown) and dehydration (loss of water).

- The "particular radiation theory" suggests that streams of electrons (-) and protons (+) passed through the cloth producing the superficial straw-colored fibers of the body image. This theory implies that during a miraculous resurrection event, the shroud collapsed through the dematerialized body of Jesus Christ supernaturally encoding the human blood markings and the body image.[3,4]
- The participants of the STURP agreed by consensus that the shroud of Turin was not a forgery.[3,4]
- Ten years following the STURP, a carbon-14 dating study[2] (1988; glossary) returned the controversial result of a "fourteenth century forgery." According to the Vatican, this important study will be repeated in 2020.[4]

The shroud of Turin is of one accord with the Old Testament scriptures, the passion narratives of the New Testament, and modern medical science. Consider the wounds that resulted secondary to SFT—the piercings of Jesus Christ (Psalm 22:16; Isaiah 53:5; Zechariah 12:10; John 19:2, 18, 34, 37; chart VI-A). First, observe the frontal view of the shroud: there is a four-inch horizontal chest wound consistent with the Roman blow of the lance[1-4,7] below the right nipple and parallel to the fifth rib interspace (John 19:33–34; figures VIII-A, X; glossary).

The blood markings caused by the BOL are present on the frontal and dorsal views of the shroud and are remarkably surrounded by the microscopic halos of serum resulting from the retraction of clotted blood (figures VIII-A, VIII-B; chapter 7).

Second, there are numerous puncture wounds on the scalp. They are consistent with the piercing wounds made by the sturdy, two-inch thorns of the Syrian Christ thornbush woven into the cap worn by Jesus (Matthew 27:29; John 19:2; chart VI-A). There are large collections of clotted blood in Jesus's ponytail and beard due to the rich blood supply of the scalp (figures VIII-A, VIII-B).

Third, the Roman nails caused four piercing wounds in the feet and wrists. The dorsal left wrist wound on the frontal image of the shroud reveals a uniquely divided blood flow pattern located directly over the space of Destot (figures VIII-A, IX; chapter 9; glossary). The shroud also confirms the nail wounds in the second metatarsal spaces of both feet consistent with Roman crucifixion (John 19:18, 23; figure VIII-B).

In conclusion, the shroud of Turin is an authentic scientific and scriptural portrayal of Jesus Christ including His passion, sacrificial death, and resurrection. It accurately portrays a severely traumatized, bloodstained, pierced, scourged, and crucified Hebrew male with multiple wounds and blood flow patterns secondary to BFT (scourging, battery, and falls) and SFT (piercings by thorns, nails, and a Roman lance). The shroud has been efficacious during my clinical assessment of Jesus Christ—His multiple wounds (chart VI-A; figures VIII-A, VIII-B) and to a lesser extent, His blood and water losses (charts I, II-B; chapter 9). It has been instructive and affirmative with respect to untangling and solving the mystery of how Jesus died.

REFERENCES

1. Barbet, P. 1950. *A Doctor at Calvary.* Indre, France: Dillon & Cie.
2. Zugibe, T. Z. 2005. *The Crucifixion of Jesus.* New York: M. Evans.
3. Antonacci, M. 2000. *The Resurrection of the Shroud.* New York: M. Evans.
4. Antonacci, M. 2015. *Test the Shroud.* St. Louis: L. E. Press.
5. Wilson, I. 1998. *The Blood and the Shroud.* New York: The Free Press.
6. Guerrera, V. 2001. *The Shroud of Turin.* Rockford, IL: Tan Books and Publishers.
7. Tribbe, F. 1983. *Portrait of Jesus.* New York: Stein and Day.

Part II
Charts and Figures

Charts

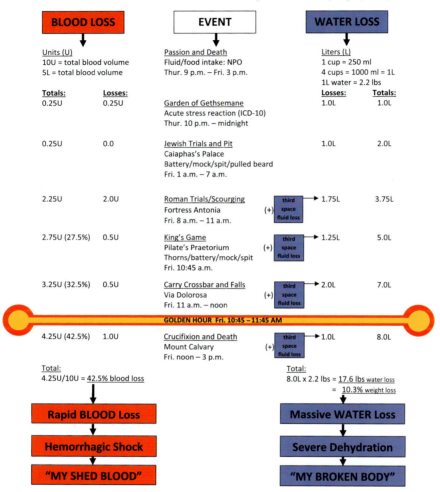

Chart I: The blood and water losses during Jesus's passion are based on scripture, modern medical science, and the shroud of Turin. Jesus's PTS resulted in His fatal losses of blood and water, severe dehydration, acute hemorrhagic shock with third space fluid loss, and His rapid demise on Calvary (Mk 15:44; charts II-B, IV-B, V, VI-A, XII; figures VIII-A, VIII-B; chapters 5, 9, 12, 13).

| CHART II-A | **NORMAL WATER BALANCE** |

INTAKE (+) 18 HRS		OUTPUT (-) 18 HRS	
WATER:	1500 mL	RESPIRATION:	500 mL
FOOD:	700 mL	SKIN:	400 mL
METABOLISM:	300 mL	URINE:	1500 mL
		FECES:	100 mL
TOTAL:	(+) 2500 mL	TOTAL:	(-) 2500 mL

Chart II-A: The estimated normal water intake (+) and output (–) is based on Jesus's age, size, and activity level during an 18 hour period. His normal intake (+) was an estimated 2,500 mL, and His normal output (–) was an estimated 2,500 mL.

| CHART II-B | **WATER BALANCE IN THE PASSION** |

(Thur. 9 p.m. — Fri. 3 p.m.)

INTAKE (+) 18 HOURS		OUTPUT (-) 18 HOURS	
WATER:	0 mL	RESPIRATIONS (hyperventilation):	1000 mL
FOOD:	0 mL	SKIN (sweat and insensible losses):	3000 mL
METABOLISM:	300 mL	URINE:	500 mL
		FECES:	0 mL
TOTAL:	(+) 300 mL	SUBTOTAL:	(-) 4500 mL
		THIRD SPACE FLUID LOSS:	
		WOUNDS (estimated 255):	800 mL
		BILATERAL PLEURAL EFFUSIONS:	2000 mL
		PERICARDIAL EFFUSION:	250 mL
		PARALYTIC ILEUS:	750 mL
		SUBTOTAL:	(-) 3800 mL
		TOTAL WATER LOSS:	(-) 8300 mL
			(+) 300 mL
		GRAND TOTAL WATER LOSSES:	(-) 8000 mL = 8.0 L
			= 17.6 lbs.
			= 10.3% body weight

Chart II-B: Jesus was NPO during the passion. He sustained severe water losses from mental afflictions in Gethsemane (hyperhidrosis), physical shock-trauma in the Roman court (battery, scourging, and piercings), and the physical and mental stress on the Via Dolorosa (hyperventilation, sweating, nausea, and vomiting). The estimated volume of third-space fluid loss—wounds (traumatic and ischemic), effusions, and paralytic ileus—are based on my analysis of the injuries (chart I; chapter 9). Jesus's total water losses—an estimated 8,000 mL (8.0 L or 17.6 lbs.)—contributed to His rapid demise (chart III). The scriptural descriptions of "broken body" and "torn flesh" represent the post-traumatic medical conditions of severe cellular dehydration, and death. Jesus did not sustain broken bones since prophetic scripture must be fufilled (Jn 19:36; charts V, VI-A, IX, see 6, 20, XII; figures VI, VII; chapter 9).

CHART III

COMPARISON – SURVIVAL TIME ON A ROMAN CROSS

	JESUS CHRIST (30 AD) 3 HOURS – "acute"	TWO REVOLUTIONARIES (30 AD) 8-10 HOURS – "routine"	SPARTACUS SLAVES (70 BC) JEWISH PRISONERS (70 AD) 5-9 DAYS – "chronic"
(1) Preliminary Traumas and Sufferings (PTS)	• Yes – severe PTS • Gethsemane — life-threatening • Scourging – fatal • Severe acute B&W losses	• Yes – mild to moderate PTS • Preparatory scourging • Mild acute B&W losses	• No PTS • No scourging • No acute B&W losses
(2) Methods	... nails; no seat	... ropes; seat; foot plate	... multiple
(3) Wounds	... 255 (estimated)	... 60 (estimated)	... none
(4) Blood Loss	... 4.25 U (estimated) – fatal	... 2.0 U (estimated)	... none
(5) Water Loss	... 8.0 L (estimated) – fatal	... 3.0 L (estimated)	... 6-10.0 L (estimated) – fatal after days

(6) Pathophysiology	• Acute stress reaction (ICD-10)
	• Multiple wounds
	• Severe blood and water losses
	• Decompensated multifactorial shock
	• Acute respiratory failure
	• Acute cardiac failure
	• Adrenal fatigue (↓ cortisol)
		• Compensated shock
		• Respiratory distress
		• Crucifracture (Jn 19:32) — fatal
		  (1) severe pain – traumatic shock
		  (2) B&W losses — multifactorial shock
		  (3) rapid death
			• Severe dehydration (days)
			• Early malnutrition (catabolism)
			• Hypovolemic shock
			• Pneumonia — sepsis
			• Heat related disease (?)
			• Kidney failure (?)
			• Electrolyte imbalances (?)
			• DVT — secondary PE (?)

(7) Postmortem	• BOL with flow of B&W (Jn 19:33-34) • Corpse: burial by the church	• Corpse: garbage dump	• Corpse: decomposition on cross

Chart III: The survival time—the length of time for death to occur on a Roman cross—was inversely proportional to the severity of the PTS. Notice the significant differences in the time of survival involving the three groups above: Jesus survived only three hours on the cross—an acute death caused by severe PTS. The two revolutionaries survived eight to ten hours on the cross—death that resulted from routine PTS and fatal crucifractures. The crucified slaves and Jewish prisoners did not sustain PTS, and many survived for days on the cross—chronic deaths from a variety of causes (chapter 5)

My conclusions are: (1) the severity of Jesus's PTS—the rapid losses of blood and water prior to His crucifixion—caused His acute death (chart I; chapter 12); (2) the Roman cross did not cause the death of Jesus (chart V; figure VI); and (3) tetany/asphyxiation is an *incorrect*, indefensible cause of Jesus's death since many of the Jewish prisoners survived for 5-9 days on their crosses. In addition, death by suffocation does not fulfill prophetic scripture (Lev 17:11; Mat 26:28; Heb 9:22; chart IX, see 6, 7, 9, 10, 20), does not satisfy the theological requirement of shed blood, and does not satisfy modern medical science (charts V, XI, XII; figures VI, VII; chapters 5, 9; glossary, "asphyxiation," "crucifixion—biomechanics").

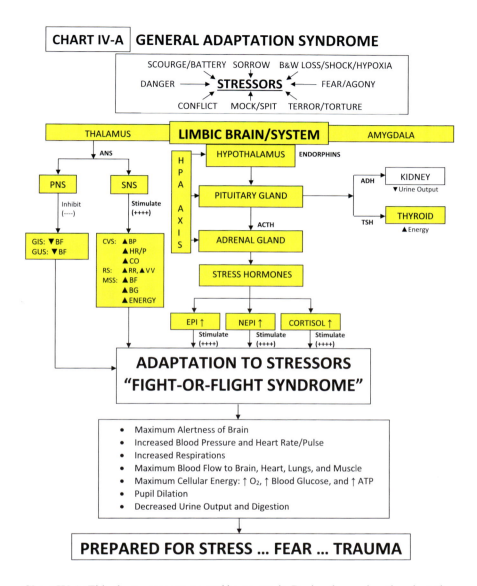

Chart IV-A: This chart represents normal homeostasis. During the passion, the adaptation to multiple stressors— mental afflictions and physical shock-trauma—was activated by the limbic brain and autonomic neuroendocrine system that prepared Jesus for survival (figure III; chapters 3, 4, 5). For the survival of the human race, the sovereign Lord and Great Physician endowed humankind with the above responses to terror, shock-trauma, fear, conflict, and pain known as the general adaptation syndrome.

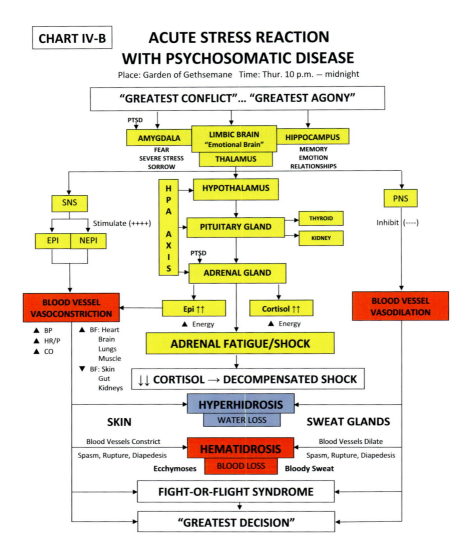

Chart IV-B: In Gethsemane, Jesus abruptly suffered His greatest conflict, greatest agony, and greatest decision—a life-threatening acute stress reaction with psychosomatic (mind-body) complications including hyperhidrosis, hematidrosis, and adrenal fatigue (↓cortisol). Jesus's overwhelming fear of separation from the Father and His impending death activated the amygdala of the limbic and autonomic neuroendocrine systems causing massive increases in the stress hormone levels (epi, nepi, and cortisol) and the nerve impulses of the SNS and the PNS (figure III). His "sorrow unto death" caused a hypertensive crisis, a racing heart, hyperventilation, and bleeding into the skin—ecchymoses, petechiae, and hematidrosis (bloody sweat). The most serious complication was adrenal fatigue and adrenal shock (↓cortisol), which hastened Jesus's demise on the cross (Mk 14:34; Lk 22:44; charts I, III, V, VII-A; figures VI, VII; chapters 4, 5, 12; glossary).

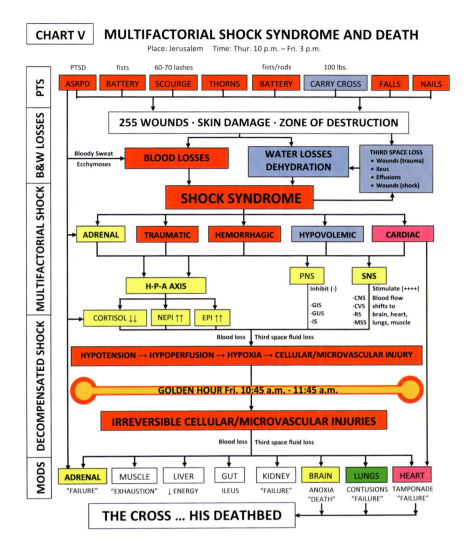

Chart V: Fatal multifactorial shock—traumatic, hemorrhagic, hypovolemic, cardiac, and adrenal—was caused by the PTS that occurred prior to the crucifixion (chart I; figure VI). Normal compensation was impossible due to the rapid and large losses of blood and water, adrenal fatigue (↓cortisol levels), and the absence of treatment during the golden hour. Decompensated shock caused the collapse of Jesus's circulatory system with severe hypotension, hypoperfusion, hypoxia, and irreversible cellular injuries (chart XI). The above pathophysiology resulted in the rapid onset of MODS and death after only three hours on the cross (charts III, VII-A, VII-B, VII-C, VII-D, XI, XII; figures IV, VI, VII; chapters 5, 9, 12, 13; glossary).

| CHART VI-A | ESTIMATED WOUNDS OF THE PASSION |

BLUNT FORCE TRAUMA (BFT)

SCOURGING/BATTERY WOUNDS: EXTERNAL — **Number**
- Lacerations/mechanical burns/skin damage (estimated) — 150
- Contusions/hematomas (estimated) — 40

SCOURGING WOUNDS: INTERNAL
- Bilateral lung contusions — (?)
- Bilateral pleural effusions — (?)
- Pericardial effusion — (?)

FOUR FALLS (Gethsemane and Via Dolorosa)
- Knees/shoulders: abrasions/contusions/hematomas (estimated) — <u>15</u>

<u>SUBTOTAL = 205</u>

SHARP FORCE TRAUMA (SFT)

- Thorn wounds (estimated) — 36
- Nail wounds — 4
- Lance wound (postmortem blow of the lance) — (1)

ECCHYMOSES/HEMATIDROSIS

- Large cutaneous bruises (estimated) — <u>10</u>

<u>SUBTOTAL = 50</u>

TOTAL (estimated) = 255

ESTIMATED MECHANICAL BURNS/SKIN DAMAGE

- Scourging burns (estimated) = 60
- Surface area of burns (estimated) = 0.5 in (width) x 4.0 in (length)
  = 2.0 in^2 (estimated area of each burn)
  = 120 in^2 ÷ 2630 (TBSA)

TOTAL SKIN DAMAGE = **4.5% of the TBSA**

Chart VI-A: The PTS of Jesus Christ caused 251 of the estimated 255 total wounds (excluding the four nail wounds). The excessive Roman scourging and battery resulted in an estimated 190 external wounds. An estimated 80% of the wounds were BFT which crushed billions of cells (third space fluid loss), lacerated millions of small blood vessels (blood loss), and damaged the skin (water loss). Jesus suffered an estimated 40 piercing wounds (SFT) resulting from the cap of thorns (36) and the nail wounds (4). The PTS caused a greater number of wounds and blood and water losses than previously reported (charts I, II-B, V; figures VI, VII; chapters 5, 9, 12). The mechanical burns/skin damage, covered an estimated 4.5% of the TBSA, and caused water losses (evaporation) and hypothermia (charts I, VII-D; glossary).

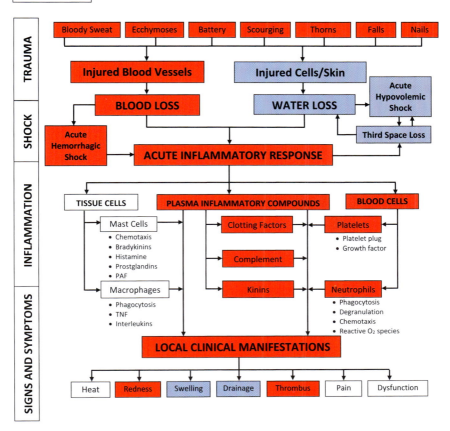

Chart VI-B: The initial phases of the acute inflammatory response took place in each of Jesus's wounds: the first responders included neutrophils, macrophages, mast cells, plasma compounds, and platelets that (1) arrest bleeding, (2) prevent infection, (3) remove dead tissue, and (4) foster healing (chart XII; glossary, "acute inflammatory response"). The clinical manifestations of acute inflammation included heat, redness, swelling, pain, and loss of function. BFT secondary to scourging, battery, and falls resulted in much greater tissue damage, cellular death, and third space water loss as compared to SFT (charts I, VI-A). The rapid demise of Jesus prevented the onset of systemic inflammatory reaction and septicemia.

| CHART VII-A | THE CAUSES OF MULTIFACTORIAL SHOCK |

ETIOLOGY	PATHOPHYSIOLOGY
Adrenal shock	Adrenal fatigue caused ↓**cortisol**, a necessary hormone for compensation during severe shock; **adrenal shock** resulted in the persistence of hypotension (↓BP) and hypoperfusion.
Traumatic shock	Multiple wounds, severe pain, and the sudden losses of B&W caused acute traumatic shock: ↓BP; ↓HR/P; and ↓CO.
Hemorrhagic shock	**BLOOD loss** = 4.25 U or 42.5% BV: Class IV **hemorrhagic shock is fatal** without treatment: the arrest of bleeding and IV blood, blood components, and crystalloid solutions.
Hypovolemic shock	**WATER loss** = 8.0 L or 17.6 lbs.: massive water losses, acute dehydration, and **hypovolemic shock are fatal** conditions without replacement with IV crystalloid solutions.
Cardiac shock	An acute pericardial effusion compressed Jesus's heart causing **cardiac tamponade, cardiac shock, and cardiac failure**: ↓BP, ↑HR/P, ↓CO, and ↓ejection fraction; emergency intervention includes needle aspiration or surgery for the decompression of the heart.

Chart VII-A: These five cardiovascular conditions caused severe multifactorial shock during the passion; the primary cause of Jesus's death was the rapid and massive losses of blood and water and decompensated hemorrhagic and hypovolemic shock (charts I, V; figures IV, VI, VII; chapters 5, 9). The presence of adrenal fatigue (↓cortisol) and secondary adrenal shock precluded normal compensation and homeostasis (charts IV-B, V; chapters 4, 5; glossary).

CHART VII-B HEMORRHAGIC SHOCK – CLASSIFICATION

CLASSIFICATION	BLOOD LOSS	BP	HR/P	RESUSCITATION FLUIDS
Class I	1.5 U = 15%	→	↑	Crystalloid solutions
Class II	2-3 U = 20-30%	↓	↑	Crystalloid and Blood
Class III	3-4 U = 30-40%	↓↓	↑↑	Crystalloid and Blood
Class IV	>4 U = >40%	↓↓↓	↑↑↑	Packed Red Cells, FFP, and Platelets: ratio is 1 to 1 to 1

Chart VII-B: Jesus lost an estimated 40 to 50% of His blood—Class IV hemorrhagic shock is fatal without treatment during the golden hour (charts I, V, XI XII). The pathophysiology of untreated hemorrhagic shock includes hypotension, hypoperfusion, severe hypoxia and acidosis, coagulopathy, irreversible cellular and microvascular injuries, and the onset of multiple organ dysfunction (chart VII-D; figures VI, VII; chapter 5; glossary).

CHART VII-C SHOCK SYNDROME – CLINICAL MANIFESTATIONS

Hypotension	↓ BP; ↓ CO	Confusion and coma	↓ BF and ↓ O_2 of the brain
Tachycardia	↑ HR/P	Weakness and fatigue	↓ BF, ↓ O_2, and ↓ BG of the muscles
Tachypnea	↑ RR	Urine output decreased	↓ BF and ↓ O_2 of the kidneys
Hypothermia	↓ T	Anxiety and restlessness	↓ BF and ↓ O_2 of the brain
Cyanosis (blue skin)	↓ P_vO_2	Cold and clammy skin	↓ BF and ↓ O_2 of the skin

Chart VII-C: The most frequent clinical manifestations (signs and symptoms) observed during shock are listed above. Tachypnea (↑RR) and tachycardia (↑HR/P) are the initial responses to shock activated by the limbic and autonomic neuroendocrine systems to restore tissue perfusion, and oxygen levels (charts I, V, XI; figures II, III; chapter 5; glossary). Urine output is an excellent clinical indicator of tissue perfusion during shock. Cyanosis is the bluish discoloration of skin caused by diminished levels of O_2 in the blood. The progression of hypoxia and acidosis during shock causes clinical tachycardia, tachypnea, confusion, fatigue, anxiety, restlessness, and ultimately coma (glossary).

| CHART VII-D | **HEMORRHAGIC SHOCK – "LETHAL TRIAD"**

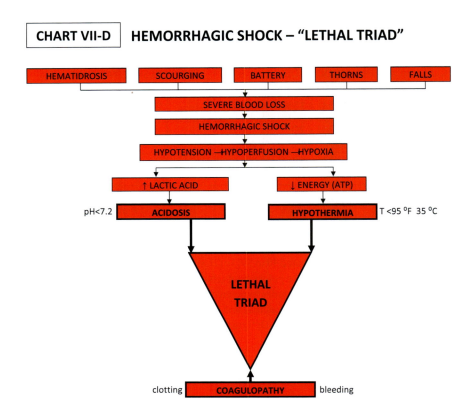

Chart VII-D: The lethal triad is a deadly complication of severe hemorrhagic shock. The three pathophysiological components consist of the following: (1) *acidosis* secondary to hypoxia ($\downarrow O_2$)—the switch to anaerobic energy ($\downarrow ATP$) with the excessive production of lactic acid ($\downarrow pH$); (2) *hypothermia* secondary to multiple wounds, blood loss, decreased energy production; and (3) *coagulopathy* secondary to the presence of the hypercoaguable state of shock-trauma—the formation of blood clots in the microcirculation of multiple organs (disseminated intravascular coagulation; chart XII). In addition, coagulopathy may be complicated by severe bleeding secondary to the consumption of platelets and fibrinogen and the activation of fibrinolysis (plasmin/plasminogen; charts V, XI, XII; glossary). Modern medical research has identified coagulopathy in more than 25 percent of patients with severe hemorrhagic shock. The lethal triad—acidosis, hypothermia, and coagulopathy—was a possible complication during Jesus's passion (chapter 5).

| CHART VIII-A | **ACUTE RESPIRATORY FAILURE IN THE PASSION**

- **Definition**: Respiratory failure is the inability of the lungs to exchange CO_2 and O_2 to sustain human life. Abnormal arterial blood gases (ABGs) establish the diagnosis: respiratory hypoxia (P_aO_2 <70 mmHg) and respiratory hypercapnia (P_aCO_2 >60 mmHg; chart XII; figures VI, VII; chapter 5; glossary).

- **Clinical Picture**: Jesus's chest wall was severely injured by excessive Roman scourging and defenseless battery resulting in multiple abrasions, ecchymoses, petechiae, lacerations, contusions, and hematomas. More importantly, He also sustained lung contusions and bilateral pleural effusions (glossary).

    On the Via Dolorosa, every breath caused sharp pleuritic chest pains. His lungs were congested by scattered areas of hemorrhage (blood) and pulmonary edema (water) resulting in "moist breath" sounds, dyspnea, and tachypnea (RR >30). His chest x-ray revealed diffuse lung bruises and bilateral pleural effusions. His ABGs were abnormal: $\downarrow P_aO_2$ = 70 mmHg, $\downarrow P_aCO_2$ = 30 mmHg (secondary to compensatory hyperventilation), and pH = 7.4 (chart XII). His clinical diagnoses included (1) chest wall and pulmonary contusions, (2) acute respiratory distress syndrome, and (3) bilateral plural effusions (glossary).

- **Pathophysiology**: The etiology of acute respiratory failure during the passion was excessive scourging, battery with rods and fists, and shock lung secondary to severe hemorrhagic shock (figures VIII-A, VIII-B; glossary). Microscopic examination of the lungs revealed disrupted and collapsed alveolar air sacs, severe congestion secondary to pulmonary edema (water), hemorrhage (blood), and an acute inflammatory response (chart VI-B).

    The abnormal presence of blood and water in the air sacs obstructed the normal exchange of CO_2 and O_2 across the alveolar-capillary membranes (CO_2 diffuses out and O_2 diffuses in). Jesus was temporarily able to compensate and exhale the excessive levels of toxic CO_2, but without medical treatment, respiratory hypercapnia ($\uparrow P_aCO_2$) and respiratory acidosis ($\downarrow pH$) ensued causing acute respiratory failure (charts V, XII; figures VI, VII; chapter 5; glossary).

- **Treatment**: Mechanical ventilation, oxygen therapy, and medications for inflammation and edema.

| CHART VIII-B | **ACUTE CARDIAC FAILURE IN THE PASSION** |

- **Definition:** Cardiac failure is the inability of the working heart to satisfy the cellular requirements for oxygen and nutrients (glossary).

- **Clinical Picture:** Jesus sustained severe BFT of His chest—scourging, defenseless battery, and several falls that resulted in injuries of the chest wall, heart, and lungs. He developed an acute pericardial effusion and a secondary cardiac tamponade with distended neck veins, muffled heart sounds, tachycardia ($\uparrow$HR/P), hypotension ($\downarrow$BP), shortness of breath ($\uparrow$RR), and acute pulmonary edema (chapters 5, 12, 13; glossary).

- **Pathophysiology:** The brutal and excessive flogging resulted in the acute inflammation of His delicate pericardial membrane or sac surrounding His heart with secondary "weeping" of 200–300 mL of serous fluid (normal <30 mL); this acute pericardial effusion compressed the heart muscle causing cardiac tamponade and acute cardiac failure with the onset of hypotension ($\downarrow$BP), hypoperfusion ($\downarrow$BF), hypoxia ($\downarrow$O$_2$), acidosis ($\downarrow$pH), and cellular dysfunction (charts V, VII-A, XI; figures VI, VII; chapter 5; glossary).

    The postmortem blow of the lance (BOL) confirmed the diagnosis of pericardial effusion with the distinct flow of blood (right atrium and ventricle) and water (serous fluid from the pericardial effusion; John 19:34; 1 John 5:6–8; figures VIII-A, X).

- **Treatment:** Once the diagnoses of acute pericardial effusion and cardiac tamponade are clinically suspected and confirmed by imaging studies, an emergency aspiration of the pericardial effusion (pericardiocentesis) or a surgical decompression (thoracotomy) is performed (glossary).

CHART IX — PROPHETIC SCRIPTURE AND THE PASSION

> "Was it not necessary that the Messiah suffer these things and enter His glory?" . . . "everything written about me in the law of Moses and in the prophets and psalms must be fulfilled." (Lk 24: 26-27, 44)

Contents

1. Jesus—The Last Adam
2. Jesus—The Protoevangelion or First Gospel
3. Jesus—The New Abel
4. Jesus—The New Isaac
5. Jesus—The New Joseph
6. Jesus—The Perfect Passover Lamb of God
7. Jesus—The New Blood Covenant of Grace
8. Jesus—The Lifted Up One
9. Jesus—The Precious Blood
10. Jesus—The Scourged One
11. Jesus—The New Job
12. Jesus—The Abandoned/Righteous One
13. Jesus—The Great High Priest
14. Jesus—The Rejected One
15. Jesus—The Suffering Servant
16. Jesus—The New Jeremiah
17. Jesus—The New Temple of God
18. Jesus—The New Jonah
19. Jesus—The Pierced One
20. Jesus—The Fulfillment of the Levitical Sacrificial System
21. Jesus—The Cursed One

CHART IX — PROPHETIC SCRIPTURE AND THE PASSION

> "Was it not necessary that the Messiah suffer these things and enter His glory?"... "everything written about me in the law of Moses and in the prophets and psalms must be fulfilled." (Lk 24: 26-27, 44)

Old Testament Prophecy...New Testament Fulfillment...Medical Science

1. Adam desired "to be like God"—yet, he became irresponsible, rebellious, and disobedient. The *original sin* of Adam resulted in the "curse" including (1) alienation of the human race from God and (2) death—physical, spiritual, and eternal (Gen 3:1-7,14-19; chart IX, see 21). Adam and Eve were immediately conscious of their guilt, shame, and fear and "sewed fig leaves to cover themselves" (Gen 3:7-10). But, the Lord God revealed the importance of *shed blood* for the forgiveness of sin by the substitution of animal garments to cover their sin (Gen 3:21; Lev 17:11,14).

    Jesus—The Last Adam. Jesus "emptied himself" (kenosis) and did "not seek equality with God" (Phil 2:6-8). He was "obedient to the will of the Father" (Jn 4:34; Heb 10:7). Adam's original sin and unrighteousness resulted in the fallen state of humankind—the curse and death. But Jesus Christ remedied and reversed this condition by His obedience, righteousness, and sacrificial death meriting infinite mercy (Tit 3:5), perfect and inexhaustible grace (Rom 5:20-21), and eternal life (Rom 6:23). "By one person's transgressions, many died in Adam; but how much more did the grace of God and His gracious gift of the one person Jesus Christ—the last Adam—overflow for the many in Christ" (Rom 5:15).

2. The Lord's curse placed enmity between Satan and the woman's offspring that began the titanic struggle of good versus evil. "[Satan] will strike your heel and you [Jesus Christ] will crush his head" (Gen 3:15 NIV).

    Jesus—The Protoevangelion or First Gospel. Jesus Christ was born of the woman as the promised Redeemer whose mission was to destroy the devil and his evil system (Gal 4:4-6; Heb 2:14-15; 1 Jn 3:8). The incarnate

Son's sacrificial death was the epic event that resulted in (1) the reversal of the curse (Gal 3:13); (2) the new blood covenant of grace that opened the heavenly sanctuary by a new and living way (Mat 26:28; Heb 9:22; 10:19-22); and (3) the freedom from sin and death, the wrath of God, and the devil. The incarnate Son's crushing defeat of Satan won the keys that unlocked the heavenly gates (Mat 16:19; Jn 12:31, 16:11; 1 Jn 4:4; Rev 3:7, 12:9-11).

3. Abel was obedient to God by offering a blood sacrifice, but his brother Cain was disobedient by "offering from his crops" which displeased the Lord. After Cain murdered Abel out of *envy*, the Lord said, "Your brother's blood cries out to me from the ground" (Gen 4:3-11).

Jesus—The New Abel. The blood of Abel "cries out for revenge" versus the blood of Jesus which "cries out for mercy" (Lk 23:24; Heb 9:22, 11:4, 12:24). The passion and sacrificial death of Jesus Christ resulted from the envy, outrage, and contempt of the Jewish religious leaders (Mat 27:23-25; Mk 15:10; Jn 19:6,15). Jesus offered the Father His "shed blood" (blood loss → acute hemorrhagic shock → death) and His "broken body"/"torn flesh" (water loss → severe dehydration → death) for the remission of sins and the eternal access into the presence of God by a new and living way (Mat 26:26-28; Heb 4:16, 6:19-20, 9:22, 10:19-22). It was *envy*—the evil of the human heart—that ultimately motivated the murders of Abel and Jesus Christ—blunt force trauma, severe losses of blood and water, and decompensated multifactorial shock (charts I, V, VI-A).

4. "Take your son Isaac, your only son whom you love, to the land of Moriah." Abraham laid the wood for the holocaust across the shoulders of his son—*the son of promise*—who willingly walked up the mountain. Later, "Abraham spied a ram caught in the thicket and offered it as a blood sacrifice"—the Lord provided the *substitute* for Isaac (Gen 22:2-3, 6, 13-14). Abraham trusted that "God was able to raise Isaac from the dead, and he received Isaac back as a symbol" (Heb 11:19).

Jesus—The New Isaac. God offered His only beloved Son—*the Son of Promise*—as the perfect and eternal blood sacrifice for the sins of the world (Jn 1:29; 3:16; Rom 8:32; 1 Jn 4:10). The wooden crossbar was laid across the shoulders of Jesus who climbed Mount Calvary in the land of Moriah. The incarnate Son willingly offered Himself as a *substitute* for humanity (Jn 10:17-18; 2 Cor 5:21). By His set plan and foreknowledge, the sovereign Lord directed these events (Jn 1:14, 3:16; Acts 2:23; Rom 8:1-2).

5. Joseph dreamed that he would "rule over his brothers." Upon hearing this, they responded with hostility, hate, envy, contempt, and violence (Gen 37:3-11). Later they mocked, rejected, stripped, imprisoned, and abandoned him in a pit: "They sold him into Egyptian slavery for twenty pieces of silver" (Gen 37:23-27). However, the sovereign Lord interceded—Pharaoh *exalted* Joseph to be in charge of his palace and the Egyptian nation (Gen 41:14-46). Following reconciliation with his Hebrew brothers, Joseph revealed the Lord's sovereignty and wisdom, "you meant this for evil, but God meant it for good" (Gen 50:20 NKJV).

Jesus—The New Joseph. Although righteous and innocent, Jesus Christ was betrayed for "thirty pieces of silver," arrested, mocked, thrown into a pit, and abandoned by His envious and outraged Hebrew brothers. (Mat 26:14-15; Mk 15:10; Lk 22:63-66, 23:35-39; Jn 1:11). During His violent death, Jesus fulfilled and perfected prophetic scripture by His words, "Father, forgive them, for they know not what they do" (the first word from the cross, Lk 23:34) . . . and "My God, My God why have you forsaken Me?" (Ps 22:1 NKJV; the fourth word from the cross, Mat 27:34). Jesus was buried and descended into the pit (Hades); however, the Father *exalted* Jesus to reign from His heavenly throne: "Jesus Christ is Lord" (Eph 4:8-10; Phil 2:5-11).

6. On the night of Passover, the Lord instructed Moses and the enslaved Israelites to sprinkle the sacrificial blood of a year-old, *unblemished* male lamb on the doorframes of their households. "*Seeing the blood, I will pass over you*" (Ex 12:3-13, 21-27, 46).

Jesus—The Perfect Passover Lamb of God. John the Baptist saw Jesus, "Behold the Lamb of God, who takes away the sins of the world" (Jn 1:29). The blood of the Passover lambs—the sacrificial animals without broken bones or deformities—redeemed and delivered Israel from Egyptian bondage. Jesus Christ fulfilled the Jewish Passover as the perfect sacrificial Lamb of

God, by offering His precious "shed blood" (blood loss) and "broken body" (water loss) as the eternal ransom that purchased humanity from the slavery to sin and death (Rom 6:17-18, 8:1-2; 1 Cor 5:7; 1 Pete 1:18-19; Rev 1:5, 5:9). Secondly, as the unblemished Lamb of God, Jesus Christ perfected and fulfilled the Hebrew Passover and Exodus—the greatest event in the Old Testament—by passing over the earth and making His exodus to the heavenly Father (Lk 9:31; Jn 13:1).

7. The ancient patriarchs of the Old Testament—Noah, Abraham, and Moses—cut and sealed divine covenants by the blood of sacrificial animals. The divine promises consisted of the sacred and eternal words known as (1) the Noahic blood covenant of new life (Gen 8:20-9:17), (2) the Abrahamic blood covenant of nation, land, and blessing (Gen 12:1-3, 22:15-18), and (3) the Mosaic blood covenant of law (Ex 19:1-24:11). The prophecies of Jeremiah (Jer 31:31-34) and Ezekiel (Ezek 36:25-27) revealed a new covenant with the future promises of the forgiveness of sin and the indwelling Spirit of God.

   Jesus—The New Blood Covenant of Grace. Jesus fulfilled and perfected the Old Testament blood covenants. He cut, sealed, and memorialized the new blood covenant of grace by His infinite, perfect, and eternal sacrificial death—His "broken body" (water loss → severe dehydration → death) and His "shed blood" (blood loss → acute hemorrhagic shock → death) (Mat 26:26-28; Heb 8:7-13, 10:14-18). He offered His life-saving blood and living water to the Father as the ransom that paid humanity's sin debt in full (Jn 19:30; 1 Tim 2:5-6; 1 Pete 1:18-19; Rev 5:6-9). The new blood covenant graciously bestows the forgiveness of sin and gloriously grants the indwelling Holy Spirit (Acts 2:38; chapter 8; glossary).

8. During their forty years in the wilderness, the Lord's chosen people were being tested regarding their unbelief and rebellion. On one occasion, "poisonous serpents" were sent to kill the people. Moses *lifted up* a bronze serpent: those who "looked upon the serpent in faith were healed and saved" (Nb 21:4-9).

   Jesus—The Lifted Up One. As He ministered, Jesus often spoke about the glory of being *lifted up*: "The Son of Man must be lifted-up so that everyone who believes in him may have eternal life" (Jn 3:14-15); "when you lift up the Son of Man, then you will realize that I AM" (Jn 8:28); and "when I am lifted up from the earth, I will draw everyone to myself" (Jn 12:32-33). The fourth gospel uniquely reveals that the lifted up One was glorified during His sacrificial death on Calvary, permitting Him to pour out the Holy Spirit on the church (Jn 7:38-39, 19:30-37). Everyone who looks upon the lifted up One in faith will be granted eternal life (Jn 3:16, 12:32, 19:30-37).

9. "Rahab the harlot" inhabited a brothel in the walls surrounding Jericho. By her faith in the Lord's "mighty deeds," she courageously hid the Israeli spies and agreed to place a "*scarlet cord* in her window" for the protection of herself, her family, and her belongings (Josh 2:12-21). During the conquest of Jericho, Joshua saw the scarlet cord and delivered Rahab—the woman of great faith (Josh 6:23-25).

Jesus—The Precious Blood. Throughout scripture, the scarlet cord of Rahab symbolizes the power, protection, purification, and healing of the precious Blood of Jesus Christ: For example, the prophetic scriptures reveal that the blood of the Passover lambs powerfully redeemed and delivered Israel from Egyptian slavery; the blood of the Levitical sacrifices atoned for sin and healed the broken friendship with Almighty God. The ancient *bloody* sacrifices were fulfilled and perfected by the precious and powerful blood of Christ: "my blood of the new covenant for the forgiveness of sins" (Mat 26:28); "justified by his blood" (Rom 5:9); "redemption by his blood" (Eph 1:7); "peace by his blood" (Col 1:20); "access to God by his blood" (Heb 10:19-20); "the blood of Jesus Christ cleanses us from all sin" (1 Jn 1:7 NKJV); "freedom by his blood" (Rev 1:5); and "the saints overcame him [Satan] by the blood of the Lamb" (Rev 12:11 NKJV).

10. "This is how Eleazar died:" Eleazar was an elderly Jewish scribe, martyred by the fatal *scourging* of the Greeks who occupied Israel (about 175 BC). Because of his obedience to the Mosaic law, "Eleazar refused to consume pork" (2 Mac 7:18-31 NAB).

Jesus—The Scourged One. Jesus sustained an estimated 60-70 brutal lashes ("three-quarters dead"). Pilate demanded this excessive scourging to pacify the envious, enraged temple aristocrats and diabolical Jewish mob. The results of this Roman overreach would be fatal—countless wounds, massive losses of blood and water, decompensated multifactorial shock, lung contusion, pleural and pericardial effusions, and paralytic ileus (Jn 19:1-12; charts I, V, VI-A; figures VI, VII, VIII-A, VIII-B; chapters 5, 10, 12; glossary). As the scourged One, Jesus fulfilled and perfected the scourging death of Eleazar. In addition, His lethal scourging fulfilled the prophetic words and actions of His "shed blood" (blood loss → acute hemorrhagic shock → death) and "broken body" (water loss → severe dehydration → death) (Mat 26:26-28; Mk 10:33-34; Lk 18:31-33, 24:44; Jn 6:51-57; 1 Cor 11:23-26; chapter 1).

11. The Sovereign Lord allowed Satan to test Job, "my blameless and upright servant," by destroying his family, home, and flocks and reputation. Secondly, Satan was permitted to afflict Job with severe mental and physical medical conditions (Job 1:13-22, 2:1-10). Job was alienated from his friends who rejected, blamed, and harshly criticized him. He was naked, powerless, abandoned, humiliated, frightened, and conflicted. He suffered from sorrow, severe anxiety, cutaneous boils, loss of teeth, severe dehydration, malnutrition, and impending doom (Job 19:13-20).

Job spoke about his mental and physical sufferings: "People jeer and laugh at me; they slap my cheek in contempt; God has handed me over to sinners; he has pierced me without mercy; and the ground is wet with my blood" (Job 16:10-15 NLT). Despite his afflictions, Job declared his innocence, did not blaspheme God, and said, "I know my Redeemer lives" (Job 19:26, 33:9 NKJV). With his spiritual eyes, Job finally saw God and repented; the Lord vindicated and exalted him, "blessing his latter days more than his earlier ones" (Job 42:1-6, 10-17).

Jesus—The New Job. The sufferings of Job were fulfilled and perfected by Jesus Christ, who suffered *mental* afflictions—paralyzing fear, severe anxiety, conflict, sorrow, and agony—caused by His impending separation from the Father and sacrificial death for the sins of the world. And like Job, Jesus was abandoned, humiliated, and powerless (Mk 14:32-42, 15:34; Lk 22:63-71, 23:33-38).

Jesus's *physical* sufferings included severe dehydration and extensive cutaneous wounds—abrasions, ecchymoses, burns, lacerations, and piercings (charts

I, VI-A). He was tempted, betrayed, and abandoned by everyone—family, disciples, and the Hebrew nation (Mat 26:39, 47-50, 70-75; Mk 14:51-52; Jn 1:11). For your sake, the Lord Jesus "became poor although He was rich, so that by His poverty you might become rich" (2 Cor 8:9; Phil 2:6-8; prologue).

During his mental and physical agonies, Jesus "did not sin" (2 Cor 5:21) and did not "return insult or threat" (1 Pete 2:21-24). As the result, Almighty God vindicated and exalted Him, "bestowing on Him the name that is above all other names" (Phil 2:9-11 NKJV). The heavenly hosts worshipped the Lamb, "You are worthy because you redeemed us by Your blood" (Rev 5:9 NKJV).

12. The Psalmist testified with regards to his mental afflictions—fear, terror, conflict, and *abandonment*—and his physical agonies of dehydration, piercings, and torture (Ps 22:1, 6-7, 12-21 NIV). Yet later, he praised, trusted, and worshiped the Lord (Ps 22:8, 22-23, 25-31 NIV; chapter 12). He was surrounded by enemies described as "fierce bulls" and "a pack of dogs" (Ps 22:12, 16 NIV): "Is this the one who relies on the Lord? Then let the Lord rescue Him" (Ps 22:8 NIV). He was frightened and tortured, "there is no one to help" (Ps 22:11, 13 NIV). He suffered from dehydration, terror, and a "melted heart" (Ps 22:14 NIV). His "hands and feet were pierced," but He sustained *no broken bones* (Ps 22:16, 17 NIV). During his apparent crucifixion, his enemies "cast lots for His garments" (Ps 22:18 NIV; chapter 10).

Jesus—The Abandoned/Righteous One. Following His betrayal and arrest in Gethsemane, Jesus was tortured, mocked, and abandoned by His disciples, Hebrew brothers and sisters, and Jewish religious authorities. Mark portrayed these acts of desertion by a "young man who ran away naked" (Mk 14:51-52). The Father temporarily *abandoned* Him during His transformation into the "sin of the world," the "curse," the "son of Satan," and "the hour of darkness." (Lk 22:53; Gal 3:13; 2 Cor 5:21). Jesus proclaimed the words of the psalmist from his holy cross, "My God, My God why have you forsaken me?" (the fourth word from the cross, Mat 27:46).

The psalmist flawlessly foreshadowed the combination of the incarnate Son's *mental* afflictions and *physical* sufferings: for example, his severe fright, overwhelming abandonment, conflict, terror, humiliation, and powerlessness (charts IV-A, IV-B) and unrelenting torture, piercings, dehydration, acute cardiac failure, and severe multifactorial shock (charts I, V; figure VI; chapter 5). Although without sin, Jesus was powerless to save Himself (Lk 23:35, 37, 39; 2 Cor 5:21; 1 Pete 2:21-23). He was continually insulted (Mat 27:39-44), but steadfastly trusted and obeyed His Father's will despite severe anguish and a "melted heart" (Mk 14:36; Heb 2:18; 5:7). Jesus sustained life-threatening scourging, battery, and piercings by thorns, nails, and a Roman lance, but sustained *no broken bones* (Jn 19:36). The Roman legionnaires fulfilled prophetic scripture by "casting lots for his garments" (Mat 27:35).

13. The sacred vestments of the Levitical High Priest included the *seamless tunic* of fine linen. It was "worn against the skin only when in the presence of God" behind the Temple veil in the Holy of Holies (Ex 28:39-40, 39:27; Lev 16:4). The psalmist wrote, "They divide My garments among them, and for My clothing [the seamless tunic], they cast lots" (Ps 22:18 NKJV).

Jesus—The Great High Priest. On Calvary, Jesus was stripped of His clothing and lifted up by the Roman legionnaires. They sat down under the cross and "cast lots for his garments" (Mk 15: 24). The beloved disciple revealed that Jesus wore the unique *seamless tunic* during His passion (Jn 19:23-25)—revelation fulfilling and perfecting the prophetic scriptures that Jesus Christ is the eternal great High Priest appointed to "offer gifts and sacrifices" (Heb 8:2, 9:11-15, 10:11-14, 20). He was our willing Victim (Jn 10:17-18) and our eternal High Priest who sacrificed Himself for the sins of the world (Jn 1:29; Gal 2:20; Eph 5:2). He graciously offered His shed blood (blood loss → acute hemorrhagic shock → death) and His broken body/torn flesh (water loss → severe dehydration → acute hypovolemic shock → death) to the heavenly Father as the ransom that merited our infinite mercy, perfect grace, eternal life, and unlimited access to God.

14. "The stone which the builders rejected has become the chief cornerstone" (Ps 118:22 NKJV). The ancient Hebrew builders placed the cornerstone at the intersection of two walls in order to align and unify the entire structure.

Jesus—The Rejected One. The "builders" represented the contentious and envious Jewish authorities and the powerful Temple aristocrats who rejected and forcefully caused the violent murder of their Messiah (Mat 21:33-42; charts I, V, VI-A; figures VI, VII, VIII-A, VIII-B). Jesus was repetitively *rejected* during his childhood years and ministry (Jn 1:10-11): For example, King Herod attempted to assassinate Jesus as an infant (Mat 2:16-18) and the Jews made numerous attempts to entrap and kill him (Lk 4:29; Jn 5:16-18, 8:59, 10:31-33). Three days following His passion and sacrificial death, Jesus was resurrected and exalted as *the Chief Cornerstone and Rock of our Christian faith* (Mat 21:41-45; 1 Pete 2:7). "At the name of Jesus every knee should bend" and "every tongue confess that Jesus Christ is Lord" (Phil 2:10-11; Rev 5:6-9). He is the foundation and the builder who unifies, stabilizes, and holds together the "living stones" of His church (Acts 4:11-12; Eph 2:20-22, 4:1-5).

15. The Suffering Servant of Isaiah is the quintessential Old Testament prefigurement of the passion and sacrificial death, "I gave my back to those who beat me [battery and scourging] and my cheeks to those who plucked my beard [taunting]" (Isa 50:6); He did not shield Himself from "buffets and spitting" (Isa 50:6); He was beaten and tortured so severely that "his appearance was beyond that of mortals" (Isa 52:14).

The Lord's Servant was "spurned" and "held without esteem"—a *man of suffering (*Isa 53:3). He suffered mentally and physically: "He bore our iniquities and our infirmities," He was "smitten and afflicted by God," and He was "crushed" (BFT) and "pierced" (SFT). The servant was "whipped"—"by his stripes [wounds] we were healed." He was "submissive" and "led like a lamb led to the slaughter." He gave His life for His own people, a "sin offering" in order to "justify many" (Isa 53:4-12 NLT; chapter 10).

Jesus—The Suffering Servant. It required centuries before the ancient church finally recognized that Jesus Christ was the fulfillment and perfection of Isaiah's Suffering Servant. Although Jesus sustained severe mental afflictions and shock-trauma, He remained obedient to the Father's perfect will—the suffering servant par excellence (Mk 9:35, 10:43-45; Jn 5:30, 6:38; Phil 2:7-8; Heb 10:5-7; chapter 1). During His trials, Jesus was mocked, spat on, beaten with rods and fists (BFT), pierced with thorns (SFT), and brutally scourged (BFT); nevertheless, he was submissive, "like a lamb being led to the slaughter" (Jn 1:29; 1 Pete 1:18-19; Rev 5:6-9).

After His betrayal and arrest, Jesus suffered repetitive episodes of defenseless battery and taunting (Mat 26:66-68, 27:26-30; Mk 14:63-65; Jn 19:1-7). Jesus sustained excessive flogging (60-70 lashes) which was the primary cause of his rapid demise on Calvary. (charts I, V, VI-A; figures VI, VII, VIII-A, VIII-B; chapter 10; glossary). The Roman legionnaires entertained themselves during the cynical, callous, and ironic king's game—spitting in His face, pulling His beard, taunting, battery, and piercings by the cap of thorns (figures VIII-A, VIII-B).

Pontius Pilate finally paraded Jesus before the mob as a helpless, bloodstained, and counterfeit King of the Jews..."Behold the man" (*Ecce Homo*; Jn 19:5); however, the chief priests were not satisfied in the least, and exhibited even greater outrage, defiance, and contempt—this man must be "lifted up" and "pierced" on a cross (Jn 19:6-8)! Jesus was afflicted mentally, physically, and spiritually, "He himself bore our sins in his body" in order that "by his wounds [stripes] you would be healed" (1 Pete 2:24).

Isaiah's prophecy of the *Man of Sorrows* was fulfilled and perfected by the incarnation, passion, and sacrificial death of Jesus Christ by the following scriptures: (1) "He loved us and gave Himself" to rescue us from sin (Gal 1:4, 2:20; Eph 5:2); (2) He bore our sins to be a "sin offering" (Heb 9:28, 10:14, 18); (3) He "justified many" by His sacrificial "broken body" and "shed blood" (Rom 5:9; Tit 3:7); and (4) He was "slain as a sacrificial lamb" and "purchased us with his blood" (Rev 5:6, 9).

16. "The word of the Lord came to Jeremiah" (Jer 1:4, 11, 2:1); yet, his Hebrew brothers *rejected* his prophetic words with contempt, mockery, and attempted murder. The weeping prophet was "betrayed" (Jer 26:4-19), like a lamb being led to the slaughter (Jer 12:19), "flogged," and "imprisoned" (Jer 37:15 NLT).

On one occasion, Jeremiah's words indicted the priests, prophets, and residents of Jerusalem; without hesitation, they mobbed and beat him shouting, "kill him!" . . . "What right do you have to prophesy that this temple will be destroyed?" (Jer 26:4-16 NLT). Jeremiah was later "thrown into a miry cistern" (pit) for boldly speaking the word of the Lord (Jer 38:4-13).

Jeremiah's preeminent revelation consisted of a future new covenant: "I will write the law on their hearts; I will forgive their evil and will remember their sin no more" (Jer 31:31-34).

Jesus—The New Jeremiah. Jesus Christ fulfilled the life and times of Jeremiah as follows: (1) He obeyed the will of God by revealing His prophetic word (Mk 1:22, 27, 14:36; Lk 24:44; Jn 6:38; Phil 2:6-8); (2) He suffered for His words and works and was *rejected* by the Jewish religious establishment (Jn 1:11, 8:59, 10:31); (3) Jesus was imprisoned in the dungeon (pit) under Caiaphas's palace and later descended to Hades (Ps 88:1-12; Eph 4:9-10; 1 Pete 3:19-20); (4) He was scourged and beaten (Jn 19:1-3); (5) His passion and sacrificial death fulfilled Jeremiah's prophecy of the new covenant: He cut and sealed the new blood covenant of grace that granted the remission of sins and the Holy Spirit (Mat 26:26-28; Acts 2:38; Heb 8:7-13, 10:14-18); (6) Jesus was like a lamb being led to the slaughter—the Lamb of God who takes away the sins of the world (Jn 1:29; 1 Cor 5:7; 1 Pete 1:19; Rev 5:6-9); and (7) during His Roman trial, the chief priests and Jewish mob shouted, "Crucify Him, crucify Him!" (Jn 19:4-6, 14-15).

The prophet Jeremiah and Jesus Christ suffered extremely severe stress, anguish, fear, violence, and sorrow. In my analysis, both suffered *post-traumatic stress disorder (ICD-10)* (glossary).

17. The Jewish tabernacle (about 1400-960 BC; Ex 25:8-22, 40:34-38) and the first Jerusalem temple of Solomon (about 960-587 BC; 1 Kgs 8:1-21; 2 Chr 36:17-21; Ezek 10:18-23) were constructed to honor the Lord's name and to provide a glorious dwelling place among His chosen people. Out of a future temple would flow rivers of living water, "Wherever the river flows, all things will live" (Ezek 47:9).

Jesus—The New Temple of God. When the Jewish religious leaders requested a sign, Jesus gave an amazing revelation, "Destroy this temple and in three days I will raise it up" (Jn 2:19-22 NKJV). He spoke of His own body, not the temple of stone—the incarnate Son *embodied* the presence and the glory of God (Mat 1:23; Jn 1:1-2,14; Heb 1:3, 2:14-18).

The Son of God was wrapped in a temple of human flesh (70% water) and human blood (93.5% water). He is the New Temple of God who fulfills, perfects, and transcends the Jewish tabernacle and the Jerusalem temple built with human hands. Jesus promised the gift of the Holy Spirit: "Out of his heart would flow rivers of living water" (Jn 7:38-39 NKJV).

From high on Calvary, the incarnate Son—the New Temple of God—was wounded by the postmortem blow of the lance that resulted in the immediate flow of His precious blood and living water that surged to the ends of the earth revealing the glorious gifts of His church (Jn 7:37-39, 19:33-37; 1 Jn 5:6-12; figure X; chapter 11). His scarlet-red blood represented the remission of sins, unlimited access to God, and the Lord's Supper/Eucharist; and His crystal-clear water symbolized the Holy Spirit, eternal life, the cleansing of the church with the word, and Christian water baptism.

18. "A large fish swallowed Jonah:" he remained "in the belly of the fish for three days and three nights" (Jon 1:17 NKJV). "Jonah *prayed*" and the Lord answered—immediately, "the fish vomited Jonah onto dry land" (Jon 2:1-10 NKJV).

    Jesus—The New Jonah. The Jewish scribes and Pharisees insisted that Jesus reveal a "heavenly sign" as proof that He was the Messiah. Jesus responded, "As Jonah was three days and three nights in the belly of the great fish, so will the Son of Man be three days and three nights in the heart of the earth" (Mat 12:38-40). Jonah's descent and exaltation in the life-saving waters of the sea and the large belly of the fish foreshadowed Jesus's passion and sacrificial death, His descent into Hades, and His resurrection three days later. From His Roman cross on Calvary, Jesus *prayed* to the Lord who glorified Him during His sacrificial death and His resurrection (Mat 27:46; Lk 23:34, 43, 46; Jn 7:39; 19:26-28, 30-37; Phil 2:6-11; figure VI; glossary, "seven words from the cross").

19. The prophecy of Zechariah revealed *that day of the Messianic Age*—revival, purification, and deliverance. "They shall look upon the one they *pierced* and mourn over him as a first-born son" (Zech 12:10 NIV). On that day,

living waters shall flow from Jerusalem— "a fountain to purify from sin and uncleanliness" (Zech 13:1; 14:8).

Jesus—The Pierced One. Jesus was *pierced* by a cap of *thorns*, *nails*, and a Roman *lance*. When lifted up on Calvary, He was looked upon and mourned by many: (1) the inhabitants of Jerusalem "returned home beating their breasts" (Lk 23:48); (2) the Roman centurion confessed, "Surely this was the Son of God" (Mk 15:39); (3) the presence of "the grieving women from Galilee" (Mat 27:55); and (4) the beloved disciple witnessed the postmortem blow of the lance that *pierced* the sacred heart of Jesus (Jn 7:38-39, 19:33-37; 1 Jn 5:6-12).

20. The Levitical sacrificial system specified that the sacrificial animals —cattle, goats, and sheep—were to be *unblemished* males (without broken bones, dislocated joints, or other deformities) (Lev 1:10, 3:6, 5:18; Dt 17:1). These animal sacrifices symbolized the moral perfection and holiness demanded by a perfect and holy God.

The Levitical law revealed the following profound truth: "The life of the flesh is in the blood for the atonement of the soul" (Lev 17:11): therefore, the life of the Jewish sinner was represented by the blood of a sacrificial animal when sprinkled on the horns, sides, and base of the altar for atonement.

On the annual Day of Atonement (Yom Kippur), the blood of a bull and goat was offered inside the holy of holies behind the temple veil and sprinkled on the mercy seat of the ark. Once each year the High Priest was permitted *access* to Almighty God to offer the sacrificial blood that temporarily covered the sins of Israel (Lev 16:1-9). The bull and goat—sin offerings—were carried outside the camp and burned (Lev 16:27 NKJV). Before reentering the camp, the Levites and priests purified themselves and their clothing with living water (Lev 16:28 NKJV).

The ancient Levitical offerings looked toward a future Redeemer based upon the Old Testament blood covenants (Gen 15:9-10; Ex 24:6-8), the daily temple sacrifices (Nb 28:3-8), the weekly Sabbath offerings (Nb 28:3-8; Lev 24:8), the blood sacrifices offered on Jewish feast days such as Passover (Ex

12:1-7,21-27), Tabernacles (Nb 29:13-28), and the Day of Atonement (Lev 16:1-19; Nb 29:7-11), and a special sin offering for the defilement by contact with a corpse which consisted of the ashes of a sacrificial red heifer taken outside the camp, mixed with "living water," and sprinkled on those who were "ceremonially unclean" (Nb 19:9-22).

Jesus—The Fulfillment of the Levitical Sacrificial System. The passion and death of the incarnate Son of God was the perfect, infinite, and eternal sacrifice for the sins of the world (Jn 1:29; 1 Pete 1:18-19; Rev 5:6-9). As the eternal High Priest, Jesus Christ entered the heavenly sanctuary with His "shed blood" (blood loss → acute hemorrhagic shock → death) and His "broken body"/"torn flesh" (water loss → severe dehydration → death). This epic, onetime event granted mankind infinite mercy (Tit 3:5), perfect and inexhaustible grace (Rom 5:20-21), and eternal access to God by a new and living way (Heb 4:16, 6:19-20, 10:19-22).

As the mediator of the new blood covenant of grace, the incarnate Son fulfilled and perfected each of the Levitical sacrificial offerings—blood, grain, oil, wine, and water. Those called and chosen by the Sovereign Lord are blessed with eternal salvation (Heb 5:9), eternal redemption (Heb 9:12), an eternal inheritance (Heb 9:15), a share in the divine nature (2 Pet 1:4), and every spiritual blessing in the heavenlies (Eph 1:3).

The atoning sacrificial death of Jesus Christ outside the gates and walls of Jerusalem perfected and fulfilled the sacrificial death of the Levitical animals; their shed blood was sprinkled on the altar and their broken bodies were burned outside the camp. Figuratively, the Christian faithful are united with Jesus Christ outside the walls since they have been separated from the sinful and corrupt world (Heb 13:10-13 NKJV).

Scripture reveals, "It is impossible for the sacrificial blood of sheep, goats, and bulls to take away sins" (Heb 10:4). As our eternal High Priest and willing Victim, Jesus Christ offered Himself for the sins of the world, making perfect those who are being consecrated (Heb 10:10-14). The sacrificial work of Jesus Christ victoriously fulfilled and perfected the Levitical sacrificial system, meriting our eternal access into the presence of Almighty God and the glorious promises and gracious spiritual blessings that the Levitical sacrificial system could *never* provide (2 Peter 1:4; Heb 10:4, 14, 19-22; chapter 1; glossary, "Christ event").

21. Following the original sin of Eden (the first garden), the Lord *cursed* the serpent (Gen 3:14-15 NKJV), the woman Eve (Gen 3:16 NKJV), the man Adam (Gen 3:17-19 NKJV), the earth (Gen 3:17-18 NKJV), and the human race (Gen 3:19, 22-24 NKJV). Our first parents had violated the law of God, "You shall not eat of the tree of the knowledge of good and evil, for in the day that you eat of it you shall surely die" (Gen 2:17 NKJV). By their disobedience and sin, Adam and Eve fell from the grace of God and were cursed with spiritual, physical, and eternal *death*, and the sufferings of life and death, eternal hell, and congenital sin disease.

Moses later wrote that anyone hanged from a tree for a crime is accursed of God (Dt 21:22-23 NKJV). Since the sovereign Lord dwelled among His chosen people and His name was to be honored, every dead body—hanged, impaled, or crucified—defiled the land and must be removed (Nb 25:33-34 NKJV).

Jesus—The Cursed One. Jesus Christ "became the curse for us" and "redeemed us from the curse of the law" (Gal 3:10, 13 NKJV). Why was this necessary? First, the human race inherited the *Adamic curse*—the inclination to sin and the curse of *death* (Rom 3:22-24, 8:1-2 NKJV; 1 Cor 15:3 NKJV; Tit 2:14 NKJV). Second, the Mosaic law was powerless to remedy and reverse the curse, deliver from sin's penalty, and impute righteousness (Rom 3:20, 28, 8:3-4 NKJV).

Therefore, the incarnate Son, in solidarity with the human race, willingly suffered His greatest conflict…His greatest agony…and His greatest decision in Gethsemane (the second garden)—a life-threatening acute anxiety reaction that was caused by His transformation into the cursed One, complicated by hematidrosis and adrenal fatigue that influenced His rapid demise on Calvary (Mk 14:33-36; Lk 22:44; Jn 19:29-37; Heb 5:7; charts IV-B, V, VI-A; figures VI, VII; chapters 4, 5; glossary).

| CHART X | **THE 10 PILLARS OF THE BLOOD AND WATER** |

1. The *scarlet cord* of Rahab is woven throughout scripture as a symbol of the *precious blood* of Christ (Joshua 2:17–18). His sacrificial blood possesses the divine power to protect, heal, forgive, redeem, justify, grant unlimited access to God, and provide freedom from sin and death, Satan, and the wrath of God.

    The rivers *of crystal-clear living water* flow across the pages of scripture as follows: the life-saving water that flowed from the living Rock in the wilderness (Exodus 17:6; 1 Corinthians 10:4), the life-giving water that flowed from the Jerusalem temple (Ezekiel 47:9), the messianic fountain that purified from the sin and uncleanness of Jerusalem (Zechariah 13:1), the immediate flow of living water from the pierced heart of Jesus Christ (John 7:38, 19:34), and the waters of eternal life flowing from the heavenly throne of God and the Lamb (Revelation 22:1–2).

    Living water symbolizes the Holy Spirit (John 4:10–14, 7:37–39), the new birth by water and Spirit (John 3:5), eternal life (John 4:10–14, 7:38, 19:34), sanctification of the church by the washing of the Word (Ephesians 5:26), and Christian water baptism (Acts 8:38). "If you thirst, come to Me and drink and I will satisfy you" (John 7:37; Revelation 22:17).

2. The sovereign Lord revealed, "The life of the flesh is in its blood for atonement on the altar" (Leviticus 17:11; figure I-A). "Without the shedding of blood there is no forgiveness" (Hebrews 9:22). The shed blood of Jesus Christ was the ransom offered to the Father for the reversal of the curse (Galatians 3:13) and the forgiveness of the sins of the world (John 1:29). Humankind has been "justified by the blood of Christ" (Romans 5:9), "redeemed by his blood" (Ephesians 1:7), and granted eternal "access to God" by the sprinkled blood of Christ (Hebrews 10:19–22). As well, "The devil is defeated by the blood of the Lamb" (Revelation 12:11).

3. The sovereign Lord reveals the *transcendency* of blood and water throughout scripture (figures I-A, I-B, I-C; chapters 1, 7). With His mighty hand, almighty God redeemed Israel by the sacrificial blood of Passover lambs and the life-saving water of the Red Sea during the Exodus.

    The Old Testament blood covenants were cut and sealed by the sacrificial shed blood of lambs, goats, and cattle (chapter 8). Israel was totally dependent on the provisional blessings from the Lord—living water for their crops and herds and blood sacrifices for their friendship. The new blood covenant of grace granted redemption and reconciliation by the shed blood (blood loss) and the broken body (water loss) of the incarnate Son.

4. The fulfillment of prophetic scripture, the theological effects of the Christ event, the transcendency of the blood and water, and the modern medical sciences solve the mystery of how Jesus died. Multiple wounds and massive losses of blood and water resulted in decompensated multifactorial shock and His rapid death (charts I, V, VI-A; chapters 4, 5, 9, 12). The *cycle of death* that transpired on Mount Calvary resulted from the preliminary traumas and sufferings: the Roman cross was Jesus's *deathbed*, not the cause of His death (figure VI).

5. The prophetic scriptures *must* be fulfilled (Matthew 5:17–18; Mark 14:49; Luke 18:31–33, 24:25–27,44; John 19:24, 28, 36–37; chart IX). The prophecies of the passion solve the mystery of how Jesus died—mental afflictions and physical shock-trauma: for example, the unblemished Passover lambs (Exodus 12:5–7, 46; chart IX, see 6); the Levitical animal sacrifices (Leviticus 1–5, 16:15–18; chart IX, see 20), the Suffering Servant (Isaiah 50:6, 52:13, 53:12; chart IX, see 15); the Abandoned/Righteous One (Psalm 22:1–28; chart IX, see 12); and the Pierced One (Zechariah 12:10; chart IX, see 19).

6. Pauline theology reveals the importance of Jesus's shed blood and broken body (1 Corinthians 10:16, 11:23–26; Hebrews 9:22, 10:5, 10, 19–22). His shed blood empowered the theological effects of the Christ event—expiation, redemption, reconciliation, salvation, justification, sanctification, glorification, new creation, transformation, freedom, peace, and access to God (glossary). The Pauline way of the passion includes co-crucifixion with Jesus Christ (Galatians 2:19–20; chapter 11).

7. The Johannine eyewitness revealed the glorious event on Calvary—"so you may also come to believe" (John 19:30–37). The postmortem BOL and the dramatic flow of the blood and water revealed the following (figure X): (1) the certain death of Jesus Christ secondary to blood and water losses; (2)

Jesus's gifts to the ancient church poured into the world—the forgiveness of sin, the access to God, the Lord's Supper/Eucharist, the Holy Spirit, eternal life, and Christian water baptism; and (3) the death of the incarnate Son will for all eternity, reflect the Father's sacrificial love for humanity (John 3:16; 1 John 4:9–10).

Finally, this testimony emphasizes the specific fulfillment of prophecy concerning the sacrificial death of Jesus (chart IX; chapter 1): the unblemished sacrificial Lamb of God—no broken bones (Exodus 12:46; Leviticus 1:10; John 19:36), the Pierced One (Zechariah 12:10; John 19:37), and the New Temple of God—His precious blood and living water flow down Calvary, through the streets of Jerusalem, and to the ends of the earth: "Let anyone who thirsts, come to me and drink" (John 7:37, 19:34; figure X).

8. Petrine theology reveals that Jesus Christ is the spotless, unblemished Lamb who offered His precious blood to the Father as the ransom for our sins (1 Peter 1:18–19). During His passion, Jesus suffered multiple wounds (255) and massive losses of blood (4.25 U and 42.5 percent) and water (8.0 L and 17.6 lbs.; charts I, II-B, VI-A)—"By his wounds you have been healed" (Isaiah 53:5; 1 Peter 2:24), "The promises of God are bestowed upon us so that we may share in the divine nature" (2 Peter 1:3–4), and "do not be led into error. But grow in grace and in the knowledge of our Lord and savior Jesus Christ" (2 Peter 3:17-18).

9. The three earthly witnesses of one accord—the Spirit, the water, and the blood—testify that Jesus is divine and has merited humankind with infinite forgiveness (1 John 1:9), freedom from sin (Revelation 1:5), and eternal life (1 John 5:6–12).

10. The new blood covenant of grace was cut, sealed, and memorialized by the perfect, infinite, and eternal sacrificial death of Jesus Christ (Matthew 26:26–28; 1 Corinthians 10:16, 11:23–26). The signs of the new blood covenant are His precious shed blood (blood loss → hemorrhagic shock) and broken body (water loss → severe dehydration; Matthew 26:26–28; Luke 22:44; John 4:10–14, 7:37–39, 19:33–34; Hebrews 9:12–14, 22, 10:19–22, 13:11–13; 1 Peter 1:19; 1 John 1:7, 5:6–12; Revelation 5:9, 7:14, 17, 12:11, 19:13, 22:1, 17; chapter 7).

| CHART XI | THE HUMAN CELL DURING THE PASSION |

NORMAL	REVERSIBLE INJURY	IRREVERSIBLE INJURY
B&W are essential for the survival of human cells.	The losses of B&W caused shock with reversible cellular injuries in multiple organs.	In the absence of treatment, decompensated shock caused irreversible cellular injuries (death) in multiple organs.
(1) cell membrane: • maintains cell integrity • pumps K^+ into the cell • pumps Na^+ out of the cell	• integrity compromised • influx of H_2O, Na^+, and Ca^{++} • swelling	• integrity lost • influx of H_2O, Na^+, and Ca^{++} • *cellular death*
(2) nucleus: • DNA (genetic code) and RNA for protein synthesis • control of cellular activity	• swelling	• "clumping" of DNA and RNA • *cellular death* • increased third space fluid loss
(3) cytoplasm: • its aqueous gel regulates levels of cellular T, pH, and concentration • contains organelles	• swelling • abnormal T, pH, and concentration	• "cloudy swelling" • cellular dysfunction • no ATP — *cellular death* • increased third space fluid loss
(4) mitochondria: • aerobic energy (ATP) • precious O_2 required for survival	• swelling/dysfunction • anaerobic energy (↓ATP)	• severe swelling/dysfunction • no ATP — *cellular death*
(5) endoplasmic reticulum and ribosomes: • protein synthesis • protein transport	• swelling/fragmenting • no growth and repair	• severe swelling/dysfunction
(6) lysosome: • contain enzymes which destroy bacteria and debris	• swelling • enzyme leakage	• "autodigestion" of cell

GOLDEN HOUR: Fri. 10:45 a.m. – 11:45 a.m.

Chart XI: The human cell is the fundamental unit of life (figure II; chapter 2). Jesus sustained multiple wounds, rapid blood and water losses, and severe multifactorial shock that resulted in irreversible cellular injuries secondary to hypotension (↓BP), hypoperfusion (↓BF), hypoxia (↓O_2), hypoglycemia (↓BG), lactic acidosis (↓pH), and decreased energy production (↓ATP). In the absence of treatment during the golden hour, billions of Jesus's cells were irreversibly injured as noted above: cloudy swelling, clumping of DNA and RNA, mitochondrial dysfunction, and cellular autodigestion. Decompensated multifactorial shock resulted in ischemic death, third space fluid loss, and the onset of multiple organ dysfunction of the lungs, liver, kidneys, heart, and brain (charts V, VII-A, VII-D; figures VI, VII; glossary).

CHART XII	ESTIMATED LABORATORY VALUES IN THE PASSION		
Blood Tests	**Normal Values**	**Via Dolorosa** Fri. 11 a.m. – noon	**Calvary** Fri. 3 p.m. (death)
[1]Hematocrit (Hct)	40-50%	30%	21%
[1]Hemoglobin (Hb)	13.5-18 g/dL	10 g/dL	7 g/dL
[1]White blood cell count	5,000-10,000/mm^3	25,000/mm^3	35,000/mm^3
[1]Neutrophils	60% of WBCs	85% of WBCs	95% of WBCs
Monocytes/Macrophages	5% of WBCs	5% of WBCs	4% of WBCs
[2]Platelets (clotting)	150,000-350,000/mm^3	70,000/mm^3	20,000/mm^3 (coagulopathy)
[2]Fibrinogen (clotting)	200-400 mg/dL	100 mg/dL	50 mg/dL (coagulopathy)
Fibrin split products	Negative	Negative (?)	Positive (coagulopathy)
D-Dimer	<300 ng/mL	>300 ng/mL (?)	>300 ng/mL (coagulopathy)
Na$^+$	136-145 mEq/L	145 mEq/L	150 mEq/L (hypernatremia)
K$^+$	3.5-5.0 mEq/L	5 mEq/L	6 mEq/L (hyperkalemia)
HCO$_3^=$	24-28 mEq/L	15 mEq/L	5 mEq/L (buffer during acidosis)
Ca^{++}	8.5-10.5 mg/dL	9 mg/dL	8 mg/dL
[3]pH (ABG)	7.4	7.4 (compensated acidosis)	<7.0 (severe acidosis)
[3]PaO$_2$ (ABG)	75-100 mmHg	70 mmHg (hypoxia)	< 50 mmHg (respiratory failure)
[3]PaCO$_2$ (ABG)	35-45 mmHg	30 mmHg (compensated)	> 60 mmHg (respiratory failure)
Lactic acid (venous)	0.6-1.7 mmol/L	>4 mmol/L	>20 mmol/L (severe acidosis)
Immunoglobulins	2-4 g/dL	3 g/dL	2 g/dL
Blood glucose (fasting)	75-110 mg/dL	>110 mg/dL	>110 mg/dL
[4]Blood urea nitrogen	7-18 mg/dL	>30 mg/dL	>50 mg/dL (dehydration)
Creatinine (kidney)	<1.2 mg/dL	>1.2 mg/dL	>3 mg/dL (kidney failure)
Bilirubin (total, liver)	0.3-1.1 mg/dL	>2 mg/dL	>5 mg/dL
Thyroxin (T$_4$, thyroid)	4-12 ug/dL	4-12 ug/dL	4-12 ug/dL
TSH (pituitary)	0.5-5.0 uIU/mL	0.5-5.0 uIU/mL	0.5-5.0 uIU/mL
[5]Cortisol (adrenal)	15-25 ug/dL	<15 ug/dL	<5 ug/dL (adrenal fatigue)
Albumen	>4 g/dL	<3g/dL	<3 g/dL

Golden Hour Station 15 Fri. 10:45 a.m. - 11:45 a.m.

Chart XII: The above laboratory values are estimated by consulting scripture and science (chapters 4, 5, 10, 12, 13). The Hct[1] and Hb[1] values were sharply decreased by the rapid and large losses of blood; the WBC count[1] was acutely elevated to 35,000/mm^3 secondary to the severity of stress, shock-trauma, and acute inflammation; and finally, the neutrophils[1] increased from 60 percent to 95 percent of the WBC count. The platelet[2] and fibrinogen[2] levels were decreased due to the extensive clotting in multiple wounds and the presence of coagulopathy. The abnormal arterial blood gases (ABGs)[3] resulted from the chest wall and lung contusions: ↓P$_a$O$_2$ (respiratory hypoxia); the initial ↓P$_a$CO$_2$ resulted from "compensatory" hyperventilation, but on Calvary, it was reversed secondary to the onset of acute respiratory failure. Severe acidosis (↓pH) was the result of respiratory acidosis (acute respiratory failure) and lactic acidosis (multifactorial shock). An elevated blood urea nitrogen[4] was caused by severe dehydration and acute kidney failure. Decreased blood cortisol[5] levels resulted from adrenal fatigue (charts I, IV-B, V, VII-D, VIII-A, XI; figures VI, VII; chapters 4, 5; glossary).

Figures

FIGURE I — THE BLOOD AND THE WATER

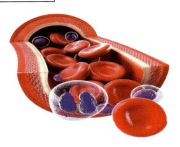

Figure I-A: Precious blood is "the life of the flesh for the atonement of sin" (Lev 17:11). The new blood covenant was cut and sealed with the shed blood of Jesus Christ—the absolute requirement for the remission of sins (Mat 26:28; Heb 9:22). The powerful blood of Jesus merits redemption, justification, reconciliation, and the unlimited access to God by a new and living way. The RBC's of the human bloodstream deliver O_2 for the production of energy; the WBCs defend against infection and cancer; and the platelets, clotting factors, and fibrinogen arrest of bleeding (chapter 7).

Figure I-B: Living water flowed from the Rock in the wilderness (Ex 17:6), the Jerusalem temple (Ezek 47:9), the heart of Jesus (Jn 7:38), and the heavenly throne of God and the Lamb (Rev 22:1). The sovereign Lord is the "source of living water" (Jer 2:13). Jesus's broken body/torn flesh resulted from His massive losses of body water and secondary cellular dehydration, dysfunction, and death (Matthew: 26:26; Hebrews 10:20; charts I, II-B). Life-giving water represents the Holy Spirit, the washing of the church by the Word of God, and eternal life. Water makes up 70% of the human body, 93.5% of blood, and 85% of the earth's surface.

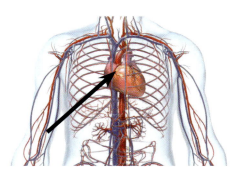

Figure I-C: The centurion's postmortem blow of the lance resulted in the flow of blood and water — blood from the right atrium and right ventricle and water (serous fluid) from the pericardial effusion (Jn 19:34; figure X; glossary). This dramatic event symbolized the massive losses of blood and water that caused Jesus's rapid death. The blood and water were the ransom Jesus offered the Father for the sins of humanity. The three witnesses—the Spirit, the water, and the blood—testify that Jesus Christ is divine and His eternal sacrifice merits infinite mercy, perfect grace, and eternal life (1 Jn 5:6-12). The incarnate Son is the New Temple of God: His blood and His water flowed down the slopes of Calvary, through the streets of Jerusalem, and to the ends of the earth. "If anyone thirsts, let him come to me and drink" (Jn 7:37; 19:34-37; Acts I:8; chart IX, see 17; chapter 11).

FIGURE II | HUMAN CELL – THE FUNDAMENTAL UNIT OF LIFE

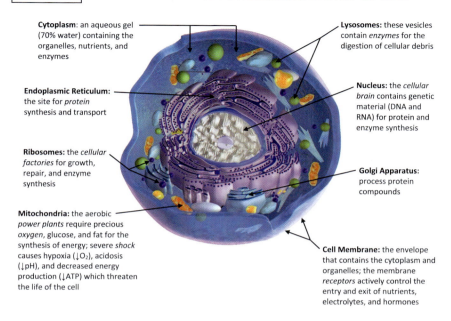

Cytoplasm: an aqueous gel (70% water) containing the organelles, nutrients, and enzymes

Endoplasmic Reticulum: the site for *protein* synthesis and transport

Ribosomes: the *cellular factories* for growth, repair, and enzyme synthesis

Mitochondria: the aerobic *power plants* require precious *oxygen*, glucose, and fat for the synthesis of energy; severe *shock* causes hypoxia ($\downarrow O_2$), acidosis ($\downarrow pH$), and decreased energy production ($\downarrow ATP$) which threaten the life of the cell

Lysosomes: these vesicles contain *enzymes* for the digestion of cellular debris

Nucleus: the *cellular brain* contains genetic material (DNA and RNA) for protein and enzyme synthesis

Golgi Apparatus: process protein compounds

Cell Membrane: the envelope that contains the cytoplasm and organelles; the membrane *receptors* actively control the entry and exit of nutrients, electrolytes, and hormones

Figure II: The humanity of Jesus Christ is described in scripture, "like his brothers in every way except sin" (Heb 2:17; 4:15). His human body—like ours—consisted of an estimated 100 trillion cells. Every type of cell possesses a unique function, size, shape, location, and life span. For example, the neutrophil (WBC) is an acute inflammatory cell that survives five to nine days, while the RBC contains Hb, a specialized protein that binds, transports, and delivers O_2 survives 120 days (figure I-A; chapters 2,7; glossary).

Jesus sustained an estimated 255 wounds, primarily BFT that lacerated and crushed billions of cells—skin, fat, muscle, tendon, and millions of small blood vessels (chart VI-A). Large losses of blood and water caused severe multifactorial shock with ischemic cellular death in multiple organs secondary to hypotension, hypoperfusion, hypoxia, acidosis, and coagulopathy (charts I, II-B, V, VII-A, VII-D). The pathophysiology of cellular death includes the following: injured cellular membranes permitted the abnormal influx of H_2O, Na^+, and Ca^{++}; clumping of nuclear DNA and RNA; inadequate synthesis of energy (ATP) by the mitochondria; and injured lysosomes caused enzymes release and cellular "autodigestion" (chart XI; figure VII; glossary).

| FIGURE III | **THE HUMAN BRAIN DURING THE PASSION** |

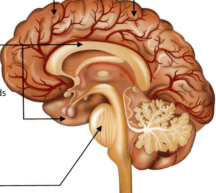

CORTICAL BRAIN

- Cognition
- Language
- Oversight
- Motor and Sensory functions
- Strategy
- Memory

LIMBIC BRAIN

- Amygdala: the nerve center that responds to fear, stress, and anxiety
- Hippocampus: the nerve center that responds to memory, emotions, and relationships
- Hypothalamus: the nerve center that activates the autonomic neuroendocrine systems of the body—the H-P-A axis, the SNS, and the PNS.

BRAINSTEM

- Respiratory center: spontaneous respiratory function
- Cardiovascular center: spontaneous cardiovascular function

Figure III: The complexities of the human brain are simplified into three neuroanatomical and neurophysiological regions: the cortical brain (cognition); the limbic brain (homeostasis); and the brainstem (life).

Jesus Christ sustained numerous stressors that activated His brain to prepare and adapt His body for survival (chart IV-A). In Gethsemane, Jesus was afflicted by life-threatening fear, sorrow, conflict, and agony (chart IV-B; chapter 4). Twelve hours later, He suffered lethal scourging, battery, and piercings (charts V, VI-A; figures VI, VII, VIII-A, VIII-B; chapters 5, 10, 13; glossary).

The psychological and traumatic episodes overwhelmed Jesus's limbic brain and autonomic neuroendocrine system including the H-P-A axis, and both the SNS, and PNS. He failed to restore homeostasis because of the rapid and extensive losses of blood and water, the absence of treatment within the golden hour, and the presence of adrenal fatigue (↓cortisol) with secondary adrenal shock (charts I, V, VII-A; glossary). The primary cause of death was decompensated multifactorial shock, cardiac arrest, and anoxia—deprivation of Jesus's vital respiratory and cardiovascular centers located in His brainstem (above).

| FIGURE IV | **MORTALITY PEAKS AFTER SEVERE TRAUMA** |

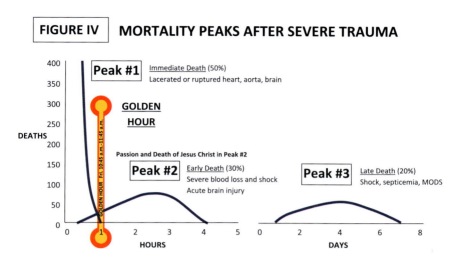

Figure IV: Major trauma is the fourth leading cause of death in the United States—60 to 70 percent of these deaths result from hemorrhagic shock. The above figure demonstrates that post-traumatic deaths fall into three mortality peaks: peak #1—the immediate deaths result within seconds or minutes after extremely violent trauma; peak #2—the early deaths result within a few hours following trauma in patients who failed to receive treatment within the golden hour (Jesus's clinical course was consistent with peak #2 since He was not treated during the golden hour, and died three hours later); and peak #3—late deaths result from serious complications that occurred days or weeks later (chart I, III, V; figure VI; chapter 13, stations 15).

In the Roman court, Jesus sustained severe scourging, defenseless battery, and piercings from the cap of thorns. He passed beyond the golden hour without treatment (Friday. 10:45 a.m.-11:45 a.m.) and survived for only three hours on the cross (Friday noon-3 p.m; figures VI, VIII-A, VIII-B). The clinical course of Jesus Christ 2000 years ago is consistent with the mortality peaks presented above (From Mulholland, M.W. et al. 2011. In *Greenfield's Surgery—Scientific Principles and Practice*. Philadelphia: Lippincott, Williams, and Wilkens, figure 17.2, 312).

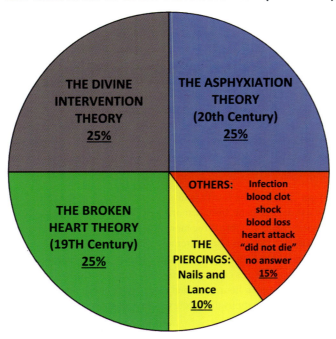

Figure V: This survey includes two hundred randomly selected Christians from all denominations. The conclusions reflect that the large majority of Christians believe in the *incorrect* causes of Jesus's death: the tetany/asphyxiation theory (about 25 percent), the broken/ruptured heart theory (about 25 percent), the divine intervention theory (about 25 percent), and the piercings by Roman nails and lance (about 10 percent). The correct causes of death include the following: acute stress reaction (ICD-10; chart IV-B); multiple wounds (chart VI-A), massive losses of blood and water (chart I), decompensated multifactorial shock (chart V), acute respiratory failure (chart VIII-A), and acute cardiac failure (chart VIII-B; glossary). Jesus arrived on Mount Calvary in critical condition secondary to the preliminary traumas and sufferings (chart III; chapter 12). Roman crucifixion did not cause the death of Jesus Christ (chart V; figure VI; chapter 13; epilogue).

The mystery of how Jesus died has been extensively investigated in this book by the following: (1) the absolute fulfillment of the prophetic scriptures (Lk 24:44; chart IX; chapters 1, 9, 12); (2) the theological effects of the Christ event, for example, "redemption by His blood" (Eph 1:7) and "access to God" by sprinkled blood and pure living water (Heb 10:19-22); (3) the transcendency of the blood and water (chart X; figures I-A, I-B, I-C; chapter 7); (4) the twenty-first-century medical sciences (charts I, III, V; figures VI, VII; chapters 4, 5); and (5) the sovereignty of our Lord and Great Physician who predetermined and coordinated the Son's incarnation, passion, and sacrificial death (Acts 2:23; chapter 13; epilogue; glossary).

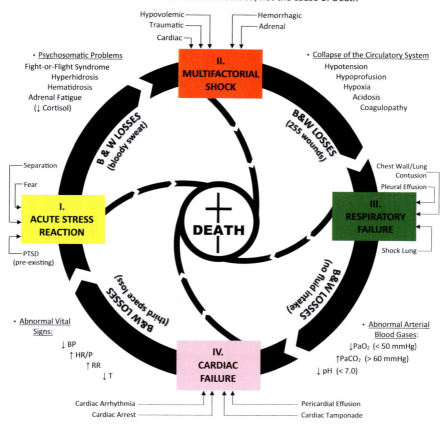

Figure VI: The death of Jesus Christ resulted from the PTS prior to His crucifixion (chapter 12). They caused four serious medical conditions (above) designated as Jesus's *cycle of death*. In Gethsemane, the life-threatening acute stress reaction was caused by the overwhelming fear of the impending separation from His Father and His violent death for the sins of the world. The lethal scourging in the Roman court caused multiple wounds, severe blood and water losses, multifactorial shock, and internal injuries of the lungs and heart (charts I, III, IV-B, V, VI-A, VII-A, VII-D, VIII-A, VIII-B, XII; figures VII, VIII-A, VIII-B; chapters 4, 5, 9, 12, 13, glossary).

| FIGURE VII | **MULTIPLE ORGAN DYSFUNCTION (MODS) IN THE PASSION**

- Multiple contusions of chest wall and lungs
- Bilateral pleural effusions
- Shock lung
- **Acute respiratory failure**

- Pericardial effusion
- Cardiac tamponade
- **Acute cardiac failure** and cardiac shock
- Cardiac arrest

- **Acute kidney failure:** was caused by rapid blood and water losses and severe multifactorial shock—hypotension, hypoperfusion, hypoxia, and decreased kidney function.

- **Blood loss:** 4-5U (estimated) caused class IV hemorrhagic shock
- **Water loss:** 8.0L (estimated) caused severe dehydration and acute hypovolemic shock
- **MODS:** decompensated multifactorial shock caused irreversible cellular/microvascular injuries and coagulopathy in **multiple vital organs**

- **Acute stress reaction:** caused secondary hematidrosis and adrenal fatigue
- The excessive **scourging, battery, and piercings** resulted in multiple wounds, partial-thickness skin damage, rapid B&W losses, and **decompensated multifactorial shock**

- The **limbic brain** was activated by multiple stressors: fear, terror, separation, trauma, blood and water losses, hypotension, and hypoxia
- The life-threatening **acute stress reaction** caused hematidrosis (blood and water losses) and adrenal fatigue (↓cortisol)

- The **pituitary gland** released ↑ACTH which exhausted the **adrenal glands** and resulted in adrenal fatigue (↓cortisol production and release)
- Scourging, battery, and piercings caused severe blood and water losses and acute multifactorial shock; **adrenal fatigue** and secondary **adrenal shock** influenced the severity of the decompensated shock and MODS.

- Abdominal scourging and severe shock caused **paralytic ileus** with third space fluid loss, abdominal swelling, and nausea and vomiting

- No broken bones (fulfillment of prophetic scripture)
- Scourging, battery, and piercings resulted in **255 wounds** and rapid losses of blood and water
- Mental and physical exhaustion resulted from severe mental afflictions and lethal shock-trauma

Figure VII: Jesus sustained shock-trauma secondary to multiple wounds, rapid and large losses of blood and water, and severe multifactorial shock—traumatic, hemorrhagic, hypovolemic, cardiac, and adrenal (charts I, V, VI-A, VII-A; figure VI; chapters 4, 5, 9, 12). In the absence of treatment, the pathophysiology was progressive—hypotension (↓BP), hypoperfusion (↓BF), hypoxia (↓O_2), and acidosis (↓pH) resulted in ischemic cellular and microvascular injuries and coagulopathy in multiple organs—lungs, heart, kidneys, liver, gut, muscle, and brain (charts VII-D, XI, XII; glossary).

The sovereign Lord and Great Physician predetermined and satisfied the modern medical sciences and choreographed the PTS, including the mental and physical afflictions that fulfilled the prophetic scriptures (charts V, IX; chapters 1, 4, 5, 12). Jesus passed beyond the golden hour on the Via Dolorosa without treatment and arrived on Mount Calvary in critical condition. His rapid demise resulted from decompensated multifactorial shock and the rapid onset of the multiple organ dysfunction syndrome (chapters 10, 13; glossary).

| FIGURE VIII-A | **SHROUD OF TURIN – FRONTAL IMAGE**

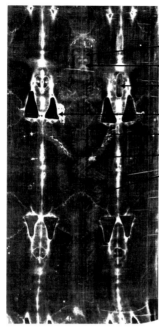

- The Shroud reveals swollen facial contusions (blood and water losses) and lacerations (blood loss); the nasal cartilage was minimally dislocated.
- Clotted blood (white) in His beard resulted from puncture wounds across the scalp (cap of thorns), and facial lacerations and nasal trauma (buffets).
- Fire damage (dated 1532).
- The centurion's BOL caused this collection of blood (white) from the right atrium/ventricle and water (serous fluid) from the pericardial effusion (figure X).
- Blood markings (white) represent clotted blood secondary to scourging, falls, and nails; microscopic haloes of serum surround each blood clot (chapter 6).
- This *divided* blood flow pattern resulted from the prominence of the ulnar styloid proximal to the Space of Destot (figure IX; chapter 9).
- Water stains from fire (dated 1532).

Figure VIII-A: This photographic negative of the shroud of Turin demonstrates the blood markings (white) and the body image (pale outline) of Jesus Christ resulting from His passion and miraculous resurrection event (chapter 6; glossary). Jesus was enshrouded with a linen burial garment according to the Jewish burial position—His wrists were secured across the groin (Mat 27:59; Jn 19:40). The lengths, ratios, and proportions of His body image are anatomically correct for the corpse of a Hebrew male—estimated to be five feet ten inches and 170 lbs. The man in the Shroud was tortured, beaten, scourged, crucified, and pierced with multiple thorns (scalp), nails (wrists and feet), and a Roman lance (right side of the chest; chart VI-A).

The large collection of blood and water (serous fluid) observed over the right chest was caused by the postmortem BOL (figure X). The divided blood flow marking on the dorsum of the left wrist is consistent with the exit wound of the Roman nail that passed through the space of Destot (figure IX). Extensive scientific research—microscope, laboratory, and computer—have authenticated the shroud of Turin as the 2,000-year-old burial cloth of Jesus Christ (chapter 6).

| FIGURE VIII-B | SHROUD OF TURIN – DORSAL IMAGE

- Multiple blood clots (white) are located over the scalp of Jesus—an estimated 36 piercing wounds caused by the cap of thorns (Chart VI-A).
- Jesus wore a ponytail.
- Prominent blood markings on the dorsal left shoulder resulted from Roman scourging (leather straps with lead dumbbells) and falls (Via Dolorosa).
- Severe Roman scourging caused multiple parallel wounds across Jesus's back—contusions, bleeding lacerations, hematomas, and mechanical burns; there were an estimated 255 wounds during the passion (chart VI-A; chapter 9).
- Dorsal pools of blood and water (serous fluid) resulted from the centurion's postmortem BOL that pierced the sacred heart of Jesus (Jn 19:34; figure X).
- Repairs from fire damage (dated 1532).

Figure VII-B: The photographic negative of the dorsal image demonstrates the multiple wounds and blood markings (white) secondary to the cap of thorns, defenseless battery (fists and rods), and excessive scourging (back, chest, abdomen, hips and legs). There were an estimated sixty to seventy lashes causing a patterned injury—repetitive stripes consisting of lacerations, abrasions, contusions, hematomas, and mechanical burns/skin damage (chart VI-A; chapter 6; glossary).

The falls on the Via Dolorosa resulted in abrasions, contusions, and sprains of His shoulders and knees. Pools of blood are identified across His lower back secondary to the postmortem blow of the lance (figure X). Blood markings (white) are visible on the sole of the right foot. The left leg appears to be shorter than the right caused by flexion of both the left knee and left hip—the result of postmortem rigor mortis (glossary).

Despite the severe trauma, the shroud of Turin does not reveal broken bones since prophetic scripture must be fulfilled—Jesus Christ is the unblemished Lamb of God (Ex 12:46; Jn 1:29, 19:36; chart IX, see 6; chapter 6).

FIGURE IX | SPACE of DESTOT — X-RAY of the LEFT WRIST

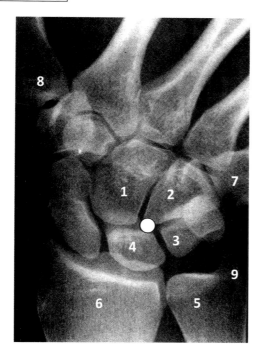

Legend

(1) Capitate ⎫
(2) Triquetrum ⎬ Space of Destot
(3) Hamate   ⎪
(4) Lunate   ⎭
(5) Ulna, left wrist
(6) Radius, left wrist
(7) Metacarpal of little finger, left hand
(8) Metacarpal of thumb, left hand
(9) Ulnar styloid, left wrist

Figure IX: This x-ray of the left wrist (palm up) demonstrates the space of Destot enclosed by four marble-sized carpal bones: capitate (1), triquetrum (2), hamate (3), and lunate (4). Together, they form a palpable anatomical depression located on the little finger side of the palmar wrist crease. The Roman executioner drove a four-sided, wrought iron nail through this space, which first expanded the space and then collapsed around the nail, providing rigid fixation between the wrist and the wooden crossbar (glossary, "crucifixion—Roman methods").

Since Roman discipline demanded assembly-line efficiency, speed, and control, the space of Destot was an excellent choice—rapid, effective, and secure. In my analysis of the shroud of Turin, the blood marking located on the dorsum of the left wrist is consistent with blood flow from the exit wound of the space of Destot (figure VIII-A); further, the divided pattern on the shroud was due to the prominent left ulnar styloid (9) observed above (chapters 6, 9; glossary; *Merriam-Webster's Medical Desk Dictionary*, 2005; Barbet, 1950).

| FIGURE X | **THE BLOW OF THE LANCE PIERCED THE HEART**

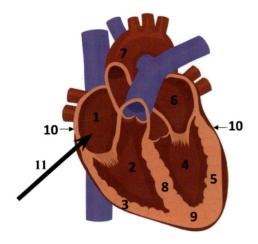

Legend
(1) Right atrium – venous blood from body
(2) Right ventricle — pumps blood to lungs
(3) Right ventricular wall (¼ inch thick)
(4) Left ventricle — pumps blood to body
(5) Left ventricular wall (1¼ inch thick)
(6) Left atrium — arterial blood from lungs
(7) Aorta – arterial blood to body
(8) Interventricular septum
(9) Apex of heart
(10) Pericardial sac — surrounds the heart
(11) The Roman lance pierced the right atrium and right ventricle

Figure X: The battlefield deathblow used by the Roman legionnaire was known as the blow of the lance (11; glossary). The approach of the lance was through the fifth rib space, just inferior to the right nipple (figure VIII-A). The right atrium (1) and the right ventricle (2) are located directly under the chest wall: note that the right ventricular wall (3) is much thinner than the left ventricular wall (5). Roman law stipulated that after crucifixion the centurion's BOL must precede the handing over of the corpse to the family for burial.

Following traumatic deaths, blood remains in its liquid state for some time due to the increasd fibrinolysin levels and the consumption platelets and clotting factors (chart XII; chapter 9); in addition, postmortem venous blood continues its return to the right atrium (1). Following the death of Jesus, the centurion's BOL resulted in the distinct flows of blood from the right atrium (1) and right ventricle (2) and water (serous fluid) from the pericardial sac (10; Jn 19:33-34). From my analysis of this episode, I believe that the presence of a pericardial effusion is the only medical condition that could have caused this unique pathophysiological phenomenon.

The sovereign Lord coordinated the postmortem flow of blood and water to reveal the following remarkable truths. First, it symbolized that the sacrificial death of Jesus Christ was caused by the losses of blood (shed blood) and water (broken body/torn flesh; Lk 22:44; Jn 6:51-58; 1 Cor 10:16; 11:23-26; 1 Jn 5:6-8). Second, it fulfilled the prophetic scripture (chart IX, see 6, 17, 19, 20): Jesus was the "unblemished Lamb of God" (the absence of broken bones), the Pierced One, and the New Temple of God (Jn 19:34-37). Third, the incarnate Son poured out His gifts on the church: His precious blood represented the forgiveness of sins, the eternal access to God, and the Lord's Supper/Eucharist and His living water symbolized the Holy Spirit, the new birth by water and Spirit, eternal life, the washing of the church by His word, and Christian water baptism.

Part III

The Passion and Death

Chapter 7

Introduction of the Blood and Water

As a specialist in orthopedic and trauma surgery, I have woven together my findings from three decades of scriptural and medical research to present an accurate and enlightening study on the nature and significance of the mental and physical sufferings inflicted on Jesus Christ. I reveal how each agonizing mental affliction and physical trauma was directly linked not only to the fulfillment and perfection of the prophetic scriptures but also to the comprehensive identification of His shed blood (blood loss) and broken body (water loss) for humankind to be redeemed from sin and restored to God.

During my analysis of the mystery of how Jesus died, I discovered that the sovereign Lord, the Great Physician, designed and directed a synergistic relationship between the fulfillment of prophetic scripture and modern medical science. When examined together, they result in a greater truth than if examined separately (Acts 2:23; charts I, IV-B, V, IX; figure VI; chapters 1, 12).

As examples, consider the sacrificial torture of the Suffering Servant (Isaiah 50:6, 52:13–14, 53:4–7, 11–12) and the Abandoned/

Righteous One (Psalm 22:1–28). The mental afflictions and physical agonies revealed in these two Old Testament prefigurements of Jesus Christ were masterfully choreographed and fulfilled in the New Testament, but they have a greater significance when considered in the light of modern medical science (chart IX, see 12, 15; chapter 10).

The blood and water are vital transcendent participants throughout the sacred scriptures (chart X; figures I-A, I-B, I-C). In the first place, the scarlet cord of Rahab is woven through God's Word and represents the power, protection, healing, forgiveness, and salvation of the sacrificial blood of Christ (Exodus 12:13; Leviticus 17:11; Joshua 2:18, 19, 6:25; Isaiah 53:5–7; Matthew 26:28; Luke 22:44; John 19:34; Hebrews 9:22;1 John 1:7; Revelation 7:14, 19:13).

Second, the crystal-clear rivers of living water flow across the scriptures symbolizing the Holy Spirit, the new birth, eternal life, and the "cleansing of the church with the washing of water by the word" (Psalm 1:3; Isaiah 44:3; Ezekiel 47:9; Zechariah 13:1; John 3:5, 4:14, 7:37–39; Ephesians 5:25–26; Revelation 22:1).

In this chapter, I discuss the exceptional roles of blood and water with reference to the medical sciences and the sacred scriptures:

1. the passion and sacrificial death included the following modern medical sciences— emergency and critical care medicine, psychiatry, surgery, and traumatology (charts I, IV-B, V, XII; figures I-A, I-B, I-C, VI, VII)
2. the fulfillments and perfections of the prophetic scriptures (chart IX; prologue; chapter 1)
3. the divine blood covenants that were cut, sealed, and memorialized with sacrificial blood and water (chapter 8)

Blood and Water

4. the theological effects of the Christ event that were empowered by the blood and life-giving water of Jesus Christ (Romans 3:25, 5:9; Ephesians 1:7; Hebrews 9:12, 22, 10:19–22)
5. the eyewitness testimony on Calvary by the beloved disciple that emphasizes the fulfillments of prophetic scripture along with the unique flow of blood and serum (water) from the pierced heart of Jesus (John 19:28, 33–37; figure X)
6. the shroud of Turin, which contains the sacrificial human blood and serum of Jesus Christ (figures VIII-A, VIII-B; chapter 6)
7. the three witnesses—the Spirit, the water, and the blood—who testified that Jesus Christ is divine meriting infinite mercy (Titus 3:5), perfect grace (Romans 5:20–21), and eternal life (Romans 6:23)

By His foreknowledge and predetermined plan, the sovereign Lord directed every episode of the passion and death: Jesus sustained a balance of mental afflictions and physical traumas that caused His rapid demise (Mark 15:44; Acts 2:23; 1 Peter 1:20).

As an example, Jesus was afflicted by a near-death experience in Gethsemane—the abrupt onset of severe fright, sorrow unto death, and conflict caused by His impending separation from the Father and His violent death for the sins of the world (Mark 14:33–36; chart IV-B; chapter 4).

Twelve hours later, He endured excessive Roman scourging, defenseless battery, piercings by thorns, and several falls on the Via Dolorosa, all of which caused multiple wounds and partial-thickness mechanical burns (chart VI-A). He also suffered massive and rapid losses of blood and water (charts I, II-B), severe multifactorial shock (charts V, VII-A), and serious internal injuries involving the lungs, heart, abdomen, and brain (charts VIII-A, VIII-B; figures VI, VII, VIII-A, VIII-B; chapter 5).

The mortal injuries that transpired *prior* to the crucifixion were the preliminary traumas and sufferings (PTS; charts III, V; chapter 12). Jesus arrived on Mount Calvary in *critical* condition prior to being lifted up. His rapid death occurred on a Roman cross but not because of the cross. This investigation reveals solid evidence beyond a reasonable doubt that the Roman cross did not kill Jesus Christ—it was His *deathbed* (figure VI).

On the night of His arrest (Thursday, 9:00 p.m.), Jesus instituted the Lord's Supper/Eucharist in the upper room to memorialize His imminent sacrificial death: the new blood covenant of grace would be cut and sealed by His shed blood (blood loss) and broken body (water loss; Matthew 28:26–28; 2 Corinthians 10:16; 11:24–26). His blood and living water were the ransom "offered" to the heavenly Father for the sins of the world (John 1:29), the eternal redemption of humanity (Hebrews 9:12), and the unlimited access to almighty God by a new and living way (Hebrews 10:19–22).

Modern trauma research reveals that arterial bleeding and hemorrhagic shock cause 60 to 70 percent of traumatic deaths (figure IV). The severity of hemorrhagic shock is based on the rate and volume of blood and water losses, the time required to arrest the bleeding, and the time required for resuscitation with blood products and crystalloid solutions.

The survival of patients with severe shock-trauma is improved significantly when treatment is initiated during the vital first hour following the trauma—the golden hour (charts I, V, VII-A, VII-B, VII-C, VII-D, XI, XII; figures VI, VII; glossary).

Major fluid losses (water) are routinely associated with severe blunt-force trauma such as the scourging, battery, and falls that occurred during the passion (chart VI-A). These losses are the result of torn and crushed flesh and lacerated blood vessels (Hebrews 2:14, 17).

Dehydration and hypovolemic shock are present in the majority of patients with shock-trauma (charts I, II-B, V, VI-A; figures VI, VII)). The scriptural terms—the "broken body" and the "torn flesh" of Jesus Christ—represent His severe cellular dehydration (John 6:53–56; 1 Corinthians 10:16; 11:24; Hebrews 10:5, 10, 20; chapter 9).

The shock-trauma sustained by Jesus Christ two-thousand years ago is comparable to the injuries treated today in level-I trauma centers with the obvious exceptions of auto crashes, explosions, and gunshot wounds. Jesus suffered multiple wounds (chart VI-A; figures IV, VIII-A, VIII-B), rapid blood and water losses (chart I), and severe multifactorial shock (chart V; chapter 5). The large third-space fluid loss resulted from

1. the initial wounds and cellular death caused by BFT (blood and water losses),
2. the bilateral pleural and pericardial effusions (water loss),
3. paralytic ileus (water loss), and
4. decompensated multifactorial shock resulted in secondary ischemic cellular death (charts I, II-B, V, XI, XII; figures VI, VII).

The destiny of the mental afflictions and shock-trauma suffered by Jesus Christ was significantly different from those patients of the modern era—the absence of emergency resuscitation, surgical intervention, and critical-care medicine in a level-I trauma center. When He arrived on Mount Calvary, Jesus had passed over the golden hour and was in *critical* condition with *irreversible* cellular and microvascular injuries. The passion and sacrificial death of the incarnate Son was predetermined and directed by the sovereign Lord and our Great Physician—His shed blood and His broken body (Acts 2:23; 1 Corinthians 11:23–26; Ephesians 1:9–10; Colossians 1:16, 20; 1 Peter 1:10–12; charts I, V, XI, XII; figures IV, VI, VII; chapters 5, 9, 12, 13).

Through His incomprehensible wisdom and knowledge, the sovereign Lord foreordained and choreographed the transcendency of blood and water throughout scripture as well as the principle cause for Jesus's death.

The Creation Story and Original Sin

Water played the prominent role in the primordial story of Creation: "In the beginning" … "formless" … and "darkness" … "the Spirit of God was hovering over the face of the waters" (Genesis 1:1–2 NKJV). God named the dry land "earth" and the basin of water the "sea" (Genesis 1:10; Job 38:4–6). The earth was formed effortlessly by the word of God (Genesis 1:6-7 NKJV; Psalm 33:4-6; Hebrews 11:3; 2 Peter 3:5).

A "stream welling up out of the earth was watering the surface of the ground and the Lord God formed man" out of water and clay (dust). The Lord God "blew into his nostrils the breath of life and so man became a living being" (Genesis 2:6–7). Our sovereign Lord and Great Physician instructed His creation, "The life of the flesh is in the blood"; the bloodstream (life) transports and delivers O_2 (breath), which creates physical life; the Spirit (God's breath) imputes the soul that creates eternal life (Genesis 2:7; Leviticus 17:11).

Following their original sin in Eden, the first garden, Adam and Eve were overcome by fear, shame, and guilt and covered themselves with fig leaves. I believe the Lord God used this unique opportunity to teach our first parents and Christians today a powerful lesson—the blood of sacrificial animals is necessary to cover sin and guilt (Genesis 3:7–21; chart IX, see 1, 2, 9, 20, 21).

Abel found favor with God by offering a blood sacrifice from his flock. By contrast, Cain offered the fruit of the soil, which displeased the Lord. Cain was downcast and filled with resentment, and he killed Abel (Genesis 4:4–8; Hebrews 11:4–5). The Lord God harshly chastened Cain, "Your brother's blood cries out to me from the soil (for revenge)" (Genesis 4:10; Hebrews 12:24).

The first recorded murder in scripture was caused by blunt-force trauma as follows: multiple wounds → blood and water losses → acute hemorrhagic shock → cardiac arrest → death. The deaths of Abel and Jesus Christ—the new Abel—were similar (charts I, V IX; figure IV).

The Ancient Patriarchs

Noah and his family were saved from the flood due to corruption and evil on earth (Genesis 6:5–8, 7:7, 17–22). The water symbolized baptism, which in turn represents salvation by the "washing of rebirth" (Titus 3:5). Christian water baptism prefigures salvation by our identification with Jesus Christ in His death and burial (down into the water) and His resurrection (rising out of the water; Matthew 3:13–17; Romans 6:3–4; 1 Peter 3:20–23 NIV).

The ancients quickly recognized the essential importance of blood and water regarding *life*.

1. Water was the most vital nutrient for survival—a provisional blessing from the Lord.

2. Pure, colorless, and active water was known as the water of life or simply living water—life-giving, lifesaving, and spiritual water.
3. The Hebrew sages and prophets revealed that almighty God was "the source of living water" (Psalm 36:10; Jeremiah 2:13, 17:13) and those who feared the Lord were "a fountain of life" (Proverbs 14:27).
4. The ancients were understandably terrified by the power and chaos of the lakes and seas that were effortlessly controlled by the authority of God's powerful word (Genesis 1:9–10, 7:6–23; Exodus 14:26–31; Job 38:8).
5. They discovered the preeminence of blood—the "shedding of blood" resulted in death (Leviticus 17:11–14).
6. Blood was the "seat and center of life"—the blood of every living creature was sacred, never to be eaten (Genesis 9:4–6; Leviticus 17:11–14; Deuteronomy 12:23–25).
7. Only blood could be offered on the Lord's altar for the atonement of sin (Leviticus 17:11; Deuteronomy 12:26–27).

The blood covenants of the great patriarchs consisted of promises, agreements, and treaties between two parties. They were sealed by mingling the blood of each participant or by the shed blood of sacrificial animals. To enter into a blood covenant or to "cut" covenant was extremely solemn since the animals that sealed the agreements were sacrificed by splitting them into two (Genesis 15:10; chapter 8; glossary); the life of each party hung in the balance. In the event of a covenant breaker, the result was that of the sacrificial animal—the "curse of death by bloodshed" (Jeremiah 34:18–20).

The new blood covenant of grace fulfilled and perfected the Old Testament blood covenants between the sovereign Lord and

Noah, Abraham, and Moses (chapter 8). This eternal covenant with humankind was cut, sealed, and memorialized by the sacrificial blood and life-saving water of Jesus Christ—our willing Victim and our eternal, great High Priest (Matthew 26:26–28; John 10:17; Hebrews 8:3, 10:11–14; chart I). He suffered and died as the sacrificial ransom offered to the Father that merited infinite mercy (Titus 3:5), perfect and inexhaustible grace (Romans 5:20–21), and eternal life (John 3:16).

The Life and Times of Israel

Yahweh's chosen people were His special possession, a kingdom of priests, and a holy nation redeemed by His powerful hand and mighty deeds (Exodus 19:5–6).

1. **The Passover.** Multitudes were freed from Egyptian slavery by the goodness, protection, and power of almighty God through the shed blood of unblemished sacrificial lambs sprinkled on the Hebrew doorframes with hyssop (Exodus 12:22). This monumental event was fulfilled and perfected 1,400 years later with the shed blood (hearts sprinkled) and pure water (bodies washed) of the perfect Lamb of God, who redeemed and freed humanity from the slavery of sin and death (John 1:29; Romans 8:1, 3, 21; Hebrews 9:12, 22, 10:22; 1 Peter 1:19; Revelation 5:6, 9; chart IX, see 6).

2. **The Exodus.** Almighty God delivered His people through the lifesaving waters of the Red Sea (Exodus 14:26–31); this was fulfilled and perfected by Jesus Christ, who passed over the earth making His exodus to the heavenly Father (Luke 9:31; John 13:1).

3. **The Mosaic Blood Covenant of Law.** Out of loving kindness, the sovereign Lord established a blood covenant with His chosen people that was mediated by Moses and ratified by the shed blood of slaughtered bulls (Exodus 24:3–8; Hebrews 9:18–22; chapter 8). The Old Testament promises were fulfilled by the new blood covenant of grace that was cut and sealed by the perfect and eternal sacrificial passion and death of Jesus Christ (1 Corinthians 11:23–26; Hebrews 9:11–15, 10:19–22, 13:11–12; chart IX, see 7).

The Day of Atonement, Yom Kippur, was a special feast day commanded by almighty God to graciously cover the sins of Israel from the previous year. Only once each year was the high priest permitted to enter the holy of holies inside the inner temple veil. He approached "the presence of almighty God" in the cloud above the mercy seat. However, he was not to enter the presence whenever he pleases: rather he must "bathe his body in water," wear the high priestly "sacred linen tunic," and bring the "sacrificial blood" of the bulls and goats with him— "otherwise he will surely die" (Leviticus 16:2-19).

The first goat was slaughtered, and its sacrificial blood was sprinkled on the mercy seat for the atonement of the nation's sins; the body was burned outside the camp (Leviticus 16:27; chart IX); the second or scapegoat was sent into the wilderness—the sins of the past year were "remembered no more" (Leviticus 16:20–22).

The sacrifices of the goats and bulls on the Day of Atonement were finite, imperfect, and temporary (Hebrews 10:1–4, 11–12). They foreshadowed the infinite, perfect, and eternal sacrificial death of Jesus Christ by His shed blood outside the gates of Jerusalem (Hebrews 13:11–14; chart IX, see 20).

As our great High Priest, the incarnate Son entered the heavenly sanctuary to offer the ransom of His precious blood and His pure, lifesaving water that graciously granted humanity's infinite forgiveness of sins (1 John 1:9) and gracious access to God by a new and living way (Hebrews 10:19–22). Since we possess this gracious access, "let us draw near by the blood of Christ" (Ephesians 2:13; Hebrews 7:19) and "let us come boldly to the throne of grace to obtain mercy and find grace in our time of need" (Hebrews 4:16 NKJV).

The remarkable story of Rahab the harlot foreshadowed the power, protection, healing, deliverance, and redemption of the sacrificial blood of Jesus Christ. The Hebrew spies were hidden, protected, and delivered by Rahab prior to the sovereign Lord's destruction of Jericho. For her own survival and that of her family as well as her belongings, Rahab fulfilled her oath by faithfully placing the scarlet cord in her window as a sign of her faithful presence (Joshua 2:17–21), and she abided under the power of that cord (Joshua 6:22–25).

About 1,400 years later, the *scarlet cord* of Rahab was fulfilled and perfected by the shed blood of Jesus Christ (Ephesians 1:7; Revelation 1:5, 5:9, 12:11). By her faith in the "mighty deeds of God" and the "scarlet cord," Rahab was honored by membership in the genealogy of Jesus Christ (Matthew 1:5) and the Hebrew hall of faith (Hebrews 11:30–31; chart IX, see 9).

Redemption and the Church Age

The sovereign Lord directed and coordinated the redemptive work of His beloved Son and the birth and growth of His faithful church by the truth, power, and conviction of the Holy Spirit (John 15:26, 16:8–15; Acts 2:23). The new blood covenant of grace was cut, sealed, and memorialized by Jesus Christ by His shed blood and broken body (Matthew 26:26–28; John 6:53–56; Hebrews 10:5, 10, 20; charts I, IV-B, V; figures VI, VII).

Following His triumphant messianic entry into Jerusalem, Jesus taught several Greek pilgrims, "And when I am lifted up, I will draw everyone to myself" (John 12:32; chart IX, see 8). When the incarnate Son of God was lifted up (Gr. *hupsóō*, "glorified") on Calvary, it represented not only His sacrificial death, but His miraculous glorification[5] that permitted Him to pour out the Spirit on the church (John 7:37–39, 19:30–34, 20:22; 1 John 5:6–12; chart IX, see 8).

There were two lethal episodes that revealed the preeminence of the blood and water during the passion—(1) the mental agony of Gethsemane complicated by hematidrosis (blood and water losses) and (2) the physical shock-trauma in the Roman court secondary to excessive scourging, defenseless battery, and piercings (severe blood and water losses; charts I, IV-B, V, VI-A, XII; figures VI, VII, VIII-A, VIII-B; chapters 4, 5, 9; glossary).

The incarnate Son was rejected, pierced, lifted up, and abandoned on His cross to fulfill the prophetic scriptures (chart IX, see 8, 12, 14, 19) and to reign majestically and gloriously from His wooden throne—the King of Kings. He spoke the seven words from His wooden pulpit—the Prophet, like Moses. And He offered Himself on His wooden altar—the eternal High Priest, like Melchizedek. Jesus Christ carried out the Father's perfect will by completing redemptive history and fulfilling prophetic scripture (Matthew 5:17-18; Luke 18:31–33; John 19:28–30, 36–37).

Prior to death, Jesus spoke these simple but extremely profound words: "It is finished" (the sixth word from the cross, John 19:30). Glorified by His sacrificial death, the incarnate Son "handed over the spirit" and poured out the Holy Spirit on the church gathered under His bloodstained and broken body (John 7:38–39, 19:30).

The wondrous drama of Mount Calvary concluded with a profound event—the centurion pierced the sacred heart of Jesus, and blood and water immediately flowed out (John 19:34; 1 John 5:6-8; figure X). His blood was symbolic of the forgiveness of sins, eternal access to God, and the Lord's Supper (chart IX, see 8, 9). His living water represented the Holy Spirit, eternal life, the washing of the church by the Word of God, and Christian water baptism.

The blood and water streamed down the rocky slopes of Calvary, through the streets of Jerusalem, across the Judean hill country, and to the ends of the earth (Acts 1:8). By His thorough identification with humanity, the incarnate Son merited infinite mercy, perfect grace, and eternal life. We are healed by His wounds, His spiritual, mental, and physical stripes. Our salvation is wholeness (Isaiah 53:5; 1 Peter 2:24).

The three witnesses of one accord—the Spirit, the water, and the blood—testified that Jesus Christ is divine (1 John 5:6–12). His divinity graciously merits infinite mercy (Ephesians 2:4), unlimited grace (Romans 5:20–21), and eternal life (Romans 6:22–23).

From Mount Calvary, the shed blood and the lifesaving, pure water of Jesus Christ continuously pour into Jerusalem and to the ends of the earth. "Let anyone who thirsts, come to me" … drink my precious blood and my life-giving water (John 4:14, 6:53–57, 7:37–39, 19:34;1 John 1:7; Revelation 7:14, 17, 21:6, 22:17).

The Last Days

The "Lamb that seemed to have been slain" is worshipped eternally by the heavenly hosts. The Lamb of God is called worthy because His precious and powerful blood "purchased the human race for [almighty] God" (Revelation 5:6–14; chart IX, see 6, 9, 20,

21). The saints "washed their robes white in the blood of the Lamb" (Revelation 7:14) and "conquered the devil by the power of the *blood* of the Lamb and the *word* of their testimony" (Revelation 12:11).

During the final judgment, the 144,000 were ransomed by the shed blood of the Lamb representing the first fruits of the human race (Revelation 14:3–5). An angel poured out God's judgment on the rivers and springs, which turned to blood since the corrupt people had "shed the blood of the holy ones and the prophets" (Revelation 16:5–7). The "great prostitute"—symbolic of the earth's evil system—was "drunk on the *blood* of the holy ones and the *blood* of the witnesses" (Revelation 17:5–6, 18).

Heaven was suddenly opened, and a white horse appeared with a rider called "Faithful and True." He wore a cloak that had been dipped in blood, and His name was "the Word of God … out of his mouth came a sharp sword to strike the nations" (Revelation 19:11–16). The New Jerusalem came down from heaven, and an eternal river of life-giving water flowed from the throne of God and the Lamb that sparkled like crystal and nourished the tree of life (Genesis 2:9, 3:22; Revelation 21:10, 22:1–2, 14). The Spirit will speak to everyone who thirsts for God: "Come …wash your robes, eat from the tree of life, and receive the gift of life-giving *water*" (Revelation 22:14, 17).

Blood

Blood (Lat. *sanguis*, Gr. *haima*) is defined by medical science as a living tissue— "the fluid that circulates through the heart, arteries, capillaries and veins, carrying nutrients and oxygen to the cells of the body."[6] Our Creator, Sovereign, and Great Physician proclaimed that blood was a vital theological and sacrificial substance, the "life of the flesh for atonement on the altar" (Leviticus 17:11–14). Since the advent of surgery, surgeons have expressed the greatest respect for blood; when a patient is clinging to life, every drop of blood is precious; it is essential for survival (figure I-A).

The bloodstream[7-9] consists of two major components: first, there are the cells—the red blood cell (RBC), the white blood cell (WBC), and the platelet (a cellular fragment). Second is the fluid component, the plasma or serum (plasma without fibrinogen), which is a mixture of water plus various ions, proteins, and other molecules (glossary).

Blood travels throughout the circulatory system, about fifty thousand miles of blood vessels consisting of the heart; the arteries that contain scarlet-red blood saturated with O_2 picked up in the lungs (chart XII); the capillaries that make up the microvascular circulation and are vital to each organ for the exchange of gases, nutrients, and waste products; and the veins that contain purplish, unoxygenated blood saturated with CO_2 returning for expiration by the lungs.

Blood is 93.5 percent water and comprises an estimated 5 to 6 percent of the human body. Jesus had an estimated blood volume of 10.0 U or 5.0 L: He lost about 4.25 U or 42.5 percent of His blood volume during the passion—a fatal condition in the absence of treatment during the golden hour (charts I, V, VII-B, XI, XII; figures IV, VII; chapter 9).

If a tube of human blood[10] is spun in a centrifuge or allowed to stand, it separates into three distinct layers.

1. The bottom layer consists of the RBCs containing hemoglobin (Hb), iron (Fe^{++}), and copper (Cu^{++}); this layer represents the Hct, normally 40 to 50 percent, and the Hb, normally 13 to 16 gm/L (chart XII).
2. The second layer or thin "buffy" coat consists of the WBCs and the platelets.

3. The superficial or amber-colored plasma layer makes up the remaining 50 to 60 percent.

The preeminent function of blood is the transport and delivery of precious oxygen to the cells throughout the body (figure I-A). In the lungs, O_2 diffuses across the alveolar-capillary membrane and binds to the Hb-iron complexes in the red blood cells. Oxygen is then delivered to the estimated one hundred trillion cells of the human body where the mitochondria—the all-important energy factories of the human cell—produce aerobic energy (ATP) by the following simplified equation (chart XI; figure II; chapter 2).

$$O_2 + fat + CHO \rightarrow ATP + CO_2 + H_2O$$

Severe multifactorial shock causes hypotension and hypoperfusion with the following serious cellular consequences: hypoxia ($\downarrow O_2$), acidosis ($\downarrow pH$), decreased energy production ($\downarrow APT$), and irreversible cellular injuries (charts V, XI). During a cardiac arrest, the neurons in the respiratory and cardiovascular centers develop severe hypoperfusion, hypoxia, and finally, anoxia; absent O_2, death will occur in about four minutes (figure III).

The importance of the perfusion of tissues with *oxygenated blood* to sustain human life cannot be overstated; for example, the absence of water intake (NPO) causes death in nine to twelve days, and the absence of food (starvation) results in death after forty to sixty days depending upon age and health.

After sustaining multiple wounds, severe blood loss, and acute hemorrhagic shock, Jesus developed critical sequelae secondary to hemorrhagic shock. First, the loss of RBCs caused a deficiency in the oxygen-carrying capacity of the blood or ischemia—cellular hypoxia, acidosis, decreased energy production, and irreversible cellular injury. Second, the loss of plasma caused a decrease in the blood volume that resulted in hypotension and hypoperfusion of the vital organs (charts I, V, VII-C, XI, XII; chapter 5; glossary). During World War II, the intravenous administration of plasma saved thousands of lives by expanding the blood volume, restoring blood pressure, and improving the perfusion of vital organs.

The WBCs defend and protect the body[6] by their unique ability to destroy and remove microorganisms (bacteria, fungus, and virus), dead tissue, foreign matter, and cancer cells. The multiple wounds sustained by Jesus were severely contaminated by a variety of foreign materials such as sand, dirt, gravel, fragments of wood, insects and their eggs, spittle, hair, feces, vomit, cloth, grass, thorns, seeds, leaves, and pollens. These pollutants along with devitalized tissues, blood clots, and plasma stimulate the first stage of immunity—the innate inflammatory response that includes the attraction of inflammatory white cells, the release of multiple inflammatory compounds (cytokines), and the arrest of bleeding by platelets, clotting factors, and fibrinogen (chart VI-B; glossary).

Within minutes, the traumatic wounds teem with neutrophils—the acute WBC response known as the storm of neutrophils. With a life span of only four days, the neutrophils diligently perform their duty to prevent infection as follows.

1. phagocytosis—engulf all foreign materials (above)
2. degranulation—release of inflammatory compounds (cytokinins) that excite the injured tissues by vasodilation (relaxing the arteries), increased vascular permeability, and diapedesis
3. chemotaxis—attract additional WBCs to the injured area such as monocytes.

During the passion, Jesus had a predictable sharp increase in His WBC count and percentage of neutrophils (chart XII; glossary).

The platelets (cellular fragments), the clotting factors (cascade of protein molecules in the plasma), and fibrinogen are present in blood to arrest hemorrhage (hemostasis) as follows.

1. The injured tissues and blood vessels stimulate the release of clotting factors.
2. The sticky platelets adhere to the injured blood vessel forming a platelet plug.
3. The clotting factors and fibrinogen construct a fibrin net that surrounds and consolidates the immature clot.
4. The platelets containing specialized elastic fibrils contract, express excess serum, and convert the platelet plug into a mature thrombus capable of preventing additional bleeding.[7–9]

Microscopic examination of the shroud of Turin demonstrates this amazing process—each blood marking (clotted blood) on the burial cloth is surrounded by a microscopic halo of serum (figures VIII-A, VIII-B; chapter 6).

An essential function of the bloodstream is to load, transport, and excrete waste products that accumulate in the body. For example, CO_2—the primary by-product of energy metabolism—must necessarily be delivered to and exhaled by the lungs. Excess nitrogen from injured and dead tissue is transported to the liver, converted to urea (BUN), cleared by the kidneys, and excreted. Severe shock causes cellular hypoxia ($\downarrow O_2$), the shift to anaerobic energy ($\downarrow\downarrow ATP$), and the production of lactic acid ($\downarrow pH$)—a toxic by-product rapidly converted to glucose. Jesus developed elevated blood levels of CO_2, BUN, and lactic acid during the passion (chart XII; glossary).

The endocrine glands produce vital hormones that are released, transported, and delivered by the bloodstream for homeostasis, energy production, growth, and repair. Hormones are molecules released by one organ, for example, the pituitary gland, which secretes ACTH into the bloodstream, which in turn stimulates a distant organ, for example, the adrenal glands.

The adrenals secrete epi, nepi, and cortisol (the stress hormones) to counter abnormal conditions, for example, the acute stress reaction and acute hemorrhagic shock. The multiple stressors that afflicted Jesus activated His limbic brain and autonomic neuroendocrine system for homeostasis and survival (charts IV-A, IV-B, V; chapters 3, 4, 5; glossary).

In conclusion, human blood is magnificent and incomparable[6-10]—the seat and center of spiritual and physical life. The shedding of blood is an absolute requirement for the forgiveness of sin (Leviticus 17:11; Romans 3:25; Hebrews 9:22;1 John 1:7). The indispensable red blood cell functions akin to a Swiss watch effortlessly loading, transporting, and delivering O_2 for the survival of trillions of cells.

Severe hemorrhage—a leak in the circulatory system—is a surgical emergency that must be arrested. Severe losses of blood and acute hemorrhagic shock are implicated in 60 to 70 percent of twenty-first-century traumatic deaths (figure IV).

The human bloodstream is a living, dynamic tissue—a system of fluid and cells in a continuous state of clotting versus bleeding. Shock-trauma interrupts this delicate balance strongly favoring a hypercoagulable state—an overactive clotting system that attempts to arrest hemorrhage versus a fibrinolytic system that dissolves clots to maintain liquidity.

For the circulatory and hematological systems, I praise the Lord along with the Virgin Mary in her *Magnificat*, "My soul magnifies the Lord" (Luke 1:46 NKJV; figures I-A, I-C).

Gary C. Hassmann, M.D.

Water

Water (Gr. *hydōr*)[6-9, 11] is the most essential nutrient for human survival. It is known as the universal solvent—unrivaled in its ability to dissolve and disperse numerous substances. The vital process of diffusion permits the rapid movement of water from one fluid compartment to another during emergencies—severe trauma, shock, dehydration, and electrolyte imbalances.

God's chosen people treasured life-giving water—the rabbis taught that living water was a provisional gift, a blessing from the Most High God of Israel. Hebrew sages contrasted the effervescent bubbles of pure, living water symbolizing wisdom, prosperity, and survival versus the stagnant, defiled waters of abandoned cisterns and contaminated ponds representing foolishness and destruction (Psalm 1:1–6, 42:1–2; Isaiah 43:20; Jeremiah 17:7–8; Ezekiel 47:9).

The healthy male body of Jesus Christ consisted of about 70 percent water. Many of His tissues and organs—like ours—contained even higher percentages, for example, the eye, blood, heart, muscles, and intervertebral disks.

The daily fluid intake for Jesus was an estimated 2.5 to 3.0 L (chart II-A). Beginning in Gethsemane, Jesus developed a negative water balance since He received nothing by mouth (NPO) and suffered large fluid losses secondary to hyperhidrosis, vomiting, hyperventilation, and third-space fluid loss (charts II-B, V, VI-A). Surgeons monitor their injured patients by carefully maintaining a twenty-four-hour record of fluid intake and output.

Water supports human life as demonstrated in the following examples.[7-9] The normal growth and development of a fetus takes place in the secure environment of amniotic fluid. Cerebrospinal fluid surrounds the brain both internally (the ventricles) and externally (the subdural space); the human brain is literally floating in the protective environment of water.

Water also provides the perfect environment for electrical currents required for nerve conduction and muscle contraction—the regular rhythm of the heart muscle, the split-second conduction of nerve impulses from the brain to the muscle receptors in the arms and legs, and the nerve impulses that proceed from the limbic and autonomic neuroendocrine systems in response to stressors such as fear, pain, blunt-force trauma, blood loss, and shock (charts IV-A, IV-B, V).

The major chamber of the human eye contains the aqueous humor, a gel-like fluid that maintains healthy levels of pressure and shock absorption. Tears moisten and lubricate the conjunctiva (the exposed outer surface).

Our joints and tendon sheaths are lubricated and nourished by the remarkable synovial fluid that affords low-friction motion. The intervertebral disk spaces of the spinal column contain a gelatinous material—the nucleus pulposus—that accommodates flexibility and shock absorption. The heart, lungs, and intestinal tract are surrounded by tissue paper–thin membranes (potential sacs) that secrete a serous lubricant that supports the gliding movements of pumping (heart), respiration (lungs), and peristalsis (intestinal muscle contractions for the movement of food, fluid, and air).

Fluid losses that are far greater than expected and unrecognized acute dehydration are frequent complications of severe blunt-force trauma. The resulting dehydration causes cellular enzyme dysfunction secondary to temperature abnormalities, acid/base imbalances, and abnormal concentration levels. In the absence of fluid replacement, dehydration and hypovolemic shock result in cellular injuries due to decreased energy production ($\downarrow$ATP; charts I, V, XI; chapter 5).

The broken body and torn flesh of Jesus Christ was the result of nothing by mouth, severe blunt-force trauma, enormous third space fluid loss, and *cellular dehydration*, dysfunction, and irreversible injury (Matthew 26:26; John 6:53–56; Hebrews 10:5, 10, 20; charts I, II-A, II-B, V, XI; figures I-B, II, VII). As the unblemished Lamb of God, Jesus did not sustain a single broken bone since the Old Testament prophetic scriptures must be fulfilled (Exodus 12:5, 46; Leviticus 4:3–5; Psalm 34:21; Luke 18:31–32, 24:44; John 19:36; 1 Peter 1:19; chart IX, see 6, 20).

This introductory chapter has highlighted the transcendent participation of the precious blood of Jesus Christ woven through the Bible as the *scarlet cord* of Rahab (Joshua 2:21; chart IX, see 9), and the *crystal-clear rivers* of living water that flow across the pages of scripture symbolizing the Holy Spirit, the cleansing of the church by the Word of God, eternal life, and Christian water baptism (Numbers 20:11; Ezekiel 47:9; Zechariah 14:8; John 4:10, 14, 7:37–39; Ephesians 5:26; Revelation 22:1).

By His set plan and foreknowledge, the sovereign Lord and Great Physician created and coordinated the transcendency of precious blood and life-giving water not only throughout the sacred scriptures, but also as the primary cause for the sacrificial death of Jesus Christ.

Consider the following mental afflictions and physical traumas.

- Jesus's bold pronouncement in the upper room, "My shed blood" (blood loss) and "My broken body" (water loss)
- the bloody sweat and ecchymoses in Gethsemane (blood and water losses)
- the onset of acute dehydration in the pit (water loss)
- the excessive scourging at the Roman pillar, battery, and piercings (fatal losses of blood and water)

- the traumatic falls, sweating, and hyperventilation occurred on the Via Dolorosa (blood and water losses)
- the postmortem blow of the lance with the immediate flow of blood and water
- the three witnesses—the Spirit, the water, and the blood—testified that our Lord and Savior Jesus Christ came by blood and water (human birth and baptism) and died by blood and water (human death).

REFERENCES

1. Harrison, R. K., editor. 1988. *Unger's Bible Dictionary.* Chicago: Moody Publishers.
2. Finegan, J. 1946. *Light from the Ancient Past.* Princeton: Princeton University Press.
3. Hengel, M. 1977. *Crucifixion in the Ancient World and the Folly of the Message of the Cross.* Philadelphia: Fortress Press.
4. Josephus, B. J. *Jewish Antiquities and the Jewish War.* Whiston, W. (Translation). 1960. Kregel Publishing. Williamson, G. A. (Translation). 1959. New York: Penguin.
5. Maloney, F. J. 1998. *The Gospel of John.* Collegeville, MN: Liturgical Press.
6. *Dorland's Illustrated Medical Dictionary.* 2012. Philadelphia: Elsevier, Saunders.
7. Gray, H. 2010. *Gray's Anatomy.* New York: Barnes and Noble.
8. Patton, K. T. and G. A. Thibodeau. 2010. *Anatomy and Physiology.* St. Louis: Mosby, Elsevier.
9. McCance, K. L. and S. E. Huether, editors. 2010. *Pathophysiology.* Maryland Heights, MO: Mosby, Elsevier.
10. Starr, D. 2000. *BLOOD.* New York: HarperCollins, Quill.
11. *Merriam-Webster's Medical Desk Dictionary.* 2005. Clifton Park, NY: Delmar.

Chapter 8

The Blood Covenants

The greatest event recorded in the Hebrew scriptures—the national epic of the Passover and the Exodus—reveals the redemption, purchase, and deliverance of God's chosen people by the sacrificial blood of unblemished lambs and the lifesaving waters of the Red Sea (Exodus 12:5–7, 21–27, 46, 14:21–22).

The Passover feast of that momentous event was celebrated 1,400 years later by Jesus Christ, who cut, sealed, and memorialized the new blood covenant of grace by His shed blood (blood loss) and His broken body (water loss). The incarnate Son fulfilled the prophetic scriptures as the perfect and eternal "Passover Lamb of God who takes away the sin of the world" (Isaiah 53:7; John 1:29; 1 Corinthians 5:7; 1 Peter 1:19; chart IX, see 6, 7, 15).

The new blood covenant (Gr. *diathēkē*, "covenant")[1–8] was mediated by the incarnate Son of God (1 Timothy 2:5; Hebrews 8:6, 9:15). He offered His sacrificial shed blood as the ransom paid to the heavenly Father meriting humankind with infinite mercy (Titus 3:5), inexhaustible and perfect grace (Romans 5:20–21), and eternal life (Romans 6:22–23).

This new blood covenant fulfilled and perfected many of the

divine promises in the Old Testament blood covenants (chart IX, see 7).

1. the Noahic blood covenant of new beginnings (Genesis 8:20–9:17)
2. the Abrahamic blood covenant of nation, land, and blessing (Genesis 12:1–3, 15:6–21, 22:15–18)
3. the Mosaic blood covenant of law (Exodus 19:1–24:11)
4. the prophetic words of the new covenant revealed by Jeremiah (Jeremiah 31:31–34) and Ezekiel (Ezekiel 36:25–27; chart IX)

We can assume the disciples were familiar with the Hebrew idiom "to cut covenant" (Heb. *berit*, "an unbreakable promise, agreement, or treaty sealed by blood"). Regardless, these Hebrew fishermen were unquestionably daunted and shocked when Jesus announced that He—not a sacrificial lamb—would cut covenant as the eternal sacrificial offering to God, pass over this world, and make His exodus to the heavenly Father (Matthew 26:26–28; Luke 9:31; John 1:29, 13:1, 3, 14:1–4; 1 Corinthians 5:7; 1 Peter 1:18–19; Revelation 5:6–9; chart IX, see 6, 7).

Ancient Africans and Syrians cut covenant to ratify or seal their solemn covenants by cutting the sacrificial animals in half and ceremonially passing between the two pieces. This was a hallowed and serious event since blood was considered sacred and synonymous with the life of every creature. If the covenant was dishonored, the covenant breaker was slaughtered as were the sacrificial animals (Genesis 9:4–5; Leviticus 17:11–14; Jeremiah 34:18–20).

Whenever two parties—friends, families, tribes, or nations—made the decision to cut covenant, a specific protocol was solemnly followed.

1. An unbreakable friendship was paramount—the sharing of similar needs and common goals.
2. The exchange of words and gifts that confirmed a lasting relationship— "What I have is yours, and what you have is mine."
3. A sacrificial ceremony sealed the blood covenant by the shedding of blood—the sacrificial animal was cut in half permitting both parties passage between the body parts thereby sealing the agreement.
4. A joyful celebration and memorial meal followed— "We are brothers of this covenant forever."
5. A landmark—a tree or pillar of stones—was established as the memorial of the covenant.

Jonathan, King Saul's eldest son, and David cut a blood covenant. Their solemn promise to each other was based on their mutual love and desire for security— "The Lord shall be between you and me, and between your posterity and mine forever" (1 Samuel 20:1–7, 41–42).

After Saul and Jonathan were killed in battle, King David honored his sacred covenantal oath by his provision for Jonathan's crippled son for the remainder of his life (2 Samuel 11:1–13).

Several unique factors underscore the solemnity, power, and eternal excellence of the *divine* blood covenants. The Lord revealed that "the life of the flesh is in the blood ... it is the blood that makes atonement for the soul ... no one among you may partake of blood" (Leviticus 17:11–14 NKJV; Deuteronomy 12:23–24).

Since blood is the seat and center of life, the Hebrew sages[2,3] concluded that the soul of a human being must reside in the lifeblood, making shed blood the absolute condition for the atonement of sin and the ratification of a covenant with almighty God (Leviticus 16:15–18, 17:14; Deuteronomy 12:23, 27).

Second, the blood covenants that originated with the sovereign Lord were far superior to those between human parties. Divine covenants do not cease to exist with the death of the human participants regardless of their stature, skill, or wealth.[2,3] Since humanity is foolish, imperfect, and temporary, it was almighty God—wise, perfect, and eternal—who stooped down in loving kindness to cut covenant with His fallen and helpless creation.

Divine blood covenants were unique in the following ways: His divine call contained an eternal purpose for His chosen people; the mandatory shedding of blood cut, sealed, and memorialized the covenant; the memorial meal and celebration; and the provision of a covenantal sign revealing the purpose and theological significance of the agreement.

The Noahic blood covenant (about 3500 BC) contained the fundamental provisions of an ancient blood covenant cut with the almighty God as follows.

1. The covenant was sovereignly designed and directed by the Lord (Genesis 9:9).
2. He alone drafted the covenantal promises— "I will never again destroy flesh with water" (Genesis 9:11).
3. God's instructions to Noah and his family were to return and repopulate the earth (Genesis 9:2, 7).
4. The *lifeblood* of every creature was to be considered as sacred, accountable to Him, and not to be eaten (Genesis 9:4–6).
5. The covenant was cut and sealed by blood sacrifices on the altar of God (Genesis 8:20).

6. The covenantal sign was given by God—a rainbow would be "set in the clouds" signifying to the people that "water will never again destroy flesh" (Genesis 9:13–17 NKJV).

The Abrahamic blood covenant (about 2000 BC) was cut and sealed between almighty God and Abraham, the revered patriarch of faith who "believed God, and it was credited to him as righteousness" (Genesis 15:6; Romans 4:3). The Abrahamic covenant contained the foundational promises that established the Old Covenant (Genesis 12:1–3, 15:9–11, 22:12–18).

The sovereign Lord's unconditional promises were made to Abraham and his descendants: first, the gift of land—the promised land known as Canaan; second, the creation of a great nation—people as numerous as the "stars in the sky" and the "sands of the ocean"; and third, eternal blessings were promised to the posterity of Abraham—they would become His "chosen people," His "royal priesthood," and His "holy nation" (Exodus 19:5–6).

However, the preeminent blessing was the Lord's promise of a descendant from Abraham's seed—the anointed One of God (Heb. Messiah; Gr. Christ; Matthew 1:1–2; Galatians 3:15–18). He would be the Son of Promise and the Redeemer who would establish the new blood covenant of grace, an infinite, perfect, and eternal covenant to be cut and sealed not by the sacrificial blood of animals split in half but by His own blood and life-giving water (Hebrews 9:11–15, 22, 10:11, 15, 19–22; chart IX, see 7).

Abraham possessed an uncompromising trust and belief in the one living God—monotheism. He obeyed God and transported his entire family to an "unseen distant land called Canaan" (Genesis 11:27–31, 12:1–6; Hebrews 11:8). By faith, Abraham cut covenant with almighty God based on the future unconditional promises of God (Genesis 12:1–3, 15:7–21).

The sign of the covenant was circumcision—the torn flesh and the blood shed that foreshadowed the death of Jesus Christ (Genesis 17:1–2; Matthew 26:26–28). Yet the new blood covenant of grace was to be a "circumcision of the heart" by the Spirit, not by law (Romans 2:29; 2 Corinthians 3:6). Abraham trusted God for the miraculous birth of Isaac, the son of promise, who would fulfill the Lord's promises and blessings (Genesis 18:9–15; Romans 4:19–22; Hebrews 11:11–12).

When tested by God in the land of Moriah, Abraham offered his only son, Isaac, whom he loved. But almighty God provided Abraham with a substitute—a sacrificial ram to be offered in the place of Isaac (Genesis 22:4–13; Hebrews 11:17–19; chart IX, see 4).

Abraham asked the Lord, "How am I to know that I shall possess the Promised Land?" The sovereign Lord cut covenant with Abraham, who split each of the sacrificial animals and birds in half and positioned the pieces opposite one another (Genesis 15:7–21; Jeremiah 34:18–20).

Alone in the darkness, almighty God passed between the carcasses—the sovereign Lord cut covenant, which included the unconditional promises for Abraham's descendants that must be fulfilled (chart IX). The pathophysiology of a sacrificial animal's death is comparable to human shock-trauma: blood shed (blood loss → acute hemorrhagic shock → death) and broken body/torn flesh (water loss → acute hypovolemic shock → death).

On Mount Sinai about three months after the Jewish Passover and Exodus, the sovereign Lord cut and sealed the Mosaic blood covenant of law with His chosen nation (Exodus 24:3–8). As the mediator, Moses sprinkled the sacrificial shed blood of young bulls first on the altar that represented almighty God and then on the people of Israel saying, "This is the blood of the covenant which the Lord has made with you" (Exodus 24:8).

Moses and the Hebrew leaders then celebrated the memorial meal in the presence of the Lord (Exodus 24:9–11 NLT). The sign of the Mosaic covenant was to keep the Sabbath day holy— "Six days you may labor and do all your work, but the seventh day is the sabbath of the Lord" (Exodus 20:8–11; Deuteronomy 5:12–15).

The new blood covenant of grace is the glorious good news of Jesus Christ, "the power of God for [our] salvation" (Romans 1:16). By His words and His works, Jesus Christ proclaimed that the signs of the new covenant were His shed blood and His broken body (chart IX, see 7).

- His greatest agony in the garden of Gethsemane was complicated by hematidrosis (blood and water losses) and adrenal fatigue (Luke 22:44; chart IV-B; chapter 4; glossary).
- He suffered brutal scourging and defenseless battery with severe blood and water losses (charts I, II-B, V, VI-A, XI, XII; figures VI, VII, VIII-A, VIII-B; chapter 12).
- He was pierced with thorns, nails, and a Roman lance causing blood and water losses (charts I, VI-A; figures I-C, VIII-A, VIII-B, IX, X; chapter 9).
- Following death, the sacred heart of Jesus was pierced by the centurion's blow of the lance with the immediate flow of blood and water, which represented (1) the cause and certainty of His death by loss of blood and water, and (2) the gracious gifts for the church (John 19:33–34; figure X; chapter 13; glossary).
- The eyewitness of the beloved disciple from Calvary— "the Spirit, the water and the blood"—testified that Jesus Christ

was divine and merited infinite mercy, perfect grace, and eternal life (John 19:29–37;1 John 5:6–12).

- The saints in heaven "conquered Satan by the blood of the Lamb" (shed blood), were washed by "the word of their testimony" (living water), and led by the Lamb "to springs of life-giving water" (John 3:5; Ephesians 5:26 NIV; Titus 3:5; Revelation 7:17, 12:11).

References

1. Tenney, M. C., editor. 1976. *The Zondervan Pictorial Encyclopedia of the Bible* (Volume I). Grand Rapids, MI: Zondervan.
2. Harrison, R. K., editor. 1988. *Unger's Bible Dictionary.* Chicago: Moody Publishers.
3. Youngblood, R. F., editor. 1995. *Nelson's New Illustrated Bible Dictionary.* Nashville: Thomas Nelson.
4. Ferguson, E., editor. 1999. *Encyclopedia of Early Christianity.* New York: Routledge, Taylor and Francis.
5. Stuhlmueller, C., editor. 1996. *The Collegeville Pastoral Dictionary of Biblical Theology.* Collegeville, MN: Liturgical Press.
6. Ferguson, S. B. and D. F. Wright, editors. 1988. *New Dictionary of Theology.* Downers Grove, IL: Intervarsity Press.
7. Kenyon, E. W. 2012. *The Blood Covenant.* Lynnwood, WA: Kenyon's Gospel Publishing Society.
8. Saia, M. R. 2007. *Understanding the Cross.* Fairfax, VA: Xulon.
9. Edersheim, A. 1961. *The Life and Times of Jesus the Messiah.* Peabody, MA: Hendrickson.
10. Swindoll, C.R. 2008. *Jesus.* Nashville: Thomas Nelson.
11. Stott, J.R.W. 1986. *The Cross of Christ.* Downers Grove, IL: Intervarsity Press.
12. Ratzinger, J. 2011. *Jesus of Nazareth (Part II).* San Francisco: Ignatius Press.
13. Sheed, F. J. 1990. *Life of Christ.* New York: Image Books, Doubleday.
14. Sheed, F. J. 1992. *To Know Christ Jesus.* San Francisco: Ignatius Press.

Chapter 9

My Challenges and Objectives

The sacred scriptures challenge us: "Do not to be led into error, but grow in grace and in the knowledge of our Lord and savior Jesus Christ" (2 Peter 3:17–18).

My great challenge and objective of the *Blood and Water* is to accurately and judiciously solve the mystery of how Jesus died by the synthesis of the following components.

1. the absolute fulfillment of the Old Testament prophetic scriptures
2. the theological effects of the Christ event, for example, freedom from sin and death and peace with God
3. the excellence of the modern medical sciences—emergency and critical care medicine, psychiatry, surgery, and traumatology
4. the transcendency of blood and water throughout the scriptures, but expressly in the passion and sacrificial death of Jesus Christ

Blood and Water

5. the sovereign Lord—our Great Physician and Surgeon—predetermined and coordinated each step and every drop of blood and water loss during the passion.

In the beginning of my studies, I was intrigued by the blood and water. My past surgical experiences and instincts persuaded me that the rapid and large losses of blood and water would solve the mystery of how Jesus died.

As my research progressed, it became increasingly obvious that the preliminary traumas and sufferings (PTS) were collectively responsible for the swift onset of His decompensated multifactorial shock and rapid demise (charts I, III, IV-B, V, VI-A, VII-A; figure VI; chapters 5, 12).

Early in the passion, the acute stress reaction in Gethsemane was complicated by two relevant and serious psychosomatic conditions: bloody sweat (blood and water losses) and adrenal fatigue (Luke 22:44; charts I, IV-B; chapter 4; glossary). The excessive scourging, defenseless battery, and piercings in the Roman court resulted in lethal shock-trauma with severe blood and water losses and injuries of the heart, lungs, abdomen and brain (John 19:1–5; charts I, V, VI-A; figures VI, VII, VIII-A, VIII-B; chapter 5).

In His foreknowledge, the sovereign Lord and Great Physician designated blood and water to be preeminent and transcendent biblical concepts (chart X; figures I-A, I-B, I-C; chapter 7). The scarlet cord of Rahab is woven throughout the sacred scriptures representing the blood of Christ—life, forgiveness, power, protection, healing, and salvation (Joshua 2:17–21, 6:22–25). The inerrant Word of God powerfully declares the preeminence of blood— "The life of the flesh is in its blood for the atonement of your soul" (Leviticus 17:11–14) and "Without the shedding of blood there is no forgiveness" (Hebrews

9:22). The rivers of living water flow across the pages of scripture from Genesis to Revelation representing the Holy Spirit, eternal life, and the washing of the church by the Word (Ezekiel 47:9; John 4:10–14, 7:38; Ephesians 5:26; Revelation 22:1). "Let anyone who thirsts come to me and drink" (John 7:37; Revelation 22:17).

After a careful analysis of the Old Testament prophetic scriptures that prefigured the passion, I was confident that both mental sufferings and physical traumas were responsible for the sacrificial death of Jesus Christ (chapters 4, 5). His rapid demise on Calvary was secondary to severe losses of blood and water, adrenal fatigue, and decompensated multifactorial shock complicated by the lethal triad. It is the *preliminary traumas and sufferings* that bear the burden of His mysterious death—not the Roman cross (Luke 18:31–33, 24:25–27, 44; charts I, II-B, III, IV-B, V, VI-A, VII-A, VII-D; figures VI, VII; chapter 12).

The following prophetic scriptures foreshadowed the death of Jesus including His mental sufferings (fear, conflict, and agony) and His physical shock-trauma (multiple wounds and massive losses of blood and water; chart IX; prologue; chapters 1, 7, 10).

1. the unblemished Levitical animal sacrifices of sheep, goats, and cattle (Leviticus 1–7; chart IX, see 20)
2. the shed blood of the Passover lambs (Exodus 12:5–7, 46; chart IX, see 6)
3. the daily and festival liquid offerings (Numbers 28–29; chart IX, see 20)
4. the Old Testament blood covenants that were cut and sealed by the blood of sacrificial animals (Genesis 15:10; chart IX, see 7; chapter 8)

Blood and Water

5. the Abandoned/Righteous One being tormented, pierced, and severely dehydrated (Psalm 22:1–28; chart IX, see 12)
6. the Suffering Servant—a lamb being led to the slaughter—who sustained wounds (stripes), contusions, multiple afflictions, and piercings (Isaiah 50:6, 52:14, 53:7; chart IX, see 15)
7. the Pierced One, who was looked upon and mourned by the inhabitants of Jerusalem (Zechariah 12:10; chart IX, see 19)
8. the slaughtered sacrificial animals offered on the Day of Atonement (Leviticus 16:1–19; chart IX, see 20)
9. the murder of Abel secondary to blunt-force trauma (Genesis 4:8; chart IX, see 3)
10. the sacrificial ram offered in the land of Moriah as a substitute for Isaac, the son of promise (Genesis 22:2–13; chart IX, see 4)
11. Job's mental afflictions and severe dehydration (Job 19:20, 30:30; chart IX, see 11)
12. The prophet Jeremiah, who was relentlessly persecuted by the Jewish religious establishment and the royal court—tortured, scourged, and thrown into a pit (Jeremiah 37:15–16 NLT; chart IX, see 16)
13. Eleazar, an elderly Jewish scribe who was fatally scourged for his uncompromising obedience to the Mosaic Law (2 Maccabees 6:28–31; chart IX, see 10).

On the night of His betrayal and arrest, Jesus boldly proclaimed that He would cut and seal the new blood covenant of grace: "my shed blood" (blood loss → acute hemorrhagic shock → death) and "my broken body" (water loss → severe dehydration → death; Matthew 26:26–28; John 6:53–56; Hebrews 10:5, 10, 20).

The signs of the new blood covenant were the precious blood and the living water of Jesus Christ (Luke 22:44; John 7:37–39, 19:34; Romans 5:9; Ephesians 1:7; Hebrews 10:19–22;1 John 1:7, 5:6–8; Revelation 5:6–9, 7:14, 17, 12:11, 22:1, 17; chapter 8).

The three witnesses of one accord—the Spirit, the water and the blood—testify that Jesus is divine meriting humanity with infinite mercy, perfect grace, and eternal life. The Spirit of truth bears witness that the incarnate Son came by blood and water (human birth and baptism) and died by blood and water (human death; John 15:26;1 John 5:6–12).

From Mount Calvary, the eyewitness testimony of the beloved disciple declared with a master's touch that the incarnate Son fulfilled and perfected the prophetic scriptures: He was the "unblemished Lamb" (Exodus 12:5–7, 46; John 19:36; chart IX, see 6), the "Pierced One" (Zechariah 12:10; John 19:37; chart IX, see 19), and the "New Temple of God" (John 2:19–22; chart IX, see 17). Blood and water dripped from the pierced heart of Jesus Christ onto the skull of Adam, flowed across the footprints of Abraham and Isaac, poured through the streets of Jerusalem, and powerfully surged to the ends of the earth (Acts 1:8). "If you thirst, come to me" ... drink my precious blood and my life-saving water (John 4:14, 6:53–57, 7:37, 19:34; Revelation 7:14, 17, 12:11, 22:17; figure X).

According to Peter, Jesus was the "unblemished lamb without spot"—His blood was the perfect and eternal ransom "offered" to the heavenly Father as payment in full for the sins of the world (1 Peter 1:18–19). His wounds (stripes) consisted of both mental and physical afflictions that grant the healing and the wholeness of our salvation (Isaiah 53:5; 1 Peter 2:24).

The apostle Paul revealed the healing power and sanctifying grace of the blood and water by his instructions concerning the Lord's

Supper or Eucharist: "shed blood" (blood loss → acute hemorrhagic shock → death) and "broken body" (water loss → severe dehydration → death; 1 Corinthians 10:16, 11:23–26). Accordingly, the theological effects of the Christ event emphasize the supernatural power and the supreme effectiveness of the blood of Christ: for example, expiation by His blood (Romans 3:25), redemption by His blood (Ephesians 1:7), and justification by His blood (Romans 5:9).

Pauline theology reveals that the blood and water of Jesus Christ merited eternal access to the Father by a new and living way— "our hearts are sprinkled" by His blood, and "our bodies are washed" by His pure and living water (Romans 5:2; Ephesians 2:13; Hebrews 4:16, 6:19-20, 10:19-22).

The shroud of Turin contains the miraculous presence of the human blood and serum (water) of Jesus Christ[1] that dramatically reveals His scourging, battery, and piercings by thorns (scalp), nails (hands and feet), and Roman lance (chest and heart). His serum may be observed on the shroud as microscopic halos surrounding each blood clot. The face cloth of Jesus contains fluid consistent with pulmonary edema[1] that drained from His mouth while in the garden tomb (Matthew 27:59; John 19:40, 20:7; figures VIII-A, VIII-B, IX, X; chapter 6).

The unlettered physicians and surgeons of the ancient era were powerless to solve the mystery of how Jesus died. Hippocrates[2] (450–370 BC) and Galen[2] (AD 129–216) were Greek physicians who established a medical regime for disease and trauma known as Galenism—an accepted form of medical practice through the eighteenth century. Dr. Galen's method strived to restore the balance of the body's four fluids or *humours*—blood, lymph (water), yellow bile (gastrointestinal system), and black bile (nervous system). By modern standards, Galenism is an archaic practice that included blood-letting (withdrawing blood) and cupping (removing water).[2]

The advancements in the medical sciences since the seventeenth century have been extraordinary particularly in those specialties identified with the passion—emergency and critical-care medicine, psychiatry, surgery, and traumatology. The following medical discoveries have supported me during my challenges and objectives to solve the mystery of how Jesus died (glossary).

1. the microscope[2] and cellular theory[2]—the cell is the fundamental unit of human life (1700; figure II; chapter 2)
2. the human body consisting of multiple organ systems (1400; figure VII)
3. humankind's survival that required the responses of homeostasis[2] (1800–2000; chapter 3)
4. the limbic brain and the H-P-A axis—the general adaptation syndrome[4] (1940s; charts IV-A, IV-B, V; figure III; chapter 4)
5. the pathophysiology[14] of the shock syndrome including third-space fluid loss, resuscitation, and blood banks[15] (1940 to the present; charts V, VII-A, VII-B; chapter 5)
6. the calculation of fluid intake and output (1900s; chart II-A)
7. intravenous blood transfusions[2,3,14,15] with whole blood and blood components—packed red cells, plasma, platelets, and fibrinogen—along with intravenous crystalloid solutions (1941 to the present; chart VII-B)
8. the acute inflammatory response[13] (1800s to the present; chart VI-B)
9. post-traumatic stress disorder (ICD-10;[3,4] 1980 to the present; chart IV-A; chapter 4)
10. the fight-or-flight syndrome[4] (1940s; chart IV-B; chapter 4)

11. pulmonary contusion, shock lung, and acute respiratory distress syndrome[3,14] (1970s; chart VIII-A; chapter 5)
12. diffuse axonal injury (concussion; 2005 to the present)
13. multiple organ dysfunction syndrome (1970s)
14. the concept of the golden hour[14] (1980s; charts I, V, XI, XII; figure IV; chapter 13)

The clinical history (subjective) and physical examination (objective) of the human Jesus were challenging (chapter 5). However, to meet this extraordinary challenge, I must understand the supreme truth—Who is Jesus Christ?

The sacred scriptures[21,22] reveal the answer to this profound question: "In the beginning was the Word...And the Word became flesh and made His dwelling among us" (John 1:1-2, 14). The Son assumed human flesh and blood and thoroughly identified with each of us to accomplish our salvation—He was "like His brothers in every way except sin" (1 Timothy 2:5–6; 1 Timothy 3:16; Hebrews 2:14–18, 4:15). The *enfleshed* Son of God is both true God and true man. However, during His passion and sacrificial death, He was in solidarity with humankind, and therefore, my assessments of His psychopathology and pathophysiology are undertaken in His humanity.

The incarnation—the first step of the passion and sacrificial death—was the unfathomable, supernatural event that sent the enfleshed Son of God to earth in the form and nature of a human being (Philippians 2:6–8; Hebrews 2:14, 10:5, 10, 20). The incarnate Son thoroughly identified with each member of the human race as He suffered from the human stressors of fear, agony, conflict, pain, wounds, hemorrhage, dehydration, decompensated shock, hypoxia, and serious internal injuries (chart IV-A). From my analysis, I concluded that the incarnate Son's mental afflictions and physical traumas were perfectly consistent with those suffered by humankind throughout medical history (figure IV).

In addition, the sovereign Lord, our Great Physician, coordinated and directed the nativity and the passion of Jesus Christ in the light of ordinary human people, places, and events—an innocent and unremarkable Hebrew girl, the small village of Bethlehem, an animal shelter with an ox and a donkey, and defiled shepherds.

In a similar manner, Jesus suffered and died from very common medical conditions in order to totally identify with His brothers and sisters—fear, agony, blunt-force trauma, blood and water losses, dehydration, hemorrhagic shock, and bruised lungs. In His foreknowledge, the sovereign Lord, the Great Physician, did not plan for the passion and death of Jesus to include rare and complex disorders such as tetany/asphyxiation, a broken/ruptured heart, and divine intervention (figure V).

Several years ago, Dr. Raymond E. Brown,[5] a prominent Christian author, wrote the following provocative challenge concerning the passion: "In my judgement the major defect of most studies of the physical death of Jesus was that they were written by doctors who did not stick to their trade" (epilogue).

I welcomed his challenge as an opportunity to utilize my spiritual gifts—a summons to action. My short answer for Dr. Brown is the research in this book. However, as you will come to appreciate, the mystery of how Jesus died is solved by much greater forces than the medical sciences by themselves. It is the synthesis of several factors—the absolute fulfillment of the prophetic scriptures, the transcendent participation of the blood and water, the effects of the Christ event, the modern medical sciences, and the sovereignty of the Lord's set plan and foreknowledge (Acts 2:23).

To collect my thoughts, I embarked on these challenges and objectives: to investigate the publications that concerned the passion, to make pilgrimages to Jerusalem and Rome to study, meditate, and personally experience the Lord's passion, and to conduct a survey of Christians' responses to the question "What caused the death of Jesus Christ?" (figure V).

The results of my survey consisted of the following answers (figure V).

1. the divine-intervention theory (25 percent)
2. the broken or ruptured heart theory (25 percent)
3. the tetany/asphyxiation theory (25 percent)
4. the piercing theory by Roman nails and lance (10 percent)
5. miscellaneous responses (15 percent)

In the following, I will discuss, debate, refute, and discredit these incorrect yet still standing causes for the death of Jesus Christ.

The divine-intervention theory was an unexpected response. Many of the participants simply answered, "God took Him to stop the intolerable pain and horrific suffering." However, there are strong theological objections to this theory, most important, the direct hindrance and opposition by almighty God make it impossible for the willing sacrificial death of Jesus Christ to forgive the sins of the world. This theory is unthinkable, beyond comprehension, impossible, and untenable! It must be strongly repudiated, rejected, and discredited since it strikes a mortal blow to the fulfillment of prophetic scripture, the effects of the Christ event, the gospel, Christology, and the redemption of humanity.

The divine-intervention theory does not fulfill the prophetic scriptures or preserve the sacred unity of the bible (Matthew 5:17-18; Luke 18:31–33, 24:25–27, 44; chart IX; chapter 1). Further, it fails to properly represent human death—a necessity since Jesus Christ *represented* humanity for the remedy of sin and death and the reversal of the curse. The incarnate Son must fulfill and perfect the Old Testament prophecies which included mental afflictions and physical sufferings such as fear, agony, abandonment, conflict, sorrow, multiple wounds, massive losses of blood and water, and decompensated multifactorial shock (charts I, IV-B, V, VI-A, IX, see 1, 2, 20, 21; figure VI).

His mental and physical agonies caused the blood and water losses required to pay the ransom for humankind's sin debt and guilt (Isaiah 53:5; Matthew 26:26–28; Mark 10:45; Hebrews 9:22, 10:19–22; 1 Peter 1:18–19, 2:24; chart I). Jesus Christ—the last Adam—was in solidarity with the human race: in Adam, "One man's sin brings condemnation and death," but in Christ, "One act of righteousness brings forgiveness, a right relationship with God, and eternal life" (Romans 5:18–21 NLT; chart IX, see 1).

The sovereign Lord sent His beloved, incarnate Son to represent each individual of the fallen human race during His passion and sacrificial death—death by His shed blood and His broken body and torn flesh to merit the following blessings.

1. infinite mercy (Titus 3:5)
2. perfect and inexhaustible favor (Romans 5:20–21)
3. eternal life (Romans 6:23)
4. the Holy Spirit for conviction, truth, sanctifying grace, and new life (John 14:25, 16:7–11, 17:17–19)
5. unlimited access to the heavenly Father by a new and living way (John 14:6; Hebrews 4:16, 10:19–22).

About 10 percent of those surveyed believed the piercings with the nails and lance caused Jesus's death. In the first place, the centurion's blow of the lance—the Roman deathblow that pierced the heart of Jesus—was a postmortem event: "When they came to Jesus, (they) saw that He was already dead" (John 19:33–34; figures VIII-A, VIII-B, X; glossary).

The well-trained Roman executioners drove their iron nails into specific, secure, and relatively safe anatomical sites such as the space of Destot to avoid major blood vessels and vital organs (figure IX). In the absence of the preliminary traumas and sufferings, routine Roman crucifixions resulted in minimal amounts of blood loss, an estimated 0.5 U. During the Jewish-Roman War (AD 70), an estimated thirty thousand Jewish prisoners were crucified without PTS, "some of whom survived for 5–9 days."[6–9] The blood markings on the shroud of Turin at the nail sites of the wrists and feet reveal minimal collections of clotted blood (figures VIII-A, VIII-B). In addition, trauma surgeons routinely insert nails, plates, rods, and screws in patients sustaining fractures; the surgical hardware is rarely if ever responsible for a significant loss of blood, shock, or death.

The broken/ruptured heart theory was introduced in the nineteenth century. This proposal consisted of the violent rupture of the myocardium (heart muscle) causing massive internal hemorrhage, cardiac arrest, and death. However, the sacred scriptures are the inerrant authority (Matthew 5:18; 2 Timothy 3:16): the presence of shed blood or external hemorrhage is a nonnegotiable requirement for the remission of sins (Leviticus 16:3,14-15,18-19; 17:11; Matthew 26:28; Hebrews 9:22, 12:24, 13:11–12).

Modern medicine teaches us that sorrow and grief do not cause the heart muscle to rupture. However, there does exist a pious, unbreakable love affair between extremely devout Christians and the Lord Jesus; they strongly believe that the heart of Jesus was literally broken on the cross caused by His heartfelt grief and profound sorrow because of humanity's sin, evil, and corruption (Proverbs 6:16–19; Romans 1:18–32; Mark 14:33–36, 15:34; Luke 22:43–44).

Dr. Stroud (1874) was a strong advocate of the broken-heart theory.[5, 10, 11] In general, he contended that the emotional grief of Jesus Christ from the reign of evil on earth predisposed the rupture of His myocardium (glossary). Stroud also theorized that after the myocardial rupture, Jesus's blood filled the pericardial sac surrounding the heart and immediately separated into red blood cells and serum; he then reasoned that the centurion's postmortem BOL resulted in the distinct flows of "blood" (red blood cells) and "water" (serum; John 19:34; figure X).

However, recent medical research has reversed this theoretical pathophysiology[6, 12–16] as follows.

1. Cardiac rupture does *not* result from psychological grief and sorrow; it is caused by a mortal myocardial injury secondary to violent trauma such as an auto crash or fall from a distance, or a massive myocardial infarction (figure IV; glossary).
2. In the event of survival from the initial event, both of these myocardial injuries are followed by an acute inflammatory response that includes the ingrowth of soft granulation tissue (capillaries and fibrous tissue).
3. A rupture is extremely rare and delayed four to five days when the tensile strength of the muscle is considerably weaker.

Regarding those patients who, similar to Jesus, die from shock-trauma, their blood does *not* immediately clot and separate into red blood cells and serum. The reasons for this are twofold: (1) there are decreased levels of circulating platelets and fibrinogen secondary to the major clotting of the multiple wounds and (2) there are elevated levels of plasmin that counter the hypercoaguable state to maintain the fluidity of the bloodstream—fibrinolysis (chart XII; chapters 5, 7; glossary). Therefore, the postmortem BOL that pierced the sacred heart of Jesus resulted in *separate* streams of (1) the blood from the right atrium and ventricle and (2) the serum (water) from the pericardial effusion (John 19:33-34; charts VII-A, VIII-B; figures I-C, VI, VII, VIII-A, X; glossary).

During the twentieth and twenty-first centuries, the most popular belief for the death of Jesus was the tetany/asphyxiation theory (figure V; glossary). This method of torture and execution originated in the German death camps[6] during World War I. Prisoners of war were hanged by their wrists some distance from the ground resulting in muscle stretching, exhaustion, and tetany that included the muscles of respiration. After two to three hours of excruciating fear, horror, and terror, a violent death resulted from *suffocation*—the inability to exhale CO_2 and inhale O_2.

Two French surgeons, Dr. Henry LeBec[17] (1926) and Dr. Pierre Barbet[6] (1950), presented their research that attempted to translate the pathophysiology of German death camp tetany/asphyxiation to the Roman crucifixion of Jesus Christ. Medical publications by Dr. R. W. Hynec[11] reported that Jesus's death was caused by tetany/asphyxiation with secondary pulmonary edema." Although never proven scientifically, this theory remains popular in the medical, ecclesiastical, and journalistic establishments (Edwards,[18] Renner,[19] O'Reilly,[20] *The Committee of Ignatius Study Bible*,[21] and the *MacArthur Study Bible*[22]).

The pathophysiology of death by tetany/asphyxiation[6,11] may be briefly summarized as follows: the victim was freely hanged by both wrists about ten inches apart and the feet about two feet above the surface. The muscles of the upper extremities, shoulders, chest, back, and abdomen (including the muscles of respiration) were rapidly compromised by prolonged stretching, intracellular chemical imbalances ($\downarrow Ca^{++}$ and $\uparrow pH$), and decreased cellular energy production ($\downarrow ATP$). As the muscle exhaustion and tetany (spasms) progressed, the victim sagged down to rest preventing the normal respiration to exhale CO_2 and to inhale O_2.

To stabilize the respiratory muscles, exhale CO_2, and finally inhale O_2, the terrified victim "pulled himself up." This human instinct to survive—the sagging down to rest and the lifting up to breathe—resulted in severe muscular fatigue, excruciating spasms and tetany, and death by asphyxiation (suffocation).

The clinical manifestations of tetany/asphyxiation as interpreted by an eyewitness[6] are summarized as follows. The execution was characterized as "horrific"—terror, agitation, abdominal distention, expansion of the chest cage, stiff and motionless legs, cyanosis, and hyperhidrosis. The corpse was described as "violet" (cyanosis) and "rigid" (tetany). The mechanism of death was similar to strangulation—the inability of the victim to exhale CO_2 (respiratory hypercapnea and acidosis) and inhale O_2 (respiratory hypoxia).

Dr. Barbet's research[6] is summarized as follows: The rapid death of Jesus Christ was caused by tetany/asphyxiation secondary to Roman crucifixion. However, during my extensive investigation, I discovered several significant discrepancies that are discussed below.

In the first place, Dr. Barbet did not introduce the fulfillment of prophetic scripture as evidence for tetany/asphyxiation. Second, many of the important medical discoveries of the late twentieth and twenty-first centuries had not yet been made available: for example, shock-trauma, third-space fluid loss, the golden hour, pulmonary contusion, coagulopathy, and adrenal fatigue. Third, Dr. Barbet incorrectly correlated the pathophysiology of German death-camp asphyxiation with his tenuous findings gleaned from the shroud of

Blood and Water

Turin as his "smoking gun" that solved the mystery of how Jesus died.

To begin, Dr. Barbet was convinced that the shroud demonstrated a "protuberant abdomen" and a "distended chest cage" concluding that both conditions were secondary to "air trapping" in the lungs. However, I disagree with his opinions based solely upon the shroud of Turin in favor of paralytic ileus—a common abdominal condition observed during shock-trauma and abdominal blunt-force trauma (chapter 5; glossary).

Based on the shroud of Turin, Dr. Barbet recognized that the blood marking on the dorsal surface of the left wrist was bifurcated—a divided pattern of blood flow (figure VIII-A). However, he erroneously concluded that with each episode of "sagging down and lifting up" during tetany/asphyxiation, Jesus's wrists rotated around the nails resulting in the divided flow of blood. In my analysis, each four-sided Roman nail was driven through the space of Destot resulting in rigid fixation without rotation (figure IX; glossary). Moreover, it was the protuberant dorsal ulnar styloid that caused the divided flow of blood (figures VIII-A, IX).

Dr. Barbet disregarded the biomechanics (the forces and the energy that work in the human musculoskeletal system) during Roman crucifixion. Let me be clear—contrary to the German death-camp victims, Jesus was not freely hanged by His wrists during the crucifixion. Rather, He was supported by a biomechanical system or machine that consisted of (1) the large foot nail or point of contact (the supporting fulcrum) and (2) the powerful muscles and bones of the lower extremities (the lever arms). This highly leveraged system maintained Jesus's body in a stable, upright position without the stretching of His muscles, tetany, exhaustion, or asphyxiation. In my judgment, this biomechanical model authoritatively *discredits* the tetany/asphyxiation theory as the cause for the death of Jesus Christ (glossary, "crucifixion— biomechanics").

A well-designed research project by Dr. Zugibe[11] demonstrated no clinical or laboratory evidence for the presence of tetany/asphyxiation during Roman crucifixion. Volunteers were secured to wooden crosses and observed. After a sufficient period of time, there were no manifestations of respiratory distress or the presence of sagging down to rest and lifting up to breathe. In addition, there was no clinical or laboratory data supporting tetany/asphyxiation or acute respiratory failure.

Finally, Dr. Barbet stated that Roman crucifracture "hastened death" secondary to tetany/asphyxiation (John 19:31–32; glossary). Crucifracture was a violent, barbaric procedure that shattered the bones of both legs and crushed the soft tissues causing death within minutes (chart III). In my clinical analysis, death by crucifracture involved victims who were near death, and then subjected to additional severe trauma as follows.

1. the sudden onset of excruciating pain and severe traumatic shock (hypotension and hypoperfusion)
2. the rapid losses of blood and water from mortal lacerations of the right and left popliteal arteries and veins (the large blood vessels directly behind the knee joints)
3. the immediate third-space fluid loss in the legs and feet
4. the rapid onset of decompensated shock including fatal levels of hypoxia ($\downarrow O_2$) and lactic acidosis ($\downarrow pH$)
5. cardiac arrest and death

The fear, horror, and terror of Roman crucifracture are comparable to bilateral, below-knee amputations in the absence of anesthesia!

Four additional publications testify against the tetany/asphyxiation theory. Dr. P. J. Smith,[6,11] a surgical colleague of Dr. Barbet, wrote the following medical opinion: "Your theory is not supported by some of the evidence set out in this book." Next, the noted Jewish historian Flavius Josephus[5,7–9] (AD 37–100) reported on thousands of Roman crucifixions during the Jewish-Roman War (AD 70)—many of these victims "lingered on their crosses for five to nine days." This extended time of survival on a Roman cross sharply contradicts the belief that Jesus died secondary to tetany/asphyxiation due to Roman crucifixion (Mark 15:44; John 19:33; chart III; figure VI).

Third, during His institution of the Lord's Supper/Eucharist, Jesus did not proclaim a death by suffocation, but rather a death secondary to His broken body and shed blood (1 Corinthians 10:16, 11:23–26; Hebrews 10:5, 10, 20, 13:11–12; charts I, V; figure VI).

Finally, death by tetany/asphyxiation does not fulfill the Old Testament prophetic scriptures or modern medical science. The unblemished Passover lambs, the Levitical sacrificial animals, the Suffering Servant, the Abandoned/Righteous One, and the Pierced One did not suffer and die secondary to suffocation (chart IX, see 6, 12, 15, 19, 20; prologue; chapters 1, 7, 10).

Dr. Edwards's[18] article was an important challenge for me since his medical publication has been the modern gold standard for the physical death of Jesus. He began with this conclusion: "The major pathophysiologic effect of crucifixion was the interference with normal respirations ... accordingly, death resulted from hypovolemic shock and exhaustion asphyxia" (tetany/asphyxiation).

Dr. Edwards disregarded the severity of the preliminary traumas and sufferings. For example, he described Gethsemane as "mental anguish" and "chills due to the cold night air." Yet the mental afflictions were life-threatening—a medical emergency. Jesus sustained an acute stress reaction with extremely serious complications—hematidrosis and adrenal fatigue, both of which influenced His rapid demise on Calvary (Mark 14:33–36; Luke 22:43–44; charts I, III, IV-B, V; figures VI, VII; chapters 4, 5, 12).

Dr. Edwards underestimated the pathophysiology of the brutal and excessive Roman scourging, defenseless battery, and bloody piercings by the cap of thorns that resulted in the following related conditions.

1. multiple wounds (chart VI-A) with rapid losses of blood and water (charts I, II-B)
2. decompensated multifactorial shock with secondary multiple organ dysfunction (charts III, V; figures VI, VII)
3. internal injuries involving the lungs, heart, abdomen, and brain (charts VIII-A, VIII-B; figures VIII-A, VIII-B).

Dr. Edwards presented a differential diagnosis or list of unrelated medical conditions including

1. "a sudden catastrophic cardiac rupture," but this condition is extremely rare, occurs four to five days following a myocardial injury, does not result in shed blood, and does not fulfill prophetic scripture.
2. "noninfective thrombotic vegetations" on the valves of the heart, but this condition rarely occurs immediately after trauma, does not result in shed blood, and does not fulfill the prophetic scriptures.
3. "exhaustion, blood loss and preshock state," but Dr. Edwards does not estimate the number and types of wounds or the losses of blood and water.

4. "exhaustion asphyxia," but as discussed above, tetany/asphyxiation does not fulfill prophetic scripture and does not satisfy modern medical science.

My most important challenge and objective was the most difficult—the analysis of the number, type, and location of the wounds and the losses of blood and water. My analysis of the multiple wounds was based on the following.

1. the prophecies (chart IX) revealed in the Old Testament scriptures (bruises, stripes, scourging, piercings, and other afflictions) and the passion narratives in the New Testament (bloody sweat, battery, scourging, and piercings)
2. the medical, psychiatric, surgical, and traumatic literature
3. the shroud of Turin (figures VIII-A, VIII-B)
4. my clinical experience and judgment

The assessment of the wounds included these parameters: the number, the cause, the force (BFT versus SFT), the type (abrasion, laceration, puncture, contusion, hematoma, and skin burns), and the location (internal versus external; charts VI-A, VI-B; glossary).

The wounds caused by blunt-force trauma (BFT) resulted from scourging, battery with rods and fists, and the falls on the stone of agony (Gethsemane) and the Via Dolorosa (glossary). These injuries accounted for an estimated 205 or about 80 percent of the wounds (chart VI-A).

BFT causes soft-tissue injuries by crushing the cells and tissues of skin, fat, muscles, and internal organs (water loss) and by tearing of the arterioles, capillaries, and venules (blood loss). In particular, the excessive Roman flogging performed by a whip with a pair of leather straps tipped with lead dumbbells resulted in an estimated 150 or more wounds—abrasions, contusions, hematomas, split lacerations, and partial-thickness mechanical burns. With remarkable accuracy, the shroud of Turin demonstrates the patterned injuries of repetitive parallel wounds secondary to the scourging.[6,11] (figures VIII-A, VIII-B; chapter 6; glossary).

The wounds caused by sharp-force trauma (SFT) resulted secondary to the piercings by thorns, nails, and the Roman lance (postmortem) and accounted for an estimated forty wounds (chart VI-A). The multiple puncture wounds of the scalp were caused by sharp thorns of the Syrian Christ thornbush[11] (Matthew 27:29; John 19:2): these sturdy, two-to-three-inch thorns pierced the highly vascular scalp causing brisk bleeding and severe pain but did not penetrate the skull or brain.

The tapered, five-to-seven-inch, wrought-iron Roman nails resulted in piercing wounds of the wrists (space of Destot) and the feet (second metatarsal space; figures VIII-A, VIII-B, IX). The four-inch transverse chest wound under the right nipple was secondary to the postmortem blow of the lance (John 19:33–34; figures VIII-A, VIII-B, X; chapter 6).

The multiple internal wounds of the lungs, heart, abdomen, and brain were caused by the violent scourging (sixty to seventy lashes), defenseless battery, and falls on the Via Dolorosa (chart VI-A; glossary, "zone of destruction"). The internal wounds that involved the pleural and pericardial membranes—the potential sacs that surround the lungs and heart—resulted in bilateral pleural and pericardial effusions that applied pressure to the lungs and heart and resulted in third space fluid loss (charts I, II-B, VIII-A, VIII-B; glossary; chapter 5).

The severity of the scourging caused diffuse bruising of the delicate lung tissues known as pulmonary or lung contusion,[3,13,16] which resulted in secondary hemorrhage (blood loss), edema[11] (water loss), and the rapid onset of hypoxia ($\downarrow P_aO_2$; charts VIII-A, XII; figures VI, VII; chapter 5).

My estimates for the blood and water losses during the passion were also challenging. The fatal losses of blood and water resulted secondary to the preliminary traumas and sufferings (prior to the crucifixion) and were responsible for the rapid demise of Jesus Christ (charts I, V; chapter 12). The brutal and excessive trauma in the Roman court caused the continuous losses of blood and water until death occurred on Calvary. In the absence of the PTS, Roman crucifixion caused minimal blood loss; for example, the nail wounds resulted in an estimated 0.25 U of blood loss (charts I, III, V; chapters 5, 12).

My analysis of Jesus's blood loss consisted of the following: the hematidrosis and ecchymosis in Gethsemane, the defenseless buffeting during the Jewish trials, the excessive and brutal scourging at the pillar, the battery (rods and fists) and piercings (thorns) during the Roman trial, the falls on the Via Dolorosa, and the nail wounds on Calvary.

In particular, the overzealous flogging (sixty to seventy lashes, "three-quarters dead"), the defenseless battery, and the multiple piercings by the thorns (thirty-six scalp wounds)—caused an estimated 3.0 U or about 30 percent of the blood volume. The total blood losses were an estimated 4.25 U or 42.5 percent of the blood volume (charts I, VII-B; figure VII; chapter 5).

Although less dramatic and more elusive than the loss of blood, the water loss was an equal threat to Jesus's life. Jesus had nothing by mouth during His eighteen-hour passion that established a negative water balance (charts I, II-A). The acute-stress reaction of Gethsemane caused large fluid losses due to hyperhidrosis (skin), hyperventilation (lungs), and vomiting (gut). The Jewish trials and overnight lockup in the pit including repetitive episodes of mocking and defenseless battery resulted in the onset of acute dehydration. The vicious scourging and battery during the Roman trial caused large and continuous losses of water and severe dehydration due to sweating, vomiting, and third-space fluid loss secondary to multiple BFT wounds with crushed, torn, and ruptured cells; bilateral pleural and pericardial effusions; pulmonary edema; and paralytic ileus (charts I, II-B).

The progressive nature of the multifactorial shock syndrome was caused by the ongoing, untreated losses of blood and water that caused hypotension, hypoperfusion, and ischemic cellular injury. The presence of decompensated multifactorial shock and coagulopathy resulted in irreversible cellular and microvascular injuries with additional third-space fluid loss in multiple organs (charts V, VII-D, XI, XII; figures VI, VII; chapter 5; glossary).

My calculations for the total third-space fluid loss were much larger than expected—an estimated 3800 mL (chart II-B). There were additional easily overlooked fluid losses secondary to evaporation (mechanical burns), sweating, hyperventilation, vomiting, and the falls that occurred during Jesus's struggle to climb Calvary bearing the heavy crossbar. The total water losses during the passion were an estimated 8.0 L or 17.6 lbs. (charts I, II-B; figure VII).

REFERENCES

1 Antonacci, M. 2000. *The Resurrection of the Shroud*. New York: M. Evans.
2 Bynum, W. and H. Bynum. 2011. *Great Discoveries in Medicine*. New York: Thames and Hudson.
3 Townsend, M., R. D. Beauchamp, B. M. Evers, and K. L. Mattox. 2012. *Sabiston Textbook of Surgery*. Philadelphia: Elsevier, Saunders.
4 Sadock, B. J. and V. A. Sadock. 2007. *Synopsis of Psychiatry*. Philadelphia: Lippincott Williams & Wilkins.
5 Brown, R. E. 1994. *The Death of the Messiah* (Volume II). New Haven: Yale University Press.
6 Barbet, P. 1950. *A Doctor at Calvary*. Indre, France: Dillon & Cie.
7 Finegan, J. 1946. *Light from the Ancient Past*. Princeton: Princeton University Press.
8 Hengel, M. 1977. *Crucifixion in the Ancient World and the Folly of the Message of the Cross*. Philadelphia: Fortress Press.
9 Josephus, B. J. *Jewish Antiquities and The Jewish War*. Whiston, W. (Translation). 1960. Kregel Publishing. Williamson, G. A. (Translation). 1959. New York: Penguin.
10 Stroud, W. A. 1874. *Treatise on the Physical Cause of the Death of Christ*. London: Hamilton and Adams.
11 Zugibe, T. Z. 2005. *The Crucifixion of Jesus*. New York: M. Evans.
12 Patton, K. T. and G. A. Thibodeau. 2010. *Anatomy and Physiology*. St. Louis: Mosby Elsevier.
13 McCance, K. L. and S. E. Huether, editors. 2010. *Pathophysiology*. Maryland Heights, MO: Mosby, Elsevier.
14 Mulholland, M. W., K. D. Lillemoe, J. M. Doherty, R. V. Maier, D. M. Simeone, and G. R. Upchurch. 2011. *Greenfield's Surgery*. Philadelphia: Lippincott Williams & Wilkins.

15 Starr, D. 2000. *BLOOD*. New York: HarperCollins, Quill.
16 Kumar, V., A. K. Abbas, and J. C. Aster. 2013. *Robbins Basic Pathology*. Philadelphia: Elsevier, Saunders.
17 LeBec, A. 1925. "The Death of the Cross, A Physiologic Study of the Passion of Our Lord Jesus Christ." *Catholic Medical Guardian* (October); 126–32.
18 Edwards, W. D., W. J. Gabel, and F. E. Hosmer. "On the Physical Death of Jesus Christ." *Journal of the American Medical Association* 1986, 255:1455–63.
19 Renner, R. 2008. *Paid in Full*. Tulsa, OK: Teach All Nations.
20 O'Reilly, B. and M. Dugard. 2013. *Killing Jesus*. New York: Henry Holt.
21 Hahn, S. and C. Mitch, editors. 2010. *The Ignatius Catholic Study Bible* (RSV). San Francisco: Ignatius Press.
22 MacArthur, J. 1997. *The MacArthur Study Bible* (NKJV). Nashville: Thomas Nelson.

Chapter 10

Fear, Horror, and Terror

Roman crucifixion grips us with fear ... horror ... and bloodcurdling terror (Lat. *crucifixus*, "the act of impaling and lifting up on a wooden cross"; Gr. *stauros*, "execution on a vertical stake").

Crucifixion was conceptualized by several ancient civilizations who impaled and "lifted up" enemies, traitors, criminals, and terrorists to remove evil from the earth and thereby please the gods (Genesis 40:22; Joshua 8:29 NLT; Esther 7:10 NLT). During the Roman era (about 100 BC–AD 500), crucifixion attained its greatest notoriety and widespread practice for the deterrence of runaway slaves and the promotion of the Pax Romana—the peace of Rome.

Fear represents the most unpleasant human emotion and can cause psychological paralysis. Fright, alarm, panic, and dread are common psychological responses to an anticipated failure, sudden danger, trauma, bleeding, severe pain, or an unfavorable medical report. Mortality continues to be the major cause of fear (Hebrews 2:14–15).

Terrorism—an event rooted in hatred and ideology—is

undertaken to create a reign of fear, horror, and terror by threats and deeds of bloodthirsty violence, torture, and carnage. The human responses to fear and terror are immediate—the limbic and autonomic neuroendocrine systems immediately adapt and prepare the human body for survival; this is known as the general adaptation syndrome (chart IV-A; figure III; chapter 3; glossary).

In the Garden of Gethsemane, Jesus Christ was abruptly afflicted and overpowered by fear, conflict, and sorrow caused by the unimaginable—His separation from the heavenly Father and His violent death for the sins of the world (Mark 14:33-36; Luke 22:43-44). Make no mistake about the fright, horror, and terror of Gethsemane. It was Jesus's greatest conflict, His greatest agony, and His greatest decision. The results were life threatening: an acute stress reaction or the fight-or-flight syndrome complicated by consequential mind-body complications—hematidrosis (blood and water losses) and adrenal fatigue (↓cortisol; chart IV-B; chapters 4, 12, 13; glossary).

About twelve hours later, Jesus persevered a second episode of extraordinary fear, horror, and terror—the brutal, bloodcurdling scourging at the Roman pillar (glossary). Pontius Pilate and Longinus, the centurion, devised a strategy to appease the outraged and envious temple aristocrats and chief priests by excessive scourging—sixty to seventy lashes, three-quarters dead. This was followed by the contemptuous and cynical king's game including defenseless battery, spitting in His face, pulling His beard, taunting, and piercings by the cap of thorns. Finally, Pilate attempted to pacify the Jewish chief priests and bloodthirsty mob by his presentation of the humiliated, beaten, and bloodied Jesus Christ—the *"Ecce Homo,"* "Behold, the man!" (John 19:1–6; glossary).

In my analysis, I concluded that Jesus arrived on Mount Calvary in critical condition secondary to the severity of the preliminary traumas and sufferings including the life-threatening acute stress reaction and the severe shock-trauma (above). The events consisting of mortal fear, terror, and torture that Jesus suffered *prior* to His crucifixion were responsible for His rapid demise on the Roman cross (Mark 15:44; John 19:33–34; charts I, III, IV-B, V, VI-A; figures VI, VII; chapters 4, 5, 9, 12, 13).

By any standard, the overreach of Roman execution by scourging and crucifixion was cruel and unusual punishment. The original objective of the Roman senate was a threefold promotion of Pax Romana: the presence of overwhelming military power; the submission to Roman authority including the public display of bloodshed and the human struggle for life; and an electric atmosphere of the general public charged with fear, horror, and terror.

However, the excessive use of force and brutality did not go unnoticed by the Roman establishment. Cicero[1] (106–43 BC), a highly gifted Roman statesman and orator, witnessed a tongue excision during a Roman crucifixion and demanded that Roman citizens be exempt from such cruel and inhumane practices. Origen[2] (AD 185–254), a prominent church father and influential author, was infuriated with his father's martyrdom by crucifixion and expressed his bitter feelings about the bloodthirsty Roman senate.

Roman crucifixion was initially designated for runaway slaves, but it rapidly became the primary method for executing traitors and revolutionaries (John 18:40, 19:17–18; chart III). The protocol for crucifixion may be summarized as follows (glossary).

1. trial and condemnation before a Roman magistrate
2. preparatory Roman scourging at the pillar—around twenty-five to thirty-five lashes—known as "half dead"

3. a heavy crossbar (100–150 pounds) laid across the back and outstretched arms, secured by heavy rope looped around the neck and abdomen, and carried through the crowded streets to an elevated location outside the city gates and walls[3–5]
4. the victim's wrists were nailed to the crossbar while flat on the ground, and both victim and crossbar were lifted onto the stationary upright forming a *T* shaped or *tau* cross
5. the quaternion of legionnaires scrupulously guarded the crucified since an escape meant their execution
6. a crucifracture in over 90 percent to prevent escape and cause immediate death
7. a declaration of death signed by the centurion in the presence of the Roman magistrate
8. the corpse discarded at a garbage dump or abandoned on the cross for decomposition and consumption by carnivores (burial by family in fewer than 1 percent of the cases; glossary, "crucifixion—Roman methods").

The "fear of the whip" was a commonly used expression throughout the Roman world. Callous, barbaric, and inhumane flogging at the Roman pillar was a savage and disgraceful method authorized by the Roman senate for one purpose—control by fear, horror, and terror.

The whip accomplished Roman justice in several circumstances: first, as a method for punishment and execution (2 Maccabees 6:27–31; Acts 5:40); second, "trial by the lash" (Acts 22:24 NKJV); and third, as a preparatory method to weaken and humiliate the condemned prior to execution (chart III; glossary).

The excessive and brutal scourging of Jesus Christ was terrifying, horrific, and outrageous—*His mortal wound.* It resulted in the following sequalae: multiple internal and external wounds (chart VI-A; figures VIII-A, VIII-B; chapter 9; glossary), the rapid and massive losses of blood and water (charts I, II-B; chapter 9), and death secondary to decompensated multifactorial shock (chart V; figure VI; chapter 5, 12, 13).

My analysis identified an excessive sixty to seventy lashes—not the routine twenty to thirty-five preparatory lashes—based upon Pontius Pilate's desire to appease the furious temple aristocrats and out of control diabolical Jewish mob. My analysis was influenced by the shroud of Turin and Jesus's rapid downhill clinical course and demise after only three hours on the cross (Mark 15:44; John 19:33; charts III, V, XI, XII; figures IV, VI, VIII-A, VIII-B; chapters 5, 6, 12, 13).

Acute complications secondary to Roman flogging were infrequent but serious and even deadly on occasion.

1. Errant lashes rarely contused, lacerated, and excised an eye, ear, or testicle.
2. The contents of the chest and abdominal cavities were rarely eviscerated (an organ herniated outside its cavity).
3. A large superficial blood vessel was rarely lacerated, and rapid hemorrhage, shock, and death ensued—the great vessels of the neck (the carotid arteries and jugular veins), the groin (the femoral arteries and veins), and the dorsal aspect of the knee joint (the popliteal arteries and veins).

The resounding thuds of the leather straps and attached lead dumbbells precipitated frightening, horrifying, and terrifying screams and groans. Each blunt-force trauma by the *flagrum* (Roman whip or scourge) crushed and lacerated the skin, subcutaneous tissue, arterioles, capillaries, venules, nerves, and muscle tissues.

The magnitude of Roman scourging resulted in severe mental and physical consequences (charts I, V, VI-A, VIII-A, VIII-B, XII; figures VI, VII, VIII-A, VIII-B).

The acute responses of the limbic and autonomic neuroendocrine systems attempted to restore equilibrium and homeostasis in response to the extremes of fear, horror, terror, destruction of tissue, losses of blood and water, and acute multifactorial shock (chart IV-A).

If the Roman trial concluded with a guilty verdict, a formal statement of condemnation was announced by the magistrate: "You are guilty of a capital crime—a threat against Rome … You will be scourged at the pillar … You will take up and bear your cross (the crossbar) … and you will be lifted up on your cross until death" (Jerusalem tour guide, 2013).

The atmosphere surrounding a Roman crucifixion was rowdy and impassioned, similar to those at the gladiatorial games. The large crowds were not simply being entertained—they were exhilarated, aroused, and addicted to the sight of human blood and the desperate struggle for human survival.

The robust Roman death squads included four well-equipped legionnaires commanded by the heart and soul of a Roman legion—an experienced, no-nonsense, pompous, and rarely challenged centurion on horseback.

The "killing field of the Roman crosses" consisted of stationary, vertical uprights on Calvary outside Jerusalem and provided the greatest possible public exposure (Jerusalem tour guide, 2013). The condemned man carried his crossbar horizontally across his upper back through the crowded streets exhibiting his bloodstained and beaten body, physical and emotional distress, and most assuredly his submission to Rome.

Sacred art concerning the passion has consistently portrayed

Jesus as bearing the entire Latin cross (around 200–300 lbs.), but historical records and traditions are conclusive—the condemned slaves, revolutionaries, and the Lord Jesus Himself carried only the horizontal crossbar (*patibulum*) of the *T*-shaped or *tau* cross[4,5] (glossary, "crucifixion—sacred art").

The sacrificial death of Jesus Christ, the Son of Promise, occurred outside the walls of Jerusalem in the land of Moriah fulfilling and perfecting prophetic scripture (Genesis 22:1–14; Exodus 29:14; Hebrews 13:11–13; chart IX, see 4). Jesus struggled to climb the Via Dolorosa bearing the Roman crossbar. His arms were extended, and His body flexed forward. He was covered head to toe with fresh streamlets of scarlet blood, purplish blood clots, and polluted sweat.

Not a single bystander had the slightest idea that this condemned, counterfeit, king of the Jews was in fact the sovereign Lord's sacrificial Passover lamb who was taking away the sins of the world and fulfilling the Hebrew scriptures (John 1:29; 1 Corinthians 5:7; 1 Peter 1:18–19; Hebrews 9:12, 13:11–14; chart IX, see 6; chapter 13).

According to the prophetic word, the Jewish Messiah, Redeemer, and Suffering Servant must be rejected, scourged, mocked and spat on, lifted up, and pierced (chart IX, see 15). Moreover, He must be afflicted by God with blood loss, a broken body, and torn flesh.

Once the naked and blood-spattered prisoner arrived on the elevated crucifixion site outside the walls, he was aggressively restrained at the foot of the stationary upright. Although rare, the ravaged, panic-stricken, and terrified victim made a last-gasp attempt to escape the madness and barbaric insanity and flail his extremities, shout threats and obscenities, break free, and spit and bite his hated Roman captors.

However, Roman discipline, intense training, and sheer power almost always prevailed; the hysterical victim was forcefully thrown to the ground and subdued against the crossbar. Several lashes with the flagellum normally ended the matter. But if the verbal abuse, spitting, and biting persisted, the executioner excised the victim's tongue. And if all else failed, the centurion drove his razor-sharp battlefield lance into the victim's heart. The Roman deathblow (blow of the lance) resulted in immediate death (figure X; glossary).

Having been lifted up, the victim sensed the reality of the moment—death was inescapable. But Jesus Christ was totally consumed by the Father's perfect will and good purpose. As He gazed at the Jerusalem temple in the distance, He was cognizant of the thousands of unblemished Passover lambs being sacrificed in preparation for the feast. He was confident that He, the incarnate Son of God, was fulfilling and perfecting the prophetic scriptures and sealing the new blood covenant of grace choreographed and coordinated by the sovereign Lord and Great Physician before the foundations of the world (Exodus 12:21–27; Matthew 26:26–29; Mark 14:49; John 1:29, 17:24, 19:14; Acts 2:23; 1 Corinthians 5:7; chart IX, see 6, 7; chapter 1).

During my assessment of the preliminary mental afflictions and physical traumas, I concluded that the Roman cross was not the cause of His rapid death (charts III, V; figure VI; chapters 4, 5, 12, 13). His survival time on the cross was only three hours (Mark 15:25, 33–34, 44; John 19:14, 33–34).

Just seconds before death, Jesus said, "It is finished"—the sixth word from the cross (John 19:29). In my mind's eye, I observed great drops of Jesus's shed blood and drops of His lifesaving water (broken body and torn flesh) falling onto the skull of Adam at the foot of the cross—the quintessential picture of the remission of sins and the reversal of the curse (Genesis 3:15; Leviticus 17:11; Matthew 26:28; Romans 5:17–19; Galatians 3:13; Hebrews 9:22; 1 John 1:7; chart IX, see 1, 21).

Jesus struggled for air. His respirations became shallow and irregular. His pulse was rapid and thready, and His abdomen was protuberant. He was severely dehydrated—His discolored tongue was swollen and adhered to His palate. His lips were parched and coated with saliva and vomitus. His urine output was decreased, dark, and concentrated. His eyes were sunken, glazed, and without expression. The mental afflictions, multiple wounds, and rapid losses of blood and water He had suffered ravaged His human mind and body—the incarnate Son had the appearance of impending doom (Isaiah 52:14, 53:5–8; Hebrews 2:14-18, 5:7-8, 12:2; chart VII-C; chapter 5).

Centuries before the passion of Jesus Christ (around 1000 BC), the psalmist wrote prophetically about the tormented Abandoned/Righteous One who reacted out of extreme fright, horror, and terror to the torture by his enemies. He was forsaken by God, mocked, threatened, bloodied, dehydrated, pierced, and surrounded by "bulls," "dogs," and "villains" (Psalm 22:1–22 NKJV; chart IX, see 12). This prophecy was fulfilled and perfected by the incarnate Son during His passion and redemptive death.

Centuries later, Isaiah wrote prophetically about the Suffering Servant of the Holy One of God (about 650 BC), the "man of sorrows" who saved and delivered his people. The Servant was the victim of severe mental afflictions and physical sufferings and reacted out of fear, horror, and bloodcurdling terror. He was wounded, scourged, pierced, spat on, and mocked; His beard was pulled, and He was marred beyond human likeness. He was crushed for our iniquities, afflicted by God, led like a lamb to the slaughter, bore our sins, and justified many (Isaiah 50:6, 52:13–53:12; chart IX, see 15). This profound prophetic scripture was fulfilled and perfected by Jesus Christ during His passion and redemptive death.

REFERENCES

1. Stott, J.R.W. 1986. *The Cross of Christ*. Downers Grove, IL: Intervarsity Press.
2. Gonzalez, J. L. 1984. *The Story of Christianity* (Volume I). New York: HarperCollins.
3. Metzger, B. M. and M. D. Coogan. 1993. *The Oxford Guide to the Bible*. New York: Oxford University Press.
4. Edwards, W. D., W. J. Gabel, and F. E. Homer. "On the Physical Death of Jesus Christ." *Journal of the American Medical Association* 1986, 255:1455–63.
5. Barbet, P. 1950. *A Doctor at Calvary*. Indre, France: Dillon & Cie.

Chapter 11

The Journey and the Way

On the night of His betrayal and arrest, Jesus addressed the twelve: "I AM the Way and the Truth and the Life. No one comes to the Father except through me" (John 14:6). This profound revelation has been called the Christian salvation formula that designates someone—the incarnate Son of God; something—the onetime sacrifice of the incarnate Son that merits infinite mercy, perfect grace, and eternal life; and someplace—unlimited access into the heavenly sanctuary.[1-7]

The incarnation, passion, and sacrificial death of Jesus Christ graciously grant our everlasting acceptance into the presence of almighty God by a new and living way: our hearts are sprinkled with His blood and our bodies washed by His pure, living water. We boldly "approach the throne of grace to receive mercy and to find grace" (Romans 5:1–2; Ephesians 2:13; Hebrews 4:16, 6:19-20, 7:19, 9:22, 10:19–22).

The impassioned journey and way of Jesus Christ was not the result of happenstance or coincidence—every mental affliction and physical agony was directed and coordinated by the sovereign Lord and Great Physician. He revealed His new and living *way* of absolute *truth* and eternal *life* by the sacrificial blood and the lifesaving water of Jesus Christ (Matthew 26:26–28; John 4:10, 14, 7:37–39; Acts 2:23; Hebrews 10:19–22; 1 Peter 1:18-20; 1 John 5:6-12; chart I).

The centurion's climactic, postmortem blow of the lance opened the sacred heart of Jesus causing the immediate flow of blood (right atrium and right ventricle) and water (serous fluid from the pericardial effusion; figure X). This dramatic episode revealed the Son's gracious gifts to the church—the forgiveness of sin, the Lord's Supper/Eucharist, the Holy Spirit, and Christian water baptism—and symbolized His mysterious death by the losses of blood and water that fulfilled prophetic scripture and satisfied modern medical science (John 19:33–37; charts I, IV-B, V, IX; prologue; chapters 5, 12).

The incarnate Son was manifested in fallen human flesh and blood allowing Him to thoroughly identify with humanity during His incarnation, passion, and sacrificial death (1 Timothy 2:5–6, 3:16; Hebrews 2:14, 17). His solidarity with humanity opened the way for our victorious Journey to Mount Calvary (Mark 1:3; Philippians 2:6–8; Hebrews 10:19–22, 12:1–3; Revelation 5:9–13). Jesus was our Victim who willingly laid down His life and our great High Priest who offered His sacrificial blood and water as the ransom that paid in full for our sin and guilt (John 1:29, 10:17–18; Hebrews 8:1–3; 1 Peter 1:18–19;1 John 1:9).

Christians are blessed by their living union with the Lord Jesus that actualizes their personal journey and way to Mount Calvary (Ephesians 1:3; Hebrews 4:16, 6:19–20, 10:19–20). We are "chosen *in* Him and adopted as sons and daughters before the foundation of the world" (Ephesians 1:4–5 NKJV), "forgiven and redeemed by His blood" (Ephesians 1:7 NKJV), "saved by His grace" (Ephesians 2:8

NKJV), and "transformed into His same image from glory to glory" (2 Corinthians 3:18 NKJV).

Every spiritual blessing and eternal promise in Him was revealed in accordance with the Lord's good purpose and perfect will "to sum up all things in Christ Jesus in heaven and on earth" (Ephesians 1:3, 9–10 NKJV).

Based on His monumental self-revelation—*I AM the only Way to God*—the Christian movement quickly became recognized as the Way (about AD 35; Acts 9:2, 22:4; Hebrews 10:19–20). By His sacrificial mental afflictions and physical agonies, Jesus Christ stands alone as "the author and finisher of our faith" (Hebrews 2:10, 12:2 NKJV; chart V; figure VI). His shed blood, broken body, and torn flesh triumphantly, graciously, and eternally granted our personal journey and way to Calvary.

By the inspiration of the Spirit of God, the authors of the Old Testament revealed two ways of life—the way of disobedience, sin, and curse versus the way of obedience, righteousness, and blessing. However, the New Testament evangelists revealed a glorious new and living way by the gracious passion and sacrificial death of Jesus Christ, whose saving work merited eternal access to the Lord and a share of His divine nature (Hebrews 4:16, 6:19–20, 10:19–22; 2 Peter 1:4).

The journey and way of life for Job consisted of a period of testing—severe mental afflictions and physical sufferings that resulted in spiritual growth. He learned to trust and obey God once he understood *who God is*. Finally, Job saw God and repented (Job 38–39, 42:5–6; chart IX, see 11)! According to the esteemed Hebrew sages, one's way of *life* includes the following: "Fear God and keep His commands, for this is man's all" (Ecclesiastes 12:13 NKJV); and your soul pursues the living God as "a deer pants for streams of living water" (Psalm 42:1-2 NIV).

There was the Abrahamic way of faith. Father Abraham "believed God and was credited with righteousness" (Genesis 15:6; Romans 4:3). By faith, Abraham—the greatest of all Hebrew patriarchs—was obedient and agreed to sacrifice his beloved son of promise trusting that almighty God would "raise him from the dead" (Genesis 22:1–15; Hebrews 11:17–19; chart IX, see 4).

There was the Mosaic way of hope. Moses was the supreme prophet, mediator, lawgiver, and deliverer of God's chosen people whose profound hope was the Lord's promise of a future Messiah and Redeemer "who would be more excellent than the treasures of Egypt" (Hebrews 6:18–19, 11:26–29). Before his death, Moses revealed the solemn words of God to his Hebrew brothers and sisters: choose between the two ways of life—obedience and life versus disobedience and death— "Choose life over death" (Deuteronomy 28:29, 30:15–16, 19).

There was the Davidic way of love. King David was "a man after God's own heart" reflected by his beautiful words, "love surrounds those who trust in the Lord" (Psalm 32:10) and "I love you Lord, you are my strength" (1 Samuel 13:14, 16:7 NKJV; Psalm 18:1).

The way of wisdom was revealed by King Solomon as follows: "The fear of the Lord is the beginning of wisdom and understanding" (Proverbs 9:10; Ecclesiastics 12:13), "There is a Way that seems right to a man, but ends in disaster" (Proverbs 14:12 NLT), and the way of "a man's words are deep waters" but "the source of wisdom is a flowing brook" (Proverbs 18:4).

The psalmist's way of prosperity and righteousness was symbolized by "a tree planted by rivers of [living] water that brings forth fruit" (Psalm 1:3, 6 NKJV). Humankind must follow the way of the Lord since He alone is the "fountain of life" (Psalm 36:9 NKJV).

The ancient church made its journey and way to Mount Calvary by daily prayer and watchfulness, meditations of the passion narratives, and the Lord's Supper/Eucharist (Mark 14:22–15:47; 1 Corinthians 11:23–26). The Markan way of the Lord's passion[8] is first and foremost servanthood: "I have come not to be served, but to serve and to give my life as a ransom for many" (Mark 10:43–45). Secondly, Mark reveals the importance of daily watchfulness with Jesus— "Could you not keep watch with me for one hour? Watch and pray that you may not undergo the test" (Mark 14:37–38).

The Lukan way must have shocked the disciples, "If anyone wishes to come after me, he must *deny* himself and take up his cross *daily* and follow me" (Luke 9:22–23). The true disciple of the Lord Jesus is an intense learner and a faithful follower. A unique characteristic of Lukan evangelism is the "journey narrative" used by Luke to reveal Jesus's most cherished parabolic words and miraculous works (Luke 9:51-19:27; 24:13-35).

1. Jesus and the disciples made the long journey from Galilee to Jerusalem, the holy city of destiny (Luke 9:51–19:27).
2. On the Via Dolorosa, Simon carried the holy cross (crossbar) and followed Jesus from behind (Luke 23:26–32).
3. On the road to Emmaus, the resurrected Jesus revealed that the prophetic scriptures written in the law of Moses and in the prophets and psalms must be fulfilled (Luke 24:25–27, 44).
4. The miraculous journey and way of the incarnate Son—His incarnation, passion, sacrificial death, and resurrection—was actualized by His exodus from the world and return to the heavenly Father (Luke 9:31).

The Lukan way to Calvary displays the profound compassion of Jesus Christ during what were His most vulnerable and humiliating eighteen hours (chapter 13).

1. He prayed for the restoration of Peter (Luke 22:31–32).
2. He healed the servant's ear (Luke 22:50–51).
3. He reconciled Pontius Pilate and King Herod (Luke 23:12).
4. He befriended and saved the Cyrenian whose family became members of the Way (Mark 15:21; Luke 23:26).
5. He consoled the crowd who "followed, mourned, and lamented Him" (Luke 23:27).
6. He comforted his virgin mother (station 12, chapter 13).
7. He consoled Veronica, who cleansed His face with the miraculous cloth (station 15, chapter 13).
8. He consoled and instructed the "Daughters of Jerusalem" (Luke 23:27–31; station 17, chapter 13).
9. He repeatedly "forgave" the Roman legionnaires, the Jewish people, and humankind (the first word from the cross, Luke 23:34).
10. He saved Dismas—the repentant revolutionary crucified on Calvary— "Today you will be in Paradise" (the second word from the cross, Luke 23:43).
11. The centurion observed the events on Calvary and glorified God by saying, "Certainly this was a righteous Man" (Luke 23:47 NKJV; station 22, chapter 13).
12. Many sorrowful Jews returned to their homes "beating their breasts" (Luke 23:48 NKJV).

The Pauline way to Mount Calvary includes our co-crucifixion with Jesus Christ: "I have been crucified with Christ and I no longer live, but Christ lives in me; my new life in the flesh is by faith in the Son of God who loved me and gave Himself for me" (Galatians 2:19–20 NKJV).

Christians are *in Christ*—the living union with the incarnate Son: "I am dead to sin and alive to God" (Romans 6:5–6, 11 NKJV). "There is no condemnation to those who are *in* Christ Jesus" (Romans 8:1–2 NKJV).

The institution of the Lord's Supper/Eucharist is an essential component of the Pauline way, His broken body and shed blood—"When you eat this bread and drink this cup, you proclaim the Lord's death" (1 Corinthians 10:16, 11:23–26 NKJV).

The great apostle also revealed, "The Gospel is the power of God to salvation" (Romans 1:16 NKJV; 1 Corinthians 15:3–4). There is divine power in the impassioned journey and sacrificial way of Jesus Christ by His broken body (mortal water loss) and His shed blood (mortal blood loss).

The theological effects of the Christ event are the signature feature of the Pauline journey and way.

- "expiation by his blood" (Romans 3:25)
- "justification by his blood" (Romans 5:9)
- "near (to God) by the blood of Christ" (Ephesians 2:13)
- "peace through his blood" (Colossians 1:20)
- the eternal access to almighty God was initiated by "a new and living way"—the "sprinkling of our hearts" with His blood and the "washing of our bodies" by His pure, living water (Hebrews 4:16, 6:19–20, 10:19–22).

The Johannine way of the passion[10] reveals the beloved disciple's climactic eyewitness testimony from Mount Calvary: "So that you also may come to believe" (John 19:35).

The apostle John initially revealed the hour of Jesus Christ as a future event (John 2:4, 7:30). But following His triumphant entry into Jerusalem, the hour became a present reality (John 12:27, 17:1): "The *hour* has come for the Son of Man to be glorified" (John 12:23)—His glorious hour to pass from this world and return to the Father in heaven (John 13:1, 3). "Unless a grain of wheat falls to the ground and dies, it remains just a grain of wheat; but if it dies, it produces much fruit" (John 12:24).

The lifting up of Jesus fulfilled and perfected prophetic scripture (Numbers 21:4–9; John 3:14, 8:28, 12:32–33) and revealed His magnificent glorification[10] by His sacrificial death for the sins of the world (John 1:29; 1 John 1:7, 9; Revelation 1:5). The exalted, lifted-up One poured out the Holy Spirit to favor, empower, and enlighten His church on Calvary (John 7:37–39, 19:30–37; 1 John 5:6–12; chart IX, see 8).

The Johannine way of the Lord's passion reveals the crucial importance of the fulfillment of prophetic scripture (John 19:24, 28, 36–37). Jesus wore "the *seamless tunic* next to His skin" since He was the great High Priest who "offered" His sacrificial blood and water to the Father (Exodus 39:27; Leviticus 8:7, 16:4; John 19:23–24; Hebrews 10:12–14, 19–22, chart IX, see 13).

The Roman legionnaires said, "Let us not tear it, but cast lots for it [the tunic]" and then "they divided My garments among them" (Psalm 22:18 NKJV; John 19:23–24).

"In order that the scripture might be fulfilled," Jesus said, "I thirst!" and "they put to his mouth a sponge soaked in wine on a sprig of *hyssop*" (Exodus 12:22; Psalm 69:21; the fifth word from the cross, John 19:29).

Jesus is the unblemished Passover Lamb of God—the Perfect One— "Not one of His bones shall be broken" (Exodus 12:5–7, 22, 46; Psalm 22:14–15; John 19:36 NKJV; chart IX, see 6, 9).

Jesus is the Pierced One— "They shall look on Him whom

they pierced" (Zechariah 12:10; John 19:37 NKJV; chart IX, see 19). The "rivers of living water" that flowed from Jesus's heart were the fulfillment and perfection of the lifesaving waters that flowed from Ezekiel's Jerusalem temple and Zechariah's messianic fountain (Ezekiel 47:9; Zechariah 13:1, 14:8; John 4:14, 7:37–39, 19:34; 1 John 5:6-8; chart IX, see 17).

The journey and way of the beloved disciple revealed his unique description of the centurion's blow of the lance with the immediate flow of blood and water (John 19:34; 1 John 5:6-12; chart VIII-B; figures VIII-A, X; glossary). The blood and water symbolized gifts for the church that poured out of Jesus's gracious heart. His blood represented the infinite forgiveness of sins (Matthew 26:28; Acts 2:38, 9:2; Hebrews 9:14, 22, 28, 12:24, 13:12), and His water symbolized the indwelling Holy Spirit (John 7:37–39; Acts 2:38; Hebrews 10:22).

The Johannine way of the passion revealed the incarnate Son as the new temple of God (chart IX, see 17). During the era of Israel's kings and prophets (about 1050 to 587 BC), the Jerusalem temple was built with human hands to honor the Lord's name and to be His dwelling place. However, this Old Testament prefigurement was fulfilled and perfected by the good news of the New Testament. The Son of God was *enfleshed* by divine hands and sent to earth in a temple of flesh and blood to offer Himself as the eternal sacrifice for the remission of sins by His shed blood and broken body (John 1:1–2, 14, 29, 2:19–22, 3:5, 16, 36, 6:40, 51–57, 19:29–37).

The psalmist revealed this same idea: "That I may dwell in the house of the Lord all the days of my life to gaze on the beauty of the Lord and to seek him in his temple" (Psalm 27:4 NIV). The first followers of the Way—those on Calvary who were gathered under the bloodstained, broken body of the new temple of God—found refuge under "the shadow of Your wings" (Psalm 36:7, 63:7 NKJV).

REFERENCES

1. Youngblood, R. F., editor. 1995. *Nelson's New Illustrated Bible Dictionary*. Nashville: Thomas Nelson.
2. Edersheim, A. 1961. *The Life and Times of Jesus the Messiah*. Peabody, MA: Hendrickson.
3. Metzger, B. M. and M. D. Coogan. 1993. *The Oxford Guide to the Bible*. New York: Oxford University Press.
4. Stuhlmueller, C., editor. 1996. *The Collegeville Pastoral Dictionary of Biblical Theology*. Collegeville, MN: Liturgical Press.
5. Brown, R. E. 1997. *An Introduction to the New Testament*. New Haven: Yale University Press.
6. Sheed, F. J. 1981. *Theology for Beginners*. Cincinnati: St. Anthony Messenger Press.
7. Tenney, M. C., editor. 1976. *The Zondervan Pictorial Encyclopedia of the Bible* (Volume V). Grand Rapids, MI: Zondervan.
8. Donahue, J. R. and D. J. Harrington. 2002. *The Gospel of Mark*. Collegeville, MN: Liturgical Press.
9. Johnson, L. T. 1991. *The Gospel of Luke*. Collegeville, MN: Liturgical Press.
10. Maloney, F. J. 1998. *The Gospel of John*. Collegeville, MN: Liturgical Press.

Chapter 12

The Preliminary Traumas and Sufferings

The severe mental afflictions and physical shock-trauma that transpired *prior* to the crucifixion are identified as the preliminary traumas and sufferings (PTS). I made two relevant discoveries during my extensive analysis of the sacred scriptures and the twenty-first century medical sciences. First, the PTS were solely responsible for the rapid demise of Jesus Christ (Mark 15:44; John 19:33–34; charts I, III, IV-B, V, VI-A; figures VI, VII); and second, the PTS fulfilled and perfected the prophetic scriptures (Matthew 5:17; Luke 18:31–33, 24:44; John 19:24, 28, 36–37; chart IX; chapters 1, 9, 10).

Jesus inaugurated His passion with the unexpected, stunning announcement that His sacrificial death would cut, seal, and memorialize the new blood covenant of grace by His broken body, torn flesh, and shed blood (Matthew 26:26–28; John 6:53–56; Hebrews 9:12, 22, 10:5, 10, 20; charts I, V, VI-A; figures VI, VII; chapter 8). The following episodes resulted in Jesus's *mortal wounds* that preceded the crucifixion on Calvary: His greatest agony in Gethsemane; His betrayal and arrest; the Jewish trials, battery, and the pit; the Roman trials, excessive scourging, battery, and piercings; and His struggles to climb Calvary (chart III; chapters 4, 5, 10, 13).

After completing my analysis of Jesus's multiple wounds (chart VI-A; figures VIII-A, VIII-B; chapter 9) and His blood and water losses (charts I, II-B, V; chapter 9), I was confident that two thousand years ago, He arrived on Mount Calvary in *critical* condition with the following diagnoses each of which fulfilled and perfected prophetic scripture (chart IX). Jesus would die on His holy cross, but Roman crucifixion was not the cause of His death (charts III, V; Figures VI, VII; chapters 4, 5, 9, 10, 13).

- The acute stress reaction in Gethsemane—predisposed by post-traumatic stress disorder—resulted from repetitive conflicts and attempts to entrap and kill Him by the Jewish authorities. During His life-threatening episode in Gethsemane, Jesus was suddenly overcome by severe fright, conflict, and agony caused by His impending separation from the Father and violent sacrificial death for the sins of the world. The resulting psychosomatic complications—hematidrosis and adrenal fatigue—influenced His rapid demise on Calvary (Mark 14:33-36; Luke 22:43-44; chart IV-B; figure VI; chapter 4; glossary).

- My analysis revealed the following: an estimated 255 wounds (charts VI-A, VI-B; figures VIII-A, VIII-B; chapter 9); an estimated blood loss of 4.25 U or 42.5 percent that resulted in class IV hemorrhagic shock, which is fatal in the absence of emergency resuscitation (charts I, III, V, VII-B, XI, XII; figure IV; chapter 9); and an estimated water loss of 8.0 L or 17.6 lbs., which is also fatal without emergency treatment (charts I, II-B, III; chapter 9).

- Decompensated multifactorial shock (traumatic, hemorrhagic, hypovolemic, cardiac, and adrenal) was the *primary* cause of Jesus's rapid demise (charts I, II-B, III, V, VII-A, VII-D). The secondary factors included (1) the absence of treatment during the golden hour (charts XI, XII; figure IV) and (2) the presence of adrenal fatigue with diminished levels of cortisol and the inability to compensate for hypotension and hypoperfusion, and the lethal triad—acidosis, hypothermia, and coagulopathy (charts IV-B, V, VII-D, XI, XII; figure VI; chapters 3, 4, 5, 10, 13; glossary).
- Acute respiratory failure caused by chest wall and pulmonary contusion, acute shock lung, and ARDS (chart VIII-A; figures VI, VIII-B, XII; chapter 5; glossary).
- Acute cardiac failure occurred secondary to acute pericardial effusion complicated by cardiac tamponade (chart VIII-B; figures VI, X; chapters 5, 13; glossary).
- Paralytic ileus resulted from the scourging that involved the abdominal wall, severe shock-trauma, and electrolyte abnormalities (charts II-B, XII; figure VIII-A; chapter 5; glossary).
- Concussion (DAI) was caused by undefended buffets of the head with a mild brain injury (chapter 5; glossary).
- The rapid onset of multiple organ dysfunction syndrome resulted from decompensated multifactorial shock, adrenal fatigue, and the lethal triad involving multiple organs (charts V, VII-A, VII-D; figures VI, VII; chapter 5; glossary).

Subsequent to the mental and physical agonies of the Roman trial, Jesus took up the Roman crossbar and turned His face toward the Via Dolorosa and Calvary. He suffered from progressive losses of blood and water, severe dehydration, and acute multifactorial shock. The contusions of His chest wall and lungs caused the immediate onset of respiratory distress. Jesus passed beyond the golden hour as Veronica cleansed His marred and bloodied face (Isaiah 52:14, 53:4, 11; charts I, V, XII; figures VIII-A, VIII-B; station 15, chapter 13).

From this moment, Jesus's downhill clinical course progressed at a rapid pace. His vital signs were as follows: dyspnea (RR >30), hypotension (BP <90/60), a racing heart (HR/P >160; glossary). He suffered from light-headedness and multiple open wounds with streams of fresh blood and scattered, purplish blood clots.

The shroud of Turin demonstrates contusions, hematomas, and lacerations involving the knees and shoulders secondary to the falls on the Via Dolorosa (figures VIII-A, VIII-B; stations 12, 16, and 18, chapter 13). In the absence of treatment, the ongoing losses of blood ("shed blood") and water ("broken body" and "torn flesh") were responsible for Jesus's rapid deterioration (Mark 15:44; Luke 23:26; John 19:33; charts I, II-B, III, V; figure VI). Under the direction of the sovereign Lord and Great Physician, Jesus fulfilled and perfected the prophetic scriptures during His sufferings on the Via Dolorosa—He was like a lamb being led to the slaughter (Isaiah 53:7; Jeremiah 12:19; John 1:29; 1 Peter 1:19; chart IX, see 15, 16).

The large estimated water losses were either underestimated or disregarded in past publications.[5–9] Further, they continued on the Via Dolorosa due to the hyperventilation, vomiting, evaporation, and sweating and third-space fluid loss from His wounds, effusions, and paralytic ileus (charts I, II-B, V; figures VI, VII).

The incarnate Son of God arrived on Calvary in critical condition secondary to the severity of the preliminary traumas and sufferings. His violent, sacrificial death took place on the preparation day for Passover during the precise hours the lambs were being slaughtered in the temple (Exodus 12:1-13; John 19:14; 1 Corinthians 5:7; 1 Peter 1:19)—a glorious example of the fulfillment of prophetic scripture (chart IX, see 6).

The majority of Christians believe that the death of Jesus Christ resulted secondary to Roman crucifixion (figure V; prologue; chapter 9). The preliminary traumas and sufferings have been *hidden* for two thousand years as the authentic etiology of Jesus's death. During my research, I discovered that the time of survival on a Roman cross was inversely proportional to the magnitude of the PTS. The severity of Jesus's preliminary agonies caused His rapid demise—not Roman crucifixion (charts I, III, IV-B, V, VI-A, VII-A, VII-D; figures VI, VII, VIII-A, VIII-B; chapters 4, 5, 9).

It has been reported[1-5] in several publications that in the absence of the PTS, "victims of Roman crucifixion lingered on their crosses for 5–9 days" (chart III; figure IV; chapters 5, 7, 9; epilogue). This is solid evidence that the severity of the preliminary traumas and sufferings resulted in the rapid demise of Jesus Christ. Nevertheless, Christian authors, biblical commentators, journalists, scripture scholars, professors, pastors, and priests continue to support, teach, and defend the incorrect causes for the death of Jesus Christ (figure V; chapter 9).

For example, in their recent publication, *Killing Jesus* (2013), journalists O'Reilly and Dugard[6] vigorously promoted the tetany/asphyxiation theory. Death on the cross is a slow journey into *suffocation*. Each time a victim takes a breath he must fight his own body weight and push his torso upward using his legs, thus allowing his lungs to expand. In time, the victim, exhausted, cannot breathe.

Rick Renner,[7] the author of *Paid in Full* (2008), passionately praised the sacrificial shed blood of Jesus, but he wrote a dramatic description of the suffocation and respiratory death of Jesus secondary to tetany/asphyxiation: Jesus was gasping for breath ... In order to breathe, he had to push himself up by his feet ... so eventually he would collapse back into the hanging position ... The victim pushed up and collapsed back down again and again ... The process of *asphyxiation* had begun.

To emphasize my research: the Old Testament prophetic scriptures and the passion narratives in the New Testament are silent concerning Jesus's death by suffocation (chart IX; prologue; chapters 1, 7, 9, 10).

In his publication *A Doctor at Calvary* (1950), Dr. Barbet[8] was the first physician to recognize the importance of the preliminary sufferings; nevertheless, he emphasized that "the primary cause for the rapid death of Jesus was asphyxia, secondary to exhaustion and tetany." His evidence was based essentially on the shroud of Turin and the German death camp executions during World War I. The incorrect conclusions made by Dr. Barbet are summarized in the following (chapter 9; glossary).

1. He disregarded the biomechanics of Roman crucifixion (glossary).
2. He underestimated the magnitude of the PTS (charts I, III, IV-B, V, VI-A, VII-A, VII-D, XI, XII; figures VI, VII; chapters 4, 5; glossary).
3. Tetany/asphyxiation does not fulfill the prophetic scriptures (Luke 18:31–33, 24:44; chart IX).
4. The words of the Lord Jesus in the upper room were not considered: "My shed blood" (blood loss) and "My broken body" (water loss) (Matthew 26:26–28).
5. The transcendency of the blood and water was not considered (Exodus 12:5–7; Leviticus 1–7, 17:11–14; Numbers 20:11; 1 Samuel 7: 5-6 NKJV; Luke 22:44; John 7:37–39, 19:34;

Romans 5:9; 1 Corinthians 10:4–5 NLT; Hebrews 9:22, 10:19–22, 13:11–12;1 John 1:7, 5:6–8; Revelation 5:6–9, 7:14, 17, 12:11, 22:1, 17; chart X; figures I-A, I-B, I-C; chapter 7).

In his publication "On the Physical Death of Jesus" (1968), Dr. Edwards[9] concluded that the death of Jesus was caused by Roman crucifixion—a ruptured heart and tetany/asphyxiation—along with several other unrelated diagnoses: noninfective vegetations on the heart valves, myocardial infarction, hypovolemic shock, and acute heart failure. In fairness to Dr. Edwards, he described that the anxiety reaction in Gethsemane and the blood losses secondary to scourging were preliminary medical conditions. Nevertheless, he mistakenly declared, "Exhaustion/asphyxiation was a primary cause in the physical death of Jesus."

During my extensive research of the Old Testament prophetic scriptures and the passion narratives in the New Testament, I discovered *no* evidence that Jesus Christ suffered and died secondary to a broken/ruptured heart or tetany/asphyxiation (chart IX). The sacrificial Levitical animals and Passover lambs did not die from internal bleeding caused by a ruptured heart, which is a cardiac death, or suffocation secondary to tetany/asphyxiation, which is a respiratory death. We must remember the sovereign Lord's instructions: "For the life of the flesh is in the *blood* and I have given it to you upon the altar to make atonement for your souls; for it is the *blood* that makes atonement for the soul" (Leviticus 17:11 NKJV).

The preliminary traumas and sufferings solve the mystery of how Jesus died; they include the following (chart I).

1. the life-threatening acute stress reaction in Gethsemane (blood and water losses)

2. the defenseless battery during the Jewish trials and the acute dehydration in the pit (blood and water losses)
3. the severe scourging, battery, and piercings during the Roman trials that resulted in multiple wounds, rapid blood and water losses, and fatal decompensated multifactorial shock
4. the hardships and falls on the Via Dolorosa (blood and water losses).
5. the arrival on Mount Calvary in critical condition

Jesus Christ arrived on Calvary, was lifted up, and survived only three hours on the holy Roman cross. The time of survival on a cross is inversely proportional to the magnitude of the PTS (chart III). He died on a Roman cross, but His death was not the result of Roman crucifixion. The mighty hand of the sovereign Lord and Great Physician coordinated and directed the perfect and eternal sacrifice of Jesus Christ by His shed blood (rapid blood loss and hemorrhagic shock) and His broken body (water loss and acute cellular dehydration). The preliminary traumas and sufferings fulfilled and perfected the Old Testament prophetic scriptures and satisfied the standards of modern medical science.

REFERENCES

1. Harrison, R. K., editor. 1988. *Unger's Bible Dictionary.* Chicago: Moody Publishers.
2. Finegan, J. 1946. *Light from the Ancient Past.* Princeton: Princeton University Press.
3. Hengel, M. 1977. *Crucifixion in the Ancient World and the Folly of the Message of the Cross.* Philadelphia: Fortress Press.
4. Josephus, B. J. *Jewish Antiquities and the Jewish War.* Whiston, W. (Translation). 1960. Kregel Publishing. Williamson, G. A. (Translation). 1959. New York: Penguin.
5. Brown, R. E. 1994. *The Death of the Messiah* (Volume II). New Haven: Yale University Press (page 1177, footnote 88).
6. O'Reilly, B. and M. Dugard. 2013. *Killing Jesus.* New York: Henry Holt.
7. Renner, R. 2008. *Paid in Full.* Tulsa, OK: Teach All Nations.
8. Barbet, P. 1950. *A Doctor at Calvary.* Indre, France: Dillon & Cie.
9. Edwards, W. D., W. J. Gabel, and F. E. Hosmer. "On the Physical Death of Jesus Christ." *Journal of the American Medical Association* 1986, 255:1455–63.

Chapter 13

The Stations of the Lord's Passion

During the Middle Ages (about 500–1500), devout Christians made the protracted and dangerous pilgrimage to Jerusalem to venerate and give thanks at the *holy sites* on the Way of the Cross (Via Crucis) and the Way of Sorrows (Via Dolorosa) that memorialize the solemn events during the Lord's passion and sacrificial death.

The fourteen original sacred stations begin with Pilate's condemnation of Jesus and conclude with His sacrificial death and resurrection. By the fourteenth century, Franciscan friars[1] had refurbished the stations of the Lord's passion and encouraged the pilgrims to reproduce the sacred shrines in their local churches.

Each station of the Lord's passion offers an exceptional opportunity to pray, meditate, praise, and worship the Lord Jesus for His sacrificial death and gracious saving work. While agonizing and fervently praying in the Garden of Olives, Jesus exhorted His disciples, "Could you not keep watch with me for one hour? Watch and pray that you will not undergo the test" (Mark 14:33–38; Luke 22:40–44; chapters 4, 11).

Blood and Water

Worship at each station begins by quieting of the mind, body, and spirit, followed by offering thanksgiving and adoration to the Lord Jesus for His infinite blessings, inexhaustible grace, and eternal promises.

Our meditations glorify the Lord's humility, servanthood, and self-sacrificial love (Mark 10:43–45; John 13:34–35; Philippians 2:5-8). Jesus was our willing Victim and great High Priest who mediated and sealed the new blood covenant of grace for our redemption and reconciliation [2,3] (Hebrews 9:15; 12:24; chart IX; see 13; chapter 8).

His precious blood and living water were the ransom presented to the Father for our transgressions and eternal access to God (Romans 6:22; 1 Corinthians 6:20; Ephesians 2:13; 1 Timothy 2:6; Hebrews 4:16, 7:19, 10:19–22; 1 Peter 1:18–19). We listen vigilantly for that still, small voice—the whisper of God— "This is the way; walk in it" (1 Kings 19:13; Isaiah 30:21; John 14:6; chapter 11).

In my analysis of both scripture and science, I discovered the mortal events that *preceded* the Roman crucifixion—the preliminary traumas and sufferings (charts I, III, IV-B, V, VI-A, VII-A, VII-D; chapter 12). These preliminary agonies—the mental afflictions in the Garden of Gethsemane (station 3; chapter 4) and the shock-trauma from the Roman trial (station 9; chapter 5)—have necessarily been added to the original Franciscan stations since they resulted in the sacrificial death and gracious redemptive work of Jesus Christ.

My revised Stations of the Lord's passion—stations 1 through 10—include the medical conditions that fulfill sacred scripture and satisfy modern medical science as follows: the multiple wounds (chart VI-A; chapter 9); the rapid loss of blood and large loss of water (charts I, II-B; chapter 9); and the decompensated multifactorial shock (charts V, VII-A, VII-B, VII-C, VII-D; figures VI, VII; chapter 5; glossary).

As predetermined and directed by the sovereign Lord, the PTS resulted in Jesus's "shed blood" (blood loss) and "broken body" (water loss)—the holy Roman cross was not the cause of His death (chapter 12; epilogue).

The Jewish people were zealous—even fanatical—concerning the advent of their Messiah King. They were looking to the future and anticipating the triumphant coming of God's Anointed One, who would redeem them from the bondage of Roman occupation and oppression. The Son of David would establish the kingdom of God and inaugurate the golden age of Israel (1 Samuel 7:12–16; Psalm 2:7–12, 89:27, 110:1–7). However, the four gospels reveal a very different divine truth. The incarnate Son was sent by the sovereign Lord to fulfill and perfect the Old Testament prophetic scriptures and to grant both Jew and Gentile infinite mercy, perfect grace, eternal life, and heavenly bliss through His passion, sacrificial death, and resurrection.

The Jewish religious and political establishment including members of the powerful Sanhedrin opposed, rejected, and attempted the murder of their Messiah on numerous occasions. Ultimately, the chief priests, elders, and scribes—consumed by contempt, envy, and rage—arrested Jesus and condemned Him to death for blasphemy. However, Pontius Pilate easily recognized the innocence of Jesus, yet for the sake of political expediency he handed Him over to be executed— "Jesus of Nazareth, King of the Jews" (John 19:15, 21).

Jesus was excessively and brutally scourged and then beaten, mocked, spat on, humiliated, and pierced. The nation of Israel has failed to accept Jesus Christ as their Messiah King despite His miraculous fulfillment and perfection of the Hebrew scriptures written centuries beforehand (Matthew 5:17–18; Luke 18:31–33, 24:26–27, 44; 1 Peter 1:10–12; chart IX).

Personal meditation, adoration, and watchfulness at each of the Lord's stations provide the unequaled opportunity to "grow in the grace and knowledge of our Lord and Savior Jesus Christ" (2 Peter 3:18 NKJV). Your personal participation in the stations will arouse a deeper appreciation of the Lord's inexhaustible mercy and self-sacrificial love. My revised stations (below) include the life-threatening mental afflictions and lethal physical agonies that fulfilled and perfected the prophetic scriptures and merit our salvation (chart IX). These sacred sites *challenge* Christians of all denominations to pray and keep watch in the presence of Jesus Christ on His way of suffering[2-12]—the heart and soul of eternal life and heavenly bliss (chapters 1, 10, 11, 12).

During our intimate encounters with the Lord, we marvel at His human virtues as recorded in Philippians 2:5–7 and 1 Peter 2:20–23).

1. meekness—His power under control
2. obedience—He trusted and obeyed the will of God
3. humility—He emptied Himself (kenosis) and stooped low (Philippians 2:7)
4. gentleness— "like a lamb being led to the slaughter"
5. patience—His self-restraint while enduring overwhelming fear and sorrow unto death
6. silence—His self-control and temperance
7. fortitude—His courage to drink the cup of divine wrath
8. prudence—His wisdom, sound judgment, and shrewdness
9. truth—He is the living Word and perfect Truth
10. love—His self-sacrificial love is revealed by His incarnation, passion, and sacrificial death
11. self-control—His self-discipline, obedience, and trust in the perfect will and good purpose of the Father

12. integrity—His upright behavior that conformed to His words
13. hope—the anchor of His human soul through His unfailing trust and belief in the promises of the Father; He endured the passion for the joy that lay before Him (Hebrews 6:19, 12:2)
14. faith—His unwavering belief in the will of the Father

A Prayer for the Stations of the Lord's Passion (modified from St. Catherine of Siena,[13] fourteenth century)

Lord, your great love for us—your creatures—was so strong that it moved you to create us out of yourself and give us your image and likeness so we might experience and share in your eternal goodness, loving kindness, and beauty. Your will and good pleasure for us is to follow the incarnate Son on the way of His passion and death and to participate in His every pain and suffering—His mental afflictions, His physical wounds, and His shed blood and His broken body. As we encounter our Lord and Savior, we humbly watch and pray for healing—physical, mental, and spiritual, amen.

Station 1: Jesus's Hour Arrives

The hour of the incarnate Son consisted of His passing over the earth and His exodus to the heavenly Father (Luke 9:31; John 13:1–3; chapter 11; glossary). He washed the feet of the disciples in the upper room to illustrate His servanthood and self-sacrificial love that would be revealed during His passion and death (John 13:3–17). Jesus was "deeply troubled" with respect to His impending betrayal, unthinkable separation from the Father, and violent death for the sins of the world (John 13:21).

Station 2: Jesus Institutes the Lord's Supper or Eucharist

Jesus celebrated the memorial meal of the new blood covenant of grace with the disciples. He "broke the bread of affliction" that represented His broken body and torn flesh. Then, He took the cup of wine saying, "This is my blood of the covenant, which will be *shed* on behalf of many for the *forgiveness* of sin" (Leviticus 17:11; Matthew 26:26–28; John 6:53–56; Hebrews 9:22, 10:10, 20). Jesus cut and sealed the new blood covenant by His sacrificial passion and death, which fulfilled the prophetic scriptures and satisfied the sovereign Lord's requirements for our redemption and reconciliation (chart IX, see 7).

Station 3: Jesus Enters the Garden of Gethsemane (the Second Garden)

This sacred station reveals the abrupt onset of a near-death medical emergency representing Jesus's greatest conflict (overpowering stress), His greatest agony (fear and sorrow unto death), and His greatest decision (trust and obedience; chart IV-B; chapter 4; glossary).

Jesus drank the "cup of divine fury" that revealed almighty God's unspeakable wrath against the sin, evil, and corruption of the world (Genesis 6:5–6; Mark 14:33–36; Romans 1:18–32). In complete solidarity with humanity, Jesus Christ willingly, yet painstakingly made the decision to bear the sins of the world and justify the many (Isaiah 53:4, 11–12; Hebrews 9:11–15, 28; chart IX, see 15). By the great hope set before Him, He was transformed into the sin of the world, the curse, the son of Satan, and the hour of darkness. This climactic decision resulted in His separation from the Father and His violent death for the sins of the world (chapter 5).

This near-death episode of the acute stress reaction was a terrifying psychopathological reaction with mind-body sequelae—hematidrosis (blood and water losses) and adrenal fatigue with decreased levels of cortisol (Luke 22:43–44; charts IV-B, V, VII-A, XII; figure VI; chapters 4, 5). Both of these complications influenced Jesus's rapid demise on Calvary (Mark 15:44; John 19:33).

Station 4: The Betrayal and Arrest of Jesus

Judas Iscariot betrayed Jesus with a diabolical, shameless, treacherous, and hypocritical kiss (Luke 22:3; John 13:30). Under the secrecy of darkness, Jesus was arrested by the sinister mob consisting of temple police and robust Roman legionnaires (John 18:3). Jesus calmly spoke, "This is your hour, the time for the power of darkness" (Luke 22:52–53). Scripture reveals that Judas had every opportunity to repent for his greedy and heinous intentions similar to other remorseful biblical characters including Job, King David, the Prodigal Son, Peter, Paul, Mary Magdalene, John Mark, Longinus (the pagan centurion under conviction who confessed on Calvary), and Dismas (the repentant revolutionary who was lifted up on Calvary).

Jesus was betrayed, arrested, and abandoned by everyone symbolized by "a certain young man" who left his linen cloth behind and "fled from them naked" (Mark 14:51–52 NKJV).

Station 5: Jewish Trials—False Witnesses, Battery, Mocking, Spitting, and Pulling His Beard

Because of their envy, contempt, and self-righteousness, the chief priests, elders, and scribes unscrupulously solicited "false testimony"

Blood and Water

in their attempt to condemn Jesus to death. At last, He spoke the words they had been waiting to hear, "I AM the Christ, the Son of the Blessed One." Without hesitation, Caiaphas, the high priest, tore his garments and convicted Jesus of "blasphemy." Members of the Sanhedrin "condemned him of deserving to die," spat on Him, and pulled His beard (flagrant insults), and the guards beat Him continuously with their fists (Isaiah 50:6; Mark 14:63–65 NIV; glossary).

Station 6: Jesus in the Pit

Jesus was shackled to the floor in the pit, a dungeon about fifty feet under Caiaphas's priestly palace. His body was covered with tender, purple ecchymosis and pinpoint, purple-red petechiae (charts IV-B; VI-A; glossary). The taunting and battery continued throughout the night. He received nothing by mouth and suffered dehydration, an estimated negative water balance of 2.0 L or 4.4 lbs. (Psalm 88:1–15 NKJV; charts I, II-A).

Station 7: Jesus Appears before the Sanhedrin

The guilty verdict of blasphemy was affirmed early on the morning of Good Friday by the members of the great council. Since Roman approval was required in capital crimes, Jesus was bound with two-inch thick rope and handed over to the Roman authorities (John 18:31, 19:7).

Jewish punishment for blasphemy was death by stoning (Leviticus 24:16). The sovereign Lord allowed the illegal actions taken by Caiaphas and the powerful temple aristocrats in order to fulfill prophetic scripture: Jesus must be *lifted up* by Roman crucifixion

(Numbers 21:4–9; John 3:14–15, 8:28, 12:32–33; chart IX, see 8) and *pierced* by thorns, nails, and a lance (Psalm 22:16; Isaiah 53:5; Zechariah 12:10; John 19:37; chart IX, see 19; figures VIII-A, VIII-B, IX, X).

Station 8: Roman Trials—Jesus Appears before Pontius Pilate

Pilate repeated his decision, "I find no guilt in him" (John 18:38; 19:6). The Roman governor recognized that Jesus of Nazareth was not a threat to the Pax Romana. Yet the furious temple aristocrats and diabolical Jewish mob were not about to rest their case—and this included extortion of the Roman governor (Mark 15:10–15; John 19:12).

Frightened and overwrought by the potential political consequences, Pilate took water and washed his hands saying, "I am innocent of this man's blood." The whole people said in reply, "His blood be upon us and upon our children" (Matthew 27:24–25). Pontius Pilate made use of every available means to release Jesus, but ultimately, exhibited his disregard for Roman law and justice when he asked Jesus the cynical question, "What is truth?" (John 18:37–38; prologue).

Station 9: The Scourging at the Pillar and the King's Game

The pathophysiology that resulted from the overreach of Roman power would prove to be fatal. Pilate and Longinus, the centurion, attempted to pacify the outraged temple aristocrats with a strategy of appeasement as follows (Mark 15:15).

1. the excessive and vicious scourging of sixty to seventy lashes ("three-quarters dead") versus the routine scourging of twenty-five to thirty-five lashes ("half dead"; Deuteronomy 25:1–3; charts I, III, V, VI-A, IX, see 10; figures VIII-A, VIII-B; chapter 5; glossary)
2. the heartless, sarcastic Roman king's game, a charade consisting of defenseless battery with fists and rods to the head, back, chest, and abdomen, frenetic mocking, spitting in His face, and pulling His beard (chart IX, see 15)
3. the piercing wounds and blood loss secondary to the cap of thorns pressed down into the highly vascular flesh of His scalp (Matthew 27:27–31; John 19:1–3; chart IX, 19)

But would this excessive use of Roman torture satisfy the deep-seated contempt, envy, and rage of the Jewish religious leaders and diabolical mob (Mark 15:10)?

Pilate's cruel and unrestrained strategy set in motion the sovereign Lord's determined plan that would fulfill prophetic scripture—multiple wounds, rapid and massive losses of blood and water, fatal multifactorial shock, and secondary internal injuries of the lungs, heart, abdomen, and brain (Acts 2:23; charts I, IV-B, V, VI-A; figures VI, VII; chapters 5, 9). The severity of the Roman scourging, battery, and piercings resulted in billions of crushed cells, small blood vessels, and tiny nerves. The types of wounds Jesus suffered included contusions, hematomas, abrasions, and piercings, an estimated 255, along with mechanical burns of the skin, an estimated 4.5 percent TBSA (chart VI-A; chapter 9; glossary). The immediate blood loss was an estimated 2.5 U or 25 percent of the blood volume, and the water loss including third-space fluid loss was an estimated 3.0 L or 6.6 lbs. (charts I, II-B, V; chapter 9). These rapid and large losses have convinced me that if the blood loss and the water loss were considered separately, each would have been fatal.

Station 10: The "Ecce Homo" and Condemnation

Pilate dramatically exaggerated the presentation of the bloodstained, bludgeoned, and humiliated "King of the Jews" with the now legendary words, "Behold, the man!" the tragic episode recognized as the *Ecce Homo* (John 19:5). In my mind's eye, time was suspended and Jerusalem fell silent. Jesus Christ was lightheaded, stunned, and disoriented, but somehow, He maintained His composure and virtuous behavior (above). His face, ponytail, beard, and body were marked with numerous streamlets of scarlet-red blood and dark purple blood clots (figures VIII-A, VIII-B).

On this first Good Friday, there would be no appeasement. The diabolical mob reacted out of fear, rage, and desperation: "Crucify Him, crucify Him!" (John 19:6 NKJV).

While standing near the historical site of the Fortress of Antonia on a pilgrimage to Jerusalem, I could hear the echoes of these words and those of Pontius Pilate as he handed over Jesus for execution, "Take up Your cross. Carry Your cross outside the walls of Jerusalem. Be lifted up on Your cross unto death" (Jerusalem tour guide, 2013).

As you meditate, keep watch, and pray on your way of the Lord's passion, carefully consider the following: the sovereign Lord allowed evil people and demonic forces to be His instruments to "accomplish all things according to the intention of His will" for the praise of His glory (Acts 2:23; Ephesians 1:11–12, 6:12; 1 Peter 1:10–12). Yet, operating within his own free will, Pilate was unaware that the overreach of his appeasement strategy would serve the Sovereign's intentions—the fulfillment of the prophetic scriptures and the pathophysiological results of the modern medical sciences as they became known (Psalm 22:12–21; Isaiah 53:4–10; Hebrews 13:11–13; charts I, V, VI-A, IX, see 8, 10, 12, 14, 15, 19, 21, XI, XII; figure VI; chapters 5, 9, 12).

Station 11: Jesus Takes up the Crossbar

The heavy patibulum (100 to 150 lbs.) was laid across Jesus's shoulders and upper back, tied with heavy rope securing His extended upper extremities, and finally looped around His neck and waist. Jesus was bent forward, top-heavy, and unsteady. He was light-headed and confused, and He collapsed several times before reaching His destination outside the Jerusalem walls (chart VII-C).

Notwithstanding, Jesus obeyed the perfect will of the Father to fulfill the prophetic scriptures and to "consecrate the people" by His sacrificial losses of precious blood and living water (Leviticus 16:27; Hebrews 10:7, 13:11–13; chart I). He departed from the Fortress of Antonia in fair medical condition.

Jesus sustained numerous abrasions, contusions, hematomas, and lacerations to His chest wall and more serious internal contusions and hematomas of His lungs (chart VIII-A; figures VIII-A, VIII-B; chapters 5, 12). As He set out for Calvary, Jesus felt sharp pleuritic chest pain with each breath. Nevertheless, it was the rapid, ongoing losses of blood and water that resulted in severe multifactorial shock and His ultimate demise (charts I, II-B, V, VII-A, XI, XII; figures VI, VII).

Station 12: Jesus Falls for the First Time

Jesus was dizzy, confused, and unsteady secondary to progressive multifactorial shock: His brain was receiving inadequate levels of precious O_2 (charts V, VII-C). He suffered a pulmonary contusion with respiratory hypoxia and a mild concussion (acute brain injury; chart XII; glossary). These post-traumatic conditions combined with bearing the heavy crossbar made the climb up Mount Calvary extremely difficult; each stumble and fall resulted in abrasions, contusions, and sprains of His shoulders and knees (chart VI-A; figures VIII-A, VIII-B).

Despite the brutal scourging, battery, piercings, and multiple falls, Jesus did not sustain a broken bone since the prophetic scriptures must be fulfilled. Jesus Christ was the unblemished sacrificial Lamb of God—the Perfect One (Exodus 12:5–7, 46; Leviticus 1:10; Luke 24:44; John 1:29, 19:34–37; 1 Peter 1:19; chart IX, see 6, 20).

Station 13: Jesus Meets His Afflicted Mother

This encounter of serenity and beauty was a striking contradiction—desperation, disappointment, and anguish versus empathy, hope, and trust. Mary's inspired words revealed her strong will, wisdom, and faithfulness: "Let it be done to me according to your word." As the "highly favored one of God," she "pondered these things in her heart" (Luke 1:30, 38, 2:19 NKJV).

Station 14: Simon Assists Jesus

The foremost obligations of centurion Longinus included the certainty his prisoner, "Jesus the Nazorean, the King of the Jews," was lifted up unto death and the declaration of death was signed in the presence of Pilate (Mark 15:44–46; John 19:19). However, based on the rapid deterioration of Jesus—labored respirations, severe blood loss, ashen skin, mental confusion, and progressive unsteadiness—the experienced centurion determined Jesus to be incapable of reaching the summit of Calvary and wisely pressed Simon, a pilgrim from Cyrene, into Roman service (Luke 23:26; charts VI-A, VII-D, XII).

According to Luke, this unsuspecting yet devout God-fearer understood the core principle of discipleship: Simon "took up the cross and followed Jesus from *behind*" (Luke 9:23, 14:27, 23:26; chapter 11). The power of the gospel was alive and well. Simon, his wife, and two sons became notable members of the ancient church (Mark 15:21; Romans 1:16, 16:13). Only by the *grace* and goodness of almighty God is it possible to deny yourself, take up your cross daily, and follow the Lord Jesus from behind!

Station 15: Veronica Wipes Jesus's Face

The church honors this impassioned woman on the way. Veronica was overcome with sorrow, kindness, and tenderness. She courageously stepped forward from her home on the Via Dolorosa and cleansed the blood and water (filthy sweat, spit, serum, and vomitus) from the beaten and disfigured face of Jesus. Suddenly, the miraculous imprint of His holy face appeared on the cloth (Isaiah 50:6, 52:14; figure VIII-A).

> Golden Hour Station 15, Friday. 10:45 a.m.–11:45 a.m.

Jesus passed the golden hour on the Via Dolorosa at station 15 (glossary). Extensive medical and surgical research[14, 15] has demonstrated that treatment received during the vital first hour is the best prognosticator for the survival of patients with shock-trauma (figure IV). The greatest challenge facing modern traumatology is to initiate lifesaving resuscitation during the golden hour: Arterial bleeding arrested and Airway secured, Breathing established, and Circulation restored (the A-A-B-C of emergency resuscitation). In the absence of emergency treatment, Jesus suffered from continuous losses of blood and water, the rapid onset and complications of decompensated multifactorial shock, and the secondary conditions involving His heart and lungs (charts I, V, VIII-A, VIII-D, XI, XII; figures IV, VI, VII; chapter 5). As Jesus crossed the golden hour, His medical condition was serious (Friday, 11:45 a.m.).

Station 16: Jesus Falls a Second Time

The continuous blood loss (shed blood) and water loss (broken body and torn flesh) resulted in severe multifactorial shock with two important sequelae[14,15] involving His circulatory system: (1) a decreased blood volume resulting in hypotension (↓BP) and hypoperfusion (↓BF), and (2) a decreased oxygen carrying-capacity—decreased RBCs that bind, transport, and deliver oxygen; (charts I, V, VII-A, VII-B, XII; chapter 5; glossary). These pathophysiological conditions resulted in cellular dehydration, hypoxia, acidosis, hypoglycemia, decreased production of cellular energy, and the probable onset of coagulopathy[14,15] (charts VII-C, VII-D, XI, XII; figures VI, VII; glossary).

In my analysis, the multiple falls that occurred along the Via Dolorosa did not cause significant injuries involving the brain, spine, lungs, and heart of Jesus—the resultant zones of destruction were insufficient (glossary).

Blood and Water

Station 17: Jesus Consoles the Daughters of Jerusalem

Despite His serious medical condition and distress, Jesus never deviated from His virtuous behavior and compassion for others. "Do not weep for me, but weep instead for yourselves and for your children" (Luke 23:27–28). Jesus also spoke prophetically to these grieving women—a warning that concerned the future Jewish-Roman War (the terror, death, and destruction of Jerusalem including the Roman crucifixions [16, 17] of more than 30,000 Jewish prisoners).

Station 18: Jesus Falls a Third Time

As Jesus continued the difficult climb of Calvary, He could observe the three stationary uprights on the summit standing about seven or eight feet above the ground—"the killing field of the crosses." His struggles on the Via Dolorosa included mental anguish, dizziness, exhaustion, dyspnea, and falls causing additional abrasions, contusions, and sprains (chart VI; figures VIII-A, VIII-B; glossary). Yet, a *grave* medical issue was looming—the ongoing, untreated water losses due to profuse sweating, hyperventilation, and vomiting and the large third-space fluid loss secondary to the initial traumatic wounds, effusions, paralytic ileus, and the progressive ischemic wounds of severe shock (charts I, II-B, V, VI, XI, XII; figures VI, VII; chapters 5, 9; glossary).

Station 19: Jesus Arrives at Mount Calvary in Critical Condition

Jesus Christ was in severe distress—confused, dyspneic, and bloodstained—"pierced for our offenses and crushed for our sins"

(Isaiah 53:5; Hebrews 9:28); "like a lamb being led to the slaughter" (Isaiah 53:7; John 1:29); and "by His stripes (wounds) we are healed" (Isaiah 53:5; 1 Peter 2:24; chart IX, see 15).

Prior to being lifted up, Jesus's vital signs were unstable (glossary): BP decreased (90/50); HR/P rapid and thready (180/minute); RR labored (35/minute); and T decreased (97°F or 36°C. He was disoriented regarding name, time, and place. His countenance was ashen and gaunt. His eyes were sunken. His tongue was swollen and stuck to His palate. His lips were parched, cracked, and coated with dried saliva, filthy sweat, and fragments of clotted blood. His neck veins were distended. Each respiration was painful and labored. His heart sounds were racing and muffled—a possible pericardial effusion with early cardiac compression and failure. His abdomen was distended, diffusely tender, and silent consistent with a paralytic ileus or an intra-abdominal injury. To sum up the clinical picture, Jesus Christ was in severe shock with the appearance of *impending doom*. The incarnate Son of God was paradoxically unable to save Himself—He was powerless, humiliated, and abandoned (Luke 23:35,37,39).

From head to toe, Jesus was covered with multiple wounds, polluted sweat and serum, vomitus, petechiae, ecchymosis, streamlets of fresh, scarlet blood, and purple blood clots. His scalp was covered with dozens of scattered puncture wounds and puddles of dark blood. His face was deformed and swollen from contusions and hematomas (Isaiah 52:14). His nasal cartilage was minimally displaced resulting from the relentless buffeting during the Jewish and Roman trials (Isaiah 50:6; Matthew 26:67, 27:30). There were patterned injuries of parallel wounds across the back, chest, abdomen, hips, and legs consistent with Roman scourging; these wounds included

Blood and Water

partial-thickness mechanical burns, contusions, hematomas, and split lacerations (chart VI-A; figures VIII-A, VIII-B; chapters 5, 9).

The bloodstained, dehydrated, and ravaged incarnate Son—the last Adam—stood naked next to the wooden upright of the Palestinian oak—the tree of eternal life. This portrait is a compelling reminder of our first parents who stood naked, frightened, and ashamed under the tree of the knowledge of good and evil—the tree of physical and spiritual death (Genesis 2:17 NIV, 3:7–12; Romans 5:17–19; Revelation 5:6–9; chart IX, see 1).

Jesus Christ reversed the original sin and the curse of Eden (the first garden) by His greatest decision—to drink the Father's cup of wrath in Gethsemane (the second garden) and to suffer and die for the sins of the world by His shed blood and broken body (chart IX, see 21). Finally, He was buried and gloriously raised to life in the Garden of Resurrection (the third garden; glossary, "gardens—the three gardens of redemption").

Station 20: Jesus Is Lifted Up

Although unstable, disoriented, and near death, the incarnate Son was lifted up and reigned from His holy cross—the eternal King sitting on His glorious wooden throne; the eternal, great High Priest offering Himself on almighty God's sacrificial wooden altar; and the eternal Prophet, like Moses, preaching the seven words from His wooden pulpit. The incarnate Son prophesied that when *lifted up* He would keep the following promises—to give eternal life to everyone who believes in Him (John 3:14–15); to reveal Himself as the great "I AM" (John 8:28); and to "draw everyone to Himself" (John 12:32; chart IX, see 8).

Station 21: Jesus Dies on His Holy Cross

By His foreknowledge and set plan, the sovereign Lord and Great Physician directed the psychopathology (chart IV-B; chapter 4) and the pathophysiology (Acts 2:23; charts I, V, VI-A; figures VI, VII; chapters 5, 9) of the passion and sacrificial death of Jesus Christ. His infinite, perfect, and eternal sacrifice was the result of the preliminary traumas and sufferings that fulfill the prophetic scriptures and satisfy the modern medical sciences (chapter 12). The PTS consisted of physical, mental, and spiritual wounds—shed blood (fatal loss of blood), broken body and torn flesh (fatal loss of water and severe dehydration), and decompensated multifactorial shock. Although Jesus was pronounced dead on His holy cross, Roman crucifixion was not the cause of his death (charts III, V; figure VI).

The postmortem blow of the lance—unique to the fourth gospel—resulted in the "immediate flow of blood and water" from the pierced heart of Jesus Christ (John 19:33–34;1 John 5:6–8; figure X; glossary). This climactic event on Mount Calvary revealed the self-sacrificial, loving heart of the Holy Trinity: God the Father—our Creator, God the Son—our Redeemer, and God the Spirit—our Sanctifier.

Station 22: Jesus Fulfills Prophetic Scripture as the Unblemished Lamb of God, the Pierced One, and the New Temple of God

The sovereign Lord linked the human sacrificial death of the incarnate Son of God to the following supernatural events.

1. darkness "from noon until three in the afternoon" (Matthew 27:45)

2. the "torn inner veil" in the temple representing the torn flesh and broken body of Jesus Christ graciously bestowed our eternal access to God by a new and living way (Leviticus 16:12–15; Matthew 27:51; Hebrews 4:16, 6:19–20, 10:19–20)
3. an earthquake "opened the tombs of many saints whose bodies were raised" (Matthew 27:51–53)
4. the Roman centurion was convicted by what he had seen and heard, and made the following heartfelt declaration of faith: "Truly this man was the Son of God" (Mark 15:39 NKJV)
5. now glorified, the lifted-up incarnate Son graciously poured out the Holy Spirit to empower and enlighten the first church on Calvary (Isaiah 52:13; John 7:38–39, 19:30;1 John 5:6–8)

The beloved disciple's eyewitness from Calvary revealed that the prophetic scriptures were fulfilled and perfected (chart IX; chapter 11).

1. Jesus is the "Perfect One"—the unblemished Lamb of God without broken bones (Exodus 12:5, 46; Leviticus 1:3, 10; John 19:36; chart IX, see 6,20).
2. Jesus is the "Pierced One"—lifted up on Mount Calvary and mourned by those who pierced Him (Zechariah 12:10; John 19:37, chart IX, see 19; figures IX, X).
3. Jesus is the "New Temple of God"—His precious blood and lifesaving water flow to the ends of the earth and satisfy all who thirst for God (1 Kings 8:6–13; Isaiah 55:1; Ezekiel 47:1-9; John 2:18–22, 7:37–39, 19:34; Acts 1:8; Hebrews 9:11–14;1 John 1:7, 5:6–12; Revelation 22:17; chart IX, see 17; figure X).

This magnificent, climactic scene on Mount Calvary—the death and the glorification of the incarnate Son—reveals for every

Christian, the most profound revelation of the Father's sacrificial love[18] (John 3:16; Romans 8:32; 1 John 4:9–10).

Station 23: Jesus Is Depositioned from the Holy Cross, Enshrouded, and Buried

The naked corpse of Jesus was immediately covered with a winding sheet. Jesus and the crossbar were depositioned and carried together by members of the first church to the stone of anointing in the Garden of Resurrection—Joseph of Arimathea, Nicodemus, the Virgin Mary, Mary Magdalene, and the disciple Jesus loved. The nails were extracted from His wrists (figure IX), the rigor mortis physically broken, and both hands were secured across His groin (figure VIII-A; glossary).

He was washed, partially anointed with myrrh and aloe, and wrapped with a vertical linen burial cloth or shroud and several horizontal bandlets (Matthew 27:57–60; John 19:38–42; figures VIII-A, VIII-B; chapter 6; glossary).

Rigor mortis[19] (stiffening of the muscles in a dead body) is demonstrated on the shroud of Turin by the flexion and rotation of the cervical spine and the flexion of the left knee (figure VIII-A; VIII-B; chapter 6; glossary). Jesus was entombed in the virgin sepulcher provided by Joseph of Arimathea (Isaiah 53:9; John 19:38).

After extensive research and meditation, I have concluded that the glorified, incarnate Son poured out the Holy Spirit while lifted up, represented by the rivers of living water that flowed from His pierced heart on Mount Calvary (Ezekiel 47:9; Zechariah 13:1, 14:8; John 7:37–39, 19:29–34;1 John 5:6–8; figure X). The grace, truth, and power of the Spirit were essential for the life of the first church on Calvary whose members were overcome by the events, potential dangers, and extreme emotions—fright, conflict, doubt, disappointment, and grief.

The members consisted of the beloved disciple, the apostle John; the Virgin Mary and Mother of God; Mary Magdalene, the demon-possessed sinner; Dismas, the repentant revolutionary who died after the crucifracture (chart III); Joseph of Arimathea, the wealthy member of the Sanhedrin and courageous secret disciple; Nicodemus, a prominent teacher and leading Pharisee, member of the Sanhedrin, and courageous secret disciple; Simon, the Cyrenian who carried the crossbar and followed Jesus from behind; Mary Salome, the mother of the apostles James and John; and Mary, the mother of James and Joseph—the four Marias on Mount Calvary (Matthew 27:56–61; Mark 15:40–47; Luke 23:26; John 19:25–27, 38–42).

Station 24: Jesus Descends to Hades, the Pit

The scriptures reveal that "the place of the dead" or Hades is also known as the grave, the netherworld, and the abyss or pit. The mysterious pit is characterized by the total absence of almighty God, utter darkness, absolute silence, isolation, despair, and terror (Psalm 16:10, 28:1, 49:15, 88:3–6; Acts 2:27, 13:35). The glorified Son descended to Hades to preach the good news of His triumphant sacrificial work, defeat Satan, take possession of the keys of heaven and hell, and victoriously release the Old Testament saints. He embraced Adam and Eve and Dismas—"Today you will be with me in Paradise"—and ascended (Luke 23:43).

Jesus escorted the saints into the presence of almighty God by a new and living way—their hearts sprinkled clean by His shed blood and their bodies washed with His pure and living water (Romans 5:2;

Ephesians 2:18, 4:9–10; 1 Peter 3:20–21; Hebrews 4:16, 6:19-20, 7:19, 10:19–22; chart I).

Station 25: The Resurrection of Jesus

The bodily resurrection of Jesus Christ is our revelation that He is the glorious, incarnate Son of God who was sent by the Father and anointed by the Spirit to redeem humanity from sin and death (Romans 3:25, 8:1–2). Jesus's passion and sacrificial death were accepted by almighty God as infinite, perfect, and eternal—the divine attributes that merit our most cherished promises of *infinite* mercy, *perfect* and unlimited grace, and *eternal* life.

Jesus Christ defeated sin and death, destroyed Satan, and revealed the glorious gospel of grace—the good news of almighty God's brilliant light, self-sacrificial love, and eternal life (1 Corinthians 15:44–45; 2 Timothy 1:10; Hebrews 2:14–15;1 John 1–5). His miraculous bodily resurrection is our promise of the blessed hope— our resurrection and eternal bliss in the exalted presence of the Holy Trinity—God the Father and God the Son and God the Spirit (Matthew 28:19; 1 Corinthians 15:53–57; 1 Timothy 6:16; Titus 2:13).

The stations of the Lord's passion fulfill and perfect the prophetic words of the incarnate Son:[8,9] "Amen, amen, I say to you, unless a grain of wheat falls to the ground and dies, it remains just a grain of wheat; but if it dies, it produces much fruit" (John 12:24).

REFERENCES

1. McBrien, R. P., editor. 1995. *The HarperCollins Encyclopedia of Catholicism.* San Francisco: HarperCollins.
2. Sheed, F. J. 1980. *To Know Christ Jesus.* San Francisco: Ignatius Press.
3. Bultmann, R. 2007. *Theology of the New Testament* (2 volumes). Waco, TX: Baylor University Press.
4. Brown, R. E. 1994. *The Death of the Messiah* (Volumes I and II). New Haven: Yale University Press.
5. Kempis, T. A. 2004. *On the Passion of Christ According to the Four Evangelists.* San Francisco: Ignatius Press.
6. Wright, N. T. 2007. *Christians at the Cross.* Ijamsville, MD: The Word Among Us Press.
7. Kenyon, E. W. 2010. *What Happened from the Cross to the Throne.* Lynnwood, WA: Kenyon's Gospel Publishing Society.
8. Benedict XVI. 2005. *Way of the Cross.* Boston: Pauline Books and Media.
9. Ratzinger, J. 2011. *Jesus of Nazareth* (Part II). San Francisco: Ignatius Press.
10. Veras, R. "Via Crucis: The Way of the Cross." *Magnificat.* 2014, 16 (1): 164–77.
11. Bishop, J. 1977. *The Day Christ Died.* New York: HarperCollins.
12. Cessario, R. 2009. *The Seven Last Words of Jesus.* New York: Magnificat.
13. Thorold, A. 2010. *The Dialogue of St. Catherine of Siena.* 2010. Charlotte: Saint Benedict Press, TAN Books.
14. Bulger, E. M. 2011. In *Greenfield's Surgery.* Philadelphia: Lippincott Williams & Wilkins.
15. Martin, M. and A. Beckley, editors. 2011. *Front Line Surgery.* New York: Springer.

16 Josephus, B. J. *Jewish Antiquities and The Jewish War*. Whiston, W. (Translation). 1960. Kregel Publishing. Williamson, G. A. (Translation). 1959. New York: Penguin.
17 Harrison, R. K., editor. 1988. *The New Unger's Bible Dictionary*. Chicago: Moody Bible Institute.
18 Balthasar, H. U. 1981. *Mysterium Paschale* (The Mystery of Easter). San Francisco: Ignatius Press.
19 Zugibe, T. Z. 2005. The *Crucifixion of Jesus*. New York: M. Evans.

Epilogue

The Mystery of How Jesus Died Is Solved by Scripture and Medical Science

Blood and Water presents original research of the sacred scriptures and the modern medical sciences that faithfully and thoughtfully deciphers and solves the mystery of how Jesus died.

My investigation puts to rest once and for all, the incorrect yet still standing causes of Jesus's death (figure V), and the provocative challenge made by the notable Raymond E. Brown[1] as follows.

In my judgment, the major defect of most of the studies I have reported on thus far is that they were written by *doctors who did not stick to their trade* and let the literalist understanding of the gospel accounts influence their judgments on the physical cause of the death of Jesus …The medical writers have expressed their conclusions without recognizing that any or all of these features might embody theological symbolism rather than historical description (chapter 9).

To properly address Dr. Brown's challenge—to update and transpose the Lord's passion into the twenty-first century medical and surgical sciences—I began my studies by addressing the most recent and relevant medical and surgical literature, for example, emergency and critical care medicine, psychiatry, surgery, and traumatology. I was careful to maintain the separation between the medical, psychiatric, and surgical sciences and the sacred scriptures including the sovereignty of God, the fulfillment of prophecy, the theological effects of the Christ event, and the biblical symbolism of the blood and water.

After many years of medical, psychiatric, surgical, and traumatic studies, I felt confident that my scientific conclusions had deciphered and solved the mystery of how Jesus died. However, I also realized that my professional analyses would spark controversy among the members of both Christian and medical communities. For example, (1) the Roman cross was Jesus's *deathbed,* not the cause of His death; (2) the episode in Gethsemane was *life-threatening* and influenced Jesus's rapid demise; and (3) the *nonexistence* of the scriptural and scientific evidence for Jesus's death by tetany/asphyxiation (suffocation), a broken heart (internal bleeding), and divine intervention (untenable theology).

Yet currently, the majority of authors, biblical commentators, professors, journalists, pastors, priests, and physicians actively support and teach that the death of Jesus Christ was caused by the Roman cross including one or more of the following medical conditions: tetany/asphyxiation, broken/ruptured heart, divine intervention, or piercings by the Roman nails and lance (figure V; prologue; chapters 5, 7, 9, 12). For the sake of the grace, the truth, and the life of the glorious gospel and the modern medical sciences, I am compelled to discredit and refute these incorrect causes of death.

In the beginning of my work, I prudently organized the passion and sacrificial death of Jesus into the following biblical episodes.

1. The life-threatening acute stress reaction in Gethsemane—His greatest agony—resulted from overwhelming fear, sorrow, and conflict, and complicated by the severe sequelae of hematidrosis (blood and water losses) and adrenal fatigue (decreased blood levels of cortisol).
2. The Jewish trials consisted of defenseless battery (blood and water losses) and imprisonment in the pit (acute dehydration).
3. The Roman trials officiated by Pontius Pilate consisted of lethal scourging at the Roman pillar (rapid and ongoing blood and water losses) plus the highly sarcastic and violent king's game that included defenseless battery (blood and water losses), pulling His beard, spitting in His face, and multiple piercings by the cap of thorns (blood and water losses).
4. The mental and physical struggles on the Via Dolorosa included several falls, sweating, vomiting, and hyperventilation plus the continuous losses of blood and water from His earlier wounds.
5. Jesus passed the golden hour without treatment and arrived at Mount Calvary in critical condition.
6. He underwent a routine Roman crucifixion on a *T*-shaped cross without crucifracture and died three hours later.

During the postmortem period, relevant episodes transpired regarding the mystery of how Jesus died. First, at the moment of Jesus's death, the inner veil of the temple was supernaturally torn, which revealed the following.

1. The torn veil represented the broken body and torn flesh of Jesus Christ caused by severe cellular dehydration—His sacrificial death provides the accessibility to almighty God for all eternity (Mark 15:36; John 14:6; Hebrews 4:16, 6:19-20, 7:19; 10:19-20).
2. Jesus fulfilled and perfected the Levitical sacrificial system (chart IX, see 20).
3. By faith in our great High Priest, we are granted eternal access into the presence of the Lord by the sprinkling of His merciful *blood* and the washing with His pure, lifesaving *water* (Hebrews 4:16, 7:19, 10:19–22; chart IX, see 13).

Second, Longinus, the pagan centurion who had witnessed the supernatural events and the glorious death of Jesus Christ, made his remarkable confession of faith: "Truly this man was the Son of God" (Mark 15:39). Third, "Pilate was amazed" when he learned that Jesus "was already dead" (Mark 15:44).

Finally, the drama on Calvary reached its magnificent conclusion—the piercing of the incarnate Son's sacred heart which caused the immediate flow of His blood—right atrium and ventricle—and His water—pericardial effusion (John 19:34;1 John 5:6–8; figures I-C, VIII-A, VIII-B, X).

The precious blood and living water that killed the incarnate Son washed the skull of Adam at the foot of the cross reversing original sin and the curse. From Calvary His blood and water poured through the streets of Jerusalem and to the ends of the earth. "If you thirst, come to Me" ... drink My precious blood—the forgiveness of sin—and My lifesaving water—the indwelling Holy Spirit (John 7:37; Acts 1:8; chart IX, see 1, 21).

To solve this two-thousand-year-old mystery without the presence of a body, I assembled my medical evidence as follows (chapters 1, 4, 5, 6, 9, 12).

1. estimates of the number, types (BFT versus SFT), and locations of the wounds (charts VI-A, VIII-A, VIII-B; figures VIII-A, VIII-B, IX, X; chapter 9))
2. estimates of the surface area of the partial-thickness mechanical burns (chart VI-A; figures VIII-A, VIII-B)
3. estimates of the blood and water losses (charts I, II-B; chapter 9).

As my research progressed, my surgical experience and instincts persuaded me that *prior* to His crucifixion, Jesus Christ had been mortally wounded—mental afflictions and physical trauma including multiple wounds, rapid and extremely large losses of blood and water, and severe multifactorial shock (charts I, II-B, III, IV-B, V, VI-A, VII-A, VII-D; figures IV, VI, VII). In the absence of modern shock-trauma resuscitation during the golden hour, Jesus suffered a rapid downhill course. I identified these fatal conditions as the *preliminary traumas and sufferings*, and I am certain that they—not Roman crucifixion—were responsible for His demise (Mark 15:44; John 19:33–34; charts I, V, XI, XII; figure VI; chapters 4, 5, 9, 12).

With solid medical evidence in hand, I was confident that I had solved the mystery of how Jesus died: *The Roman cross did not kill Jesus Christ—it was His deathbed.*

Yet, over the course of my journey and way to decipher the mystery of how Jesus died, I struggled to maintain the separation (above) between the medical sciences and the sacred scriptures. Ultimately, I was convicted by the following persuasive words from the Lord, *"My word is powerful, inspired, and flawless!"* I was impressed to make a pilgrimage for the sole purpose of inquiring of the Lord.

Subsequently, in the Garden of Gethsemane while mediating in His presence,[4] I heard that still, small voice of almighty God: "Doctor, I AM that I AM!" The word of the Lord blazed across my mind: "With God, all things will be possible" (Luke 1:37); "the Spirit of truth will guide you into all truth" (John 16:13); "My strength is made perfect in your weakness" (2 Corinthians 12:9).

The sovereign Lord revealed to me that He—the great I AM, sovereign Lord, and Great Physician—created, predetermined, and coordinated *everything* that exists including the modern medical sciences, the fulfillment of prophetic scripture, the theological effects of the Christ event, and the transcendency of the blood and water.

As faithful Christians, we trust and obey our monotheistic, Triune God.[2,3] The infinite power and eternal wisdom of the sovereign Lord had determined the incarnate Son's passion and sacrificial death directing His mental afflictions—fright, sorrow, terror, conflict, and agony—and His physical traumas—multiple wounds, severe blood and water losses, and decompensated multifactorial shock.

The omnipotent and omniscient God is our Source—Creator, Redeemer, and Great Physician and Surgeon. By His Word, He effortlessly spoke the billions upon billions of solar systems into existence. He designed, created, and breathed life into the magnificent human body consisting of more than one hundred trillion living cells including the complexities of molecular biology, the genome, and the circulatory system consisting of an unimaginable fifty thousand miles of blood vessels. As our Savior and Lord, He is the Originator of every spiritual blessing—our light, self-sacrificial love, and eternal life (Ephesians 1:3;1 John 1–5).

I often reflect on the limits and restraints I had placed on the sovereign Lord's infinite power and perfect wisdom. But, was it not the great I AM who wove the scarlet cord of Rahab through the pages of scripture to reveal the blood of Christ? And was it not He who revealed the crystal-clear rivers of living water that flowed from the pierced heart of the incarnate Son representing the Holy Spirit, the washing of the church by His Word, the new birth by water and Spirit, and eternal life (chart X; figures I-A, I-B, I-C; chapter 7)?

I have come full circle during my personal and spiritual journey and my way to Mount Calvary! The Author of sacred scripture and sovereign Originator of all things—seen and unseen—revealed to me that the fulfillment of prophetic scripture, the theological effects of the Christ event, and the transcendent participation of the blood and water were synergistically synthesized with the medical sciences to solve the mystery of how Jesus died.

On the night of His betrayal and arrest, Jesus shocked the twelve when He proclaimed that He—the perfect Lamb of God and not a sacrificial animal—would cut, seal, and memorialize the new blood covenant of grace by His sacrificial death and the shedding of His blood and His broken body. His precious blood and lifesaving water are eternal and transcendent themes that robustly flow through the pages of sacred scripture from Genesis to Revelation (chart X; figures I-A, I-B, I-C; prologue; chapters 1, 7).

Under the direction of the sovereign Lord, the preliminary traumas and sufferings resulted in the *mortal wounds* of Jesus Christ—His fatal losses of blood and water, and His decompensated, multifactorial shock. The passion and sacrificial death of Jesus Christ— "delivered by the determined purpose and foreknowledge of God"—consisted of the following events (Acts 2:23).

1. In Gethsemane, the sequelae of the acute stress reaction were hematidrosis and ecchymosis (blood and water losses) and *adrenal fatigue* (decreased cortisol levels).

2. The Jewish trials included relentless battery and mocking and the lockup in the pit—*acute dehydration* (water losses).
3. The *fatal scourging*, battery, and piercings during the Roman trial resulted in severe, ongoing blood and water losses.
4. The mental afflictions and physical agonies on the Via Dolorosa exacerbated the blood and water losses.
5. Jesus arrived on Mount Calvary in *critical* condition *prior* to His crucifixion primarily due to the continuous blood and water losses (charts I, II-B, III, IV-B, V, VI-A, VII-A, VII-D, XI, XII; figures VI, VII, VIII-A, VIII-B; chapters 4, 5, 10, 12, 13).

The three witnesses were of one accord— "the Spirit, the water and the blood" (1 John 5:6–8)—testify that the incarnate Son of God was *enfleshed* with blood and water. He was *baptized* in living water and *died* by the losses of blood and water. His precious blood and lifesaving water flow eternally from His sacred heart down the rocky slopes of Mount Calvary, into the narrow streets of Jerusalem, and to the ends of the earth. "If your soul thirsts, come to me and drink" and my lifesaving blood (forgiveness) and cleansing water (Holy Spirit) will satisfy you (John 7:37–39, 19:33–34; Revelation 22:17). We must hold dearly to the promises of God and share in His divine nature (2 Peter 1:4).

The sovereign Lord—our Great Physician and Surgeon—directed every step of the passion and sacrificial death by the synthesis of modern medical science and sacred scripture including the absolute fulfillment and perfection of prophecy, the theological results of Christ's perfect and eternal sacrifice by His shed blood and His broken body, and the transcendency of His precious blood and living water. The Christian's journey and way to Mount Calvary is by the incarnate Son's precious and powerful blood and His crystal-clear living water.

REFERENCES

1. Brown, R. E. 1994. *The Death of the Messiah* (Volume II). New Haven: Yale University Press (pages 1089, 1092).
2. Bultman, R. 2007. *Theology of the New Testament* (2 volumes). Waco, TX: Baylor University Press.
3. Sheed, F. J. 1981. *Theology for Beginners.* Cincinnati: St. Anthony Messenger Press.
4. Young, S. 2011. *Jesus Calling.* Nashville: Thomas Nelson.

Glossary

abrasion: Scrape or scratch of the skin or other organ.

acid/base balance: A pH of 7.4 is the optimal value for the function of cellular enzymes; for example, the synthesis of cellular energy (ATP) requires a pH of 7.4 (chart XII; chapter 7).

acidosis: The accumulation of excessive acid (hydrogen ions) along with the depletion of buffers (bicarbonate; chart XII). Lactic acidosis (pH <7.4) results during hemorrhagic shock, cellular hypoxia ($\downarrow O_2$), and the switch to anaerobic energy production ($\downarrow$ATP; $\uparrow$lactic acid). Respiratory acidosis (pH <7.4) results secondary to acute respiratory failure. The presence of severe cellular acidosis causes cellular enzyme dysfunction and cellular death (charts I, V, VII-D, VIII-A, XI, XII).

acute: The sudden onset of a medical, psychological, or traumatic condition, for example acute stress reaction, acute hemorrhagic shock, and acute respiratory failure.

acute inflammatory response: The innate immune response to trauma and infection that sequesters, dilutes, and removes bacteria, foreign matter, and dead cells. Each wound sustained by Jesus initiated an acute inflammatory response (charts VI-A, VI-B).

acute respiratory distress syndrome: ARDS is a serious lung condition characterized by the following pathophysiology: injury of the alveolar-capillary membranes (the site of gas exchange), acute inflammatory response, and abnormal arterial blood gases; for example, lung contusion is one cause of ARDS (charts VI-B, VIII-A, XII; chapter 5).

acute stress reaction with psychosomatic disease: The acute stress reaction or fight-or-flight syndrome is a psychopathological condition caused by stressors such as sudden danger, conflict, pain, anxiety, fear, and sorrow. The life-threatening acute stress reaction in Gethsemane was complicated by the psychosomatic conditions (mind-body disorders) of hematidrosis (bloody sweat) and adrenal fatigue ($\downarrow$cortisol) that influenced Jesus's rapid demise (charts IV-B, VII-A; figures III, VI, VII; chapters 4, 5).

adenosine triphosphate (ATP): A complex molecule containing high-energy phosphate bonds necessary for cellular life. Aerobic energy (ATP) is synthesized by O_2, CHO, and fat—a life-sustaining function that is threatened during multifactorial shock (charts V, VII-D, XI; chapters 5, 7).

adrenal fatigue: The exhaustion of the adrenal glands caused by one or more episodes of severe anxiety, fear, or conflict resulting in decreased levels of blood cortisol, the crucial hormone necessary for compensation (homeostasis) during anxiety reactions, stress, and shock-trauma (charts IV-A, IV-B, V, VII-A; chapters 3, 4, 5).

adrenal glands: Small endocrine organs located on the superior domes of the kidneys (suprarenal glands); as members of the H-P-A axis, they secrete the stress hormones—epi, nepi, and cortisol—in response to disorders such as the acute anxiety reaction and shock-trauma (charts IV-A, IV-B, V; chapters 3, 4, 5).

adrenocorticotropic hormone: The pituitary gland—activated by the hypothalamus—secretes ACTH in response to stressors such as fear, anxiety, pain, shock-trauma, and hypoxia, which in turn stimulates the adrenal glands (H-P-A axis) for the release of *cortisol* (charts IV-A, IV-B, V; figure III; chapter 4).

aerobic energy: In the presence of *oxygen,* the cellular mitochondria produce ATP—the energy sufficient to sustain cellular life (chart XI; figure II; chapters 2, 7).

albumen: An important plasma protein that helps to maintain the fluid content of the intravascular space.

alveolar air sac or alveolus of the lungs: The tiny air sacs of the lungs vital for gas exchange—O_2 inhaled and CO_2 exhaled.

amino acid: The basic unit of protein molecules—uniquely containing nitrogen—required for growth and repair and the synthesis of antibodies, enzymes, and albumen.

amygdala: An almond-sized nerve center in the subcortical limbic brain; if activated by stressors such as fear, anxiety, and conflict, the amygdala stimulates the autonomic neuroendocrine system for homeostasis (charts IV-A, IV- B; figure III; chapters 3, 4).

anabolism: The constructive or anabolic state of the body that includes a positive nitrogen (protein) balance.

anaerobic energy: In the absence of *oxygen* during severe hemorrhagic shock or strenuous physical exercise, the production of cellular energy is insufficient to sustain life ($\downarrow$ATP; charts V, XI; figure II; chapter 7).

anemia: A low RBC count defined by Hct <30 percent and Hb <10 gm/dL (chart XII).

Annas: The powerful high priest of Israel (AD 6–15) who preceded his son-in-law Caiaphas (AD 15–36; John 18:19–24).

anoxia: The absence of oxygen that results in rapid cellular death.

anticoagulants: Chemical compounds—aspirin, heparin, and warfarin—inhibit the formation of blood clots.

anxiety: The stressful state of conflict, apprehension, anguish, and sorrow. During episodes of anxiety, conflict, and stress, the limbic brain activates (1) the autonomic nervous system (SNS and PNS) and (2) the endocrine system (release of stress hormones) which cause an increase in blood pressure, pulse rate, sweating, fatigue, and nervousness (charts IV-A, IV-B; chapters 3, 4).

apostle: Jesus "called out" many disciples—learners and followers: He later "sent out" His twelve apostles to preach the gospel (Matthew 10:1–7, 28:19–20).

appeasement strategy: The self-serving plan of Pilate and centurion Longinus to pacify the furious and defiant temple aristocrats and diabolical Jewish mob during Jesus's Roman trials. The strategy included excessive scourging (sixty to seventy lashes, or "three-quarters dead") and the violent king's game. Pilate unsuccessfully presented Jesus as a severely beaten, bloodstained, and pathetic counterfeit king (the *Ecce Homo*) in an attempt to appease the Jewish mob, prevent the execution of an innocent man, and save his political career (John 19:1–7; chapters 5, 9, 10, 12, 13).

arrhythmia: An irregular rhythm and rate of the heart.

asphyxiation: An *incorrect,* but still standing theory that Jesus Christ died from suffocation secondary to Roman crucifixion—the cross allegedly caused muscle tetany (contractions and spasms), exhaustion, and the inability to exhale CO_2 and inhale O_2. Tetany/asphyxiation is an *untenable* theory discredited in this book since it does *not* fulfill prophetic scripture and does *not* satisfy medical science (charts III, V; figures V, VI; chapters 5, 9, 12; epilogue).

atonement: Reconciliation or "at-one-ment" with God by the sacrificial death of Jesus Christ. The Old Testament Levitical animal sacrifices were an imperfect and temporary cover for the sins of Israel that foreshadowed the onetime atoning sacrifice of the incarnate Son that grants infinite mercy, perfect grace, and eternal life (Leviticus 23:28; John 3:16; Romans 5:10–11, 8:1-2; Ephesians 2:8-9).

battery: The use of force with fists or rods to beat, attack, and assault the opposition.

blasphemy: The dishonoring, insulting, or defiling of God. Jesus was condemned to death by the Jewish Sanhedrin for blasphemy after

He proclaimed His equality to almighty God (Leviticus 24:16; Mark 14:61–64).

blood components and products: The constituents of whole blood that are separated for specific medical treatments; for example, the current resuscitation of severe hemorrhagic shock includes the administration of three or more components of whole blood—packed red blood cells, fresh frozen plasma, and platelets (chart VII-B; chapters 5, 7, 13).

blood covenant: The solemn agreements and sacred promises made between two parties or nations or between humankind and God; they were cut and sealed by a blood sacrifice. To cut covenant indicated that *blood*—that is, your life—hung in the balance (Genesis 15:9-10; Leviticus 17:11; Exodus 24:3–8; Matthew 26:26–28; Hebrews 8:7–13, 9:15–22, 10:16–17; chapter 8).

blood markings—shroud of Turin: The human blood (type AB) of Jesus Christ was encoded on His burial garment—the result of a miraculous resurrection event (Antonacci 2015). These markings are the actual blood from His multiple wounds—battery, scourging, and piercings by thorns, nails, and lance. Microscopic examinations demonstrate the amazing presence of anatomical blood flow patterns and perfectly formed blood clots with normal halos of serum (chart VI-A; figures VIII-A, VIII-B; chapter 6).

blood transfusion: The infusion of whole blood or blood components directly into the venous system for the treatment of shock-trauma or other medical conditions.

blow of the lance: Roman legionnaires underwent basic training with a Roman lance to "open the side" of an enemy combatant. The approach of the BOL or Roman deathblow was through the right fifth rib space of the chest wall piercing the heart (right atrium and right ventricle) and causing immediate death. The standard Roman lance was seven to nine feet in length with a razor-sharp blade about twelve inches long and three inches wide (figures I-C, VIII-A, X; chapter 11; station 21, chapter 13).

blunt-force trauma: The application of unsharpened, mechanical forces to the body—rods, fists, falls, and whip with attached lead dumbbells that crush and tear human tissue; BFT results in greater tissue damage, acute inflammatory responses, and third-space fluid loss than does sharp-force trauma. The majority of Jesus's wounds—an estimated 80 percent—were secondary to BFT (charts VI-A, VI-B; figures VIII-A, VIII-B; chapter 9).

body image—shroud of Turin: The perfect, visible image of a crucified, Hebrew male miraculously encoded on the burial garment of Jesus Christ (figures VIII-A, VIII-B; chapter 6; Antonacci 2015).

broken/ruptured heart: A popular theory that Jesus died from a broken heart during His crucifixion secondary to overwhelming sorrow, grief, and despair; however, grief and sorrow do *not* cause the human heart to rupture. Moreover, the scriptures reveal that *shed blood*—that is, external hemorrhage—is an absolute requirement for the remission of sins. The broken/ruptured heart theory is an incorrect cause of Jesus's death and is discredited in this book (Leviticus 17:11; Matthew 26:26–28; Hebrews 9:12–13, 22, 10:19–22, 13:11–12; figure V; chapter 9; epilogue).

buffet: To strike repetitive violent blows.

Caiaphas: The Jewish high priest (AD 15–36) and president of the Sanhedrin who exerted his powerful influence for the crucifixion of Jesus Christ during the Jewish and Roman trials. Crucifixion was necessary during the passion since "lifting up"—the lifted up One—and "piercing"—the Pierced One—fulfilled the prophetic scriptures (Numbers 21:8–9; Psalm 22:16 NLT; Isaiah 53:5 NLT; Zechariah 12:10; John 3:14, 12:32–33, 18:32, 19:37; chart IX, see 8, 19; chapter 11).

capillaries: The microscopic blood vessels for the critical *exchange* of gases, nutrients, electrolytes, and important molecules that takes place between the blood and the cells (figure II).

cap of thorns, crown of thorns: Branchlets of the *Syrian Christ thornbush* were woven into the cap worn by Jesus during the king's game. The sharp, sturdy two-inch thorns pierced the highly vascular tissues of the scalp, yet did not penetrate the skull or brain (Matthew 27:29; John 19:2; chart VI-A; figures VIII-A, VIII-B; station 9, chapter 13).

carbohydrate: Glucose—the basic unit of CHO—is the universal fuel for cellular energy (ATP). Blood glucose levels are elevated by stress hormones to increase energy production during periods of danger, shock-trauma, and severe anxiety (charts IV-A, XII; chapter 3).

carbon dioxide: CO_2 is the toxic by-product of energy production that must be transported to the lungs and exhaled. Elevated $PaCO_2$

is present during respiratory failure (charts VIII-A, XII; figure VII; chapter 5).

carbon-14 dating: The scientific method that measures the date of an archeological relic by the assessment of carbon-14 losses over time (chapter 6).

cardiac arrest: The abrupt cessation of cardiac function causing the precipitous loss of blood pressure, heart-beat, and cardiac output (*Merriam-Webster's Medical Dictionary* 2005).

cardiac ejection fraction: A measurement of cardiac function in patients with possible heart failure—the ratio of the volume of blood the heart empties during systole to the volume of blood at the end of diastole expressed as a percentage. The normal ejection fraction is about 55 to 75 percent. Jesus developed acute cardiac failure with an estimated ejection fraction of less than 50 percent on Calvary (chart VIII-B; figures VI, VII; chapters 5, 12; *Merriam-Webster's Medical Dictionary* 2005).

cardiac failure: The inability of the heart to pump adequate volumes of blood to satisfy the oxygen and nutritional requirements of the tissues (chart VIII-B; chapter 5).

cardiac output: The volume of blood pumped by the heart per minute—the normal CO is about 5 L/minute.

cardiac shock: The failure of the heart to adequately perfuse the organs with oxygen and essential nutrients (charts VII-A, VIII-B; figure VI; chapter 5).

cardiac tamponade: Compression of the heart muscle by a pericardial effusion causing cardiac failure and shock (charts V, VII-A; VIII-B; figures VI, VII, X; chapter 5).

catabolism: The breakdown of tissues (catabolic state) reflected by a negative nitrogen (protein) balance and a negative calorie (energy) balance.

catecholamines: Important stress hormones—epi and nepi—are instantly released into the bloodstream in response to stressors such as pain, danger, anger, fear, shock-trauma, bleeding, and sudden hypotension; they prepare the body for emergencies by increasing cardiovascular performance and energy production (charts IV-A, IV-B, V; chapters 4, 5).

cell: The fundamental unit of life—the smallest anatomical structure capable of sustaining life. The life of a human cell can be threatened during shock-trauma and acute dehydration by hypotension, hypoperfusion, hypoxia, and acidosis, resulting in cellular injury and dysfunction (charts V, XI; figure II; chapter 2).

Christ event: The incarnation, passion, sacrificial death, and resurrection of Jesus Christ which grants the following Christological effects—expiation, redemption, reconciliation, justification, sanctification, glorification, salvation, freedom, transformation, new creation, peace, access to God, and a share of the divine nature (glossary, "theological effects of the Christ event").

Christology: The study of the person and the redemptive work of Jesus Christ.

chronic: A medical condition that persists for days, weeks, or years.

church: The living body of Jesus Christ made up of those delivered from the power of darkness and transferred to the kingdom of the beloved Son of God: The redeemed and reconciled *faithful* who are under the headship of the Lord Jesus Christ (Ephesians 1:22–23, 4:12; Colossians 1:13-14).

clinical course: The observed direction of a patient with disease or trauma; for example, Jesus Christ had a rapid, downhill clinical course secondary to the preliminary mental afflictions and shock-trauma arriving on Mount Calvary in critical condition (charts I, III, IV-B, V; figure VI; chapters 10, 12, 13).

clinical manifestations: These include the patient's signs (objective findings) such as vital signs, bleeding, wounds, and laboratory values (chart XII) and symptoms (subjective complaints), for example, fear, pain, and dizziness (chart IV-A).

coagulopathy, diffuse intravascular coagulopathy (DIC): Severe hemorrhagic shock and septicemia are complicated by coagulopathy in about 25 percent of patients. Coagulopathy results in (1) widespread intravascular blood clots, (2) consumption of platelets and fibrinogen with potential secondary bleeding, (3) disruption of blood flow causing tissue ischemia, and (4) severe inflammation and cellular death in multiple organs—lungs, liver, and kidneys (charts VII-D, XII; chapter 5).

coma: The state of profound unconsciousness without a response to voice or pain stimulation.

concussion or diffuse axonal injuries (DAI): An acute brain injury caused by BFT with the following clinical manifestations: alterations in the level of consciousness (name, address, and date), retrograde amnesia, confusion, blurred vision, headache, and ringing in the ears. Research demonstrates that inflammation and swelling of the axons are the primary pathophysiology (chapter 5).

contusion or bruise: The result of BFT that causes the crushing of cells (water loss and swelling) and the tearing of capillaries (blood loss and swelling); contusions involve the skin, subcutaneous tissue, muscle, and internal organs, for example, the lungs, brain, kidneys, and bone.

cortisol: An important stress hormone synthesized by the adrenal glands (H-P-A axis) and secreted in response to stress, danger, or medical emergencies, for example severe anxiety, fear, conflict, alarm, pain, shock-trauma, hemorrhage, hypotension, and inflammation. Cortisol reduces inflammation, increases energy production, and supports *epinephrine* for the compensation of hypotension during shock (charts IV-A, IV-B, V). Jesus suffered adrenal fatigue and secondary adrenal shock (resistant hypotension) due to the inadequate levels of cortisol (charts V, VII-A, XII; figures VI, VII; chapters 4, 5).

creatinine: A plasma protein marker that assesses kidney function (chart XII).

crucifixion—archeology: The bones of a crucified Jewish male (dated AD 7) were discovered in 1968 during the excavation of a cemetery at Giv'at ha Mivtar, Old City Jerusalem. The skeletal remains in a Jewish ossuary with the Hebrew name "Yehohanan" revealed valuable forensic evidence of a first-century Roman crucifixion including large iron nails placed in the forearms and heels and crucifractures of both lower extremities. However, according to the fourth gospel, (1) the crucifixion of Jesus involved His wrists and not His forearms (John 20:25–28; figures VIII-A, IX) and (2) Jesus did not sustain Roman crucifractures (John 19:33) since the prophetic scriptures must be fulfilled: "Not a bone of it will be broken" (Exodus 12:5, 46; Leviticus 1:10; Luke 24:44; John 19:31–36; chart IX, see 6, 20).

crucifixion—biomechanics: The study of biomechanics—the application of mechanical laws that govern a living body—shines a bright light on the following critical question (chapter 9): Can the death of Jesus Christ by Roman crucifixion be translated into death by tetany/asphyxiation that occurred in the German death camps of World War I? First, the prisoners were *freely* hanged by their wrists (the feet were some distance from the ground). In contrast, Jesus was *supported* by a large Roman nail in both feet—the fulcrum (point of contact) that permitted the lever arms (the lower extremities) to generate leverage (large forces for support).

Second, the respiratory muscles (chest, abdomen, and diaphragm) of Jesus were stabilized by the fulcrum (the large nail in the feet) and the powerful lever system (bones and muscles of the lower extremities) permitting normal respirations. The *contrast* between Roman crucifixion and death camp execution is profound: the prisoners were freely hanged by their wrists at some distance from the ground and developed muscle stretching, tetany, exhaustion, and death by suffocation. The biomechanics of Roman crucifixion provide strong evidence against tetany/asphyxiation (figure V; chapter 9; Barbet 1950; Zugibe 2005).

crucifixion—Roman methods: Roman crucifixion consisted of twelve steps (glossary, "instruments of Roman crucifixion").

1. The condemned was stripped while standing alongside the stationary upright.
2. The condemned was secured by the legionnaires on the ground with his arms extended flat against the crossbar.
3. A capped, four-sided, eight-inch-long, wrought-iron nail was driven through the right wrist—the space of Destot—and the wood of the crossbar (figure IX).
4. The left wrist was nailed to the crossbar.
5. The condemned was lifted into a standing position.
6. The condemned was *lifted up*—the hollowed cavity or "groove" of the crossbar was placed over the "tongue" of the upright using ladders, stools, ropes, and wooden forks; a heavy mallet secured the two pieces of the *T* (*tau*) cross.
7. Both feet were nailed against the wood of the upright with thirty degrees of knee flexion and forty degrees of ankle plantar flexion (downward); a larger nail was driven first through the second metatarsal space of the left foot, and then into the right foot; both feet—left over right—were rigidly nailed to the wooden upright.
8. The titulus was fastened to the crossbar above the victim's head.
9. The centurion and the quaternion of legionnaires guarded the victim until death.
10. Crucifractures were performed in greater than 90 percent of Roman crucifixions using a forty-pound iron bar to smash the bones and soft tissues of both legs.

11. The centurion signed the declaration of death in the presence of a Roman magistrate.
12. The disposition of the corpse: abandoned for decomposition and consumption by carnivores, carried to the city dump, or buried by the family (less than 1 percent).

crucifixion—sacred art: My investigation was enhanced by the study of sacred art, for example, the suffering in Gethsemane, the scourging at the Roman pillar, the *Ecce Homo,* the bearing of the cross and falls on the Via Dolorosa, and the crucifixion on Mount Calvary (glossary, "instruments of Roman crucifixion").

The works of sacred art have been arbitrarily divided into three historical periods. The Roman era or period of absence (about AD 33–500) was characterized by the shame and scandal associated with the passion—the violent Roman execution of the Jewish Messiah King was a contradiction. Sent by the sovereign Lord to save the world from sin and evil, Jesus Christ was brutally tortured and died a humiliating death on the wood of a Roman cross. Both Jew and Gentile considered this to be a ridiculous event—foolish, absurd, and impotent. A humiliated, abandoned, powerless, and bloodstained Messiah was a strange and paradoxical subject for sacred art. A good example representing this period is the graffiti discovered on the walls of a Roman villa portraying Jesus as a crucified donkey (about 150).

The Middle Ages or period of the glorified Christ (about 500–1400) was characterized by a handsome, well-dressed, and exalted Messiah who stood comfortably on a large foot plate while crucified: there was no evidence of distress, wounds, or major bleeding. The church and artists refused to portray the violence, affliction, and agony present during the passion. The best example for this historical period is the San Damiano crucifix or the cross of St.

Francis (around 1200); this revered work of art reveals no evidence of trauma or suffering. Jesus was adorned with a glorious halo and dressed in a luxurious linen loincloth. He appears calm, is in stable condition, and is surrounded by angels, the virgin Mary, and Longinus, the centurion. The twelve apostles are observed in the heavenlies worshipping the Father in the presence of the Holy Spirit.

The Renaissance era or period of the suffering Christ (about 1500–1800) provided realistic portraits of Jesus in critical condition—severe distress, multiple wounds, hemorrhage, soft-tissue swelling, ashen skin and wearing a cap of sharp thorns. In my analysis, the renowned German painter, Matthias Grunewald (1455-1528) captured the human agony, horror, and terror, of the Messiah during His sacrificial death; he skillfully portrayed the flow of blood, muscle spasms, extreme exhaustion, and the presence of impending doom. The artist poignantly included cutaneous *buboes*—the offensive pustular lesions of the bubonic plague that ravaged the sixteenth-century church—were being offered to almighty God by the Son, who was in solidarity with humanity.

crucifracture: Bilateral crucifractures were routinely carried out in more than 90 percent of Roman crucifixions. Both legs distal to the knee joints (tibia and fibula) or proximal (femur) were violently smashed and shattered with a forty-pound iron bar. This barbaric spectacle resulted in mortal wounds of the femoral or popliteal vessels with severe arterial and venous hemorrhage, third-space fluid loss, and rapid death secondary to traumatic, hemorrhagic, and hypovolemic shock and cardiac arrest. Roman crucifracture caused cruel and rapid death, prevented escape, and aroused the crowd with inhuman violence, horror, and terror (chart III; chapter 10, 13).

crystalloid solutions—salt and glucose: Isotonic solutions—the human concentrations of 0.9 percent—are administered during the resuscitation of acute hemorrhagic shock and severe dehydration for the purpose of fluid replacement and restoration of the circulating blood volume. Hypertonic solutions (2.5 to 7.5 percent) are effective during resuscitation by the reduction of third-space fluid loss (chart VII-B; chapter 5).

cytokines: Inflammatory compounds released by acute inflammatory cells—neutrophils, macrophages, and mast cells—combat infection and initiate the healing process (chart VI-B; chapter 7).

day of preparation for Passover: On the afternoon that preceded the Jewish Passover—the day of preparation—thousands of unblemished Passover lambs were sacrificed in the Jerusalem temple by the priests and Levites. On the afternoon of Good Friday (between noon and 3:00 p.m.), Jesus Christ died on Calvary as the infinite, perfect, and eternal Passover Lamb of God. The sovereign Lord directed the fulfillment of prophetic scriptures and satisfied the modern medical sciences (John 1:29, 19:14; 1 Corinthians 5:7; Acts 2:23; 1 Peter 1:18–19; chart IX, see 6; chapter 5).

death: Medical science defines death as "the cessation of spontaneous cerebral, respiratory, and circulatory functions." Scripture defines death as "the separation of the eternal soul from the temporary physical body" (Philippians 1:21; Dorland 2012).

deep-vein thrombosis: DVT is the formation of venous blood clots generally occurring in the deep veins of the lower extremities following trauma, surgery, or prolonged immobilization; the primary complication of untreated DVT is life-threatening pulmonary embolism (chart III; chapter 5).

degranulation: During the acute inflammatory response, the WBCs release granules (enzymes) that destroy foreign matter, dead tissue, and bacteria (chart VI-B).

dehydration: A serious negative water balance resulting from decreased fluid intake, increased fluid losses, or both (charts I, II-A, II-B). Severe dehydration causes cellular dysfunction, injury, and ultimately cellular death. During the passion of Jesus Christ, the presence of *cellular dehydration* signifies His "broken body" and "torn flesh" (Matthew 26:26; John 6:53-56; 1 Corinthians 10:16, 11:24; Hebrews 10:5, 10, 20; charts III, V; figure VII; chapters 5, 7, 9, 12, 13).

***Diagnostic and Statistical Manual of Mental Disorders**: **IV Text Revision**:* The *DSM-IV-TR* is the official coding system edited in the United States for psychiatric diseases.

diapedesis: The migration of blood cells across the capillary walls during acute inflammatory responses and the hematidrosis (bloody sweat) and ecchymosis (bruised skin) in Gethsemane (charts IV-B, VI-A, VI-B).

diffuse axonal injury or concussion: The descriptive name for the inflammation and swelling that occurs in the axons following concussions.

diffusion: The passive movement of water and gases O_2 and CO_2 across cell membranes from higher to lower concentrations.

disciples: The original followers and students of Jesus who later became His apostles—commissioned and sent out to "make disciples of all nations" (Matthew 10:1–15, 28:19).

drink or liquid offerings: The Levitical sacrificial system included daily, monthly, and festival offerings of water, broth, and wine (Numbers 28:7, 14–15; Judges 6:20; 1 Chronicles 11:17–19; chart IX, see 20).

dyspnea: Difficult or painful respirations; shortness of breath.

Ecce Homo— "Behold, the man" (John 19:5): Pilate's grand presentation of Jesus Christ to the Roman court after life-threatening scourging, piercings, and defenseless battery; however, the defiant chief priests and diabolical Jewish mob were not impressed or appeased by Pilate's brutal and excessive punishment. Furthermore, they demanded that Jesus be lifted up and pierced, oblivious to the fact their demands were fulfilling and perfecting the prophetic scriptures (chart IX, see 8, 19).

ecchymosis: A purplish patch of blood or a bruise limited to the skin (charts IV-B, VI-A).

ecclesiology: The theological study of the church.

edema: The abnormal collection of fluid in the interstitial spaces between the cells and capillaries: edema results during shock-trauma as third-space fluid loss during (1) the initial blunt-force trauma phase (crushed cells) and (2) the ischemic phase (hypotension, hypoperfusion, hypoxia, and cellular death). Pulmonary edema resulted during the passion secondary to lung contusion, shock lung, and acute cardiac failure (charts I, II-B, V, VI-A, VIII-A, VIII-B; figures VI, VII; chapter 9).

effusion: The inflammatory response secondary to trauma (scourging) or disease (infection) that causes the collection of bodily fluids (serum, plasma, or blood) in the pleural membranes (sacs) surrounding the lungs and the pericardial membrane (sac) surrounding the heart. Effusions are capable of causing large losses of fluid and compressing the underlying organ (chart II-B).

electrolytes: Minerals in solution dissociate into ions with positive or negative charges; for example, sodium (Na^+), potassium (K^+), chloride (Cl^-), bicarbonate (HCO_3^-), magnesium (Mg^{++}), and calcium (Ca^{++}); electrolytes generate electrical currents for heart rhythm, muscle contraction, and nerve conduction; they also support fluid concentrations necessary for normal cellular enzyme activity (chart XII; chapter 5).

endocrine system: The glandular organs such as the pituitary gland (brain), adrenal glands (abdomen), and thyroid gland (neck); each secretes a hormone, ACTH, cortisol, and thyroxin respectfully, into the bloodstream with specific effects on specific distant organs (charts IV-A, IV-B, V; figures III, VII). The limbic brain is activated by stressors (fear, conflict, or shock) which stimulate the endocrine system to restore homeostasis.

endorphin: A potent hormone released for analgesia and euphoria by the hypothalamus (limbic brain) in response to pain, trauma, and strenuous physical exercise (chart IV-A).

enzyme: Protein catalysts that accelerate chemical reactions; for example, the enzymes required for cellular energy (ATP) and growth and repair. Shock-trauma and dehydration inhibit enzyme function by *abnormal* temperature, acid/base balance, and fluid concentration resulting in cellular dysfunction, injury, and death (chart XI).

epinephrine: Epi (adrenalin) is a powerful stress hormone secreted into the bloodstream by the adrenal glands in response to stressors such as fear, stress, agony, bleeding, shock-trauma, and hypotension. To properly prepare, adapt, and compensate, epi activates maximum performance by the circulatory, respiratory, and cellular energy systems (charts IV-A, IV-B, V).

eschatology: The theological study of the end times including the second advent, the general resurrection, judgment, and heaven and hell.

essential nutrients: There are more than forty nutrients necessary for human survival and wellness: water, carbohydrates (1), fats (2), protein (9 amino acids), minerals (16) and vitamins (13).

etiology: The cause of medical, psychological, and traumatic conditions; for example, the etiology of shock following BFT is the loss of blood and water, and the etiology of an acute stress reaction is fear, anxiety, and violence.

exacerbation: The patients' symptoms and signs become more severe.

fear: The unpleasant emotional state and psychological response to a threatening event that activates the general adaptation syndrome (chart IV-A). Upon entering Gethsemane, Jesus was abruptly overwhelmed by extreme fright secondary to His separation from the Father and His sacrificial death for the sins of the world (chart IV-B; chapter 4).

fibrin: The final step in the clotting of blood is the activation of plasma fibrinogen into fibrin which surrounds the platelet plug creating a thrombus (charts VI-B, XII; chapter 7; *Merriam-Webster's Medical Dictionary* 2005).

fibrinolysin: Plasma enzymes such as plasmin and heparin dissolve fibrin to preserve the fluid state of the bloodstream. The overactivation of plasmin during shock-trauma and coagulopathy can result in severe hemorrhage (charts VII-D, XII; chapter 7).

fight-or-flight syndrome: The strong psychopathological response to an emotional crisis or sudden danger synonymous with the general adaptation syndrome (Chart IV-A) and the acute stress reaction (ICD-10; chart IV-B).

gardens—the three gardens of redemption: The Garden of Eden (original sin and curse)—sin; the Garden of Gethsemane (greatest conflict, greatest agony, and greatest decision)—death; and the Garden of Resurrection (victory over death)—life.

glucose: The basic unit of CHO—the universal fuel for energy production (ATP): the normal BG level is 75 to 110 mg/dL (chart XII; chapter 3).

golden hour: The vital first hour following shock-trauma, heart attack, and stroke. Medical treatment during the vital golden hour significantly lowers the morbidity and mortality rates—life versus death (charts I, V, XI, XII; figure IV; station 15, chapter 13).

gospel: The good news of salvation in and through Jesus Christ—His passion, sacrificial death, and resurrection (Mark 1:1, 14–15, 10:45; Luke 2:11, 19:10; Romans 1:16–17, 8:1–2; 1 Corinthians 15:3–4).

hematidrosis: Jesus sustained a life-threatening acute stress reaction in Gethsemane complicated by the excretion of blood or blood pigments through the skin. Hematidrosis or bloody sweat is a rare and serious medical condition that was uniquely described by Dr. Luke, a Greek physician. The sovereign Lord and Great Physician predetermined and directed this affliction to reveal (1) the severity of Jesus's mental sufferings; (2) the role of blood and water in the passion, and (3) the scriptural transcendency of blood and water (Mark 14:33–34; Luke 22:43–44; chart IV-B; figures VI, VII; chapter 4; *Merriam-Webster's Medical Dictionary* 2005).

hematocrit: Hct is the measure of packed red blood cells; normal Hct = 40 to 50 percent (chart XII).

hematoma: An abnormal collection of blood in the soft tissues or an enclosed space.

hemoglobin: Hb is the unique protein contained in the RBCs that binds, transports, and delivers O_2 throughout the body for the production of energy; normal Hb = 13–16 g/dL or about 33 percent of the Hct (chart XII).

hemostasis: The arrest of bleeding by the physiologic processes of vasoconstriction and clotting or by surgical pressure, packs, and clamps.

histamine: An inflammatory compound (cytokine) released by mast cells in wounds causing vasodilation, increased vascular permeability, and diapedesis (chart VI-B).

holocaust: A burnt offering of the Levitical sacrificial system that signifies one's total dedication and consecration to almighty God. First, the animal's sacrificial blood is "sprinkled around the altar" (Leviticus 1:5); then "the priest shall burn the whole offering on the altar" as a sweet-smelling aroma to the Lord (Leviticus 1:9).

homeostasis: The dynamic neuroendocrine process that restores the body's equilibrium and steady state in response to external stressors (trauma or danger) or internal stressors (fear or hypoxia). This involuntary preparation and adaptation of the body are necessary responses for human survival (charts IV-A, IV-B, V; chapter 3).

hormone: Chemical compounds such as ACTH, epi, and cortisol are the products of the endocrine system secreted into the blood stream by the glandular cells. Hormones target distant organs to stimulate specific functions (charts IV-A, IV-B, V; figure VII; chapters 3, 7).

hour—the hour of Jesus Christ: The incarnate Son's future hour of destiny (John 2:4) including His glorification and fulfillment of Old Testament prophecy by His passion, sacrificial death, and resurrection; ultimately He passed over the world and made His exodus to the heavenly Father (Luke 9:31; John 13:1, 3, 17:1; chart IX, see 6; chapters 11, 13).

human body: The temporary flesh (70 percent water) and blood (93.5 percent water) of the human body consists of an estimated one hundred trillion cells: It is supported by fifty thousand miles of blood vessels and organized into multiple complex organ systems. Jesus Christ— "like His brothers in every way except sin"—thoroughly identified Himself with each member of the human race during His passion and sacrificial death. Yet, it is the human soul created by almighty God that provides human life and bestows eternal life (John 1:14, 3:16; Hebrews 2:14–18, 4:15).

hypercapnia: The elevation of $PaCO_2$ observed during respiratory failure (charts VIII-A, XII).

hyperhidrosis: Excessive sweating (water loss) that occurred to Jesus during the acute stress reaction in the Garden of Gethsemane (Luke 22:44; charts I, IV-B; chapter 4).

hyperkalemia: An elevated blood level of potassium (K^+) secondary to shock-trauma, dehydration, and acute kidney failure (charts III, XII; chapter 5).

hypernatremia: An elevated blood level of sodium (Na^+) secondary to dehydration (charts III, XII; chapter 5).

hypertension: The abnormal elevation of BP >125/80.

hyperthermia—heat exhaustion and heat stroke: The serious but rare medical conditions that occur during strenuous physical exercise and elevation of the environmental temperature characterized by high fever >102°F (39°C), severe dehydration, and weight loss (chart III; chapter 5).

hyperventilation: An increased volume of air flowing in and out of the alveolar air sacs of the lungs leading to the abnormal loss of carbon dioxide (↓$PaCO_2$)—observed during strenuous physical exercise, severe shock, and lung contusion (charts V, XII; chapters 3, 5; *Merriam-Webster's Medical Dictionary* 2005).

hypoperfusion: A decrease in the blood flow through an organ causing inadequate levels of O_2 and nutrients for cellular survival. During severe shock, hypoperfusion causes ischemia of the vital organs—hypoxia, acidosis, dysfunction, and irreversible cellular and microvascular injuries and secondary third-space fluid loss. The hallmark of hemorrhagic shock is *hypoperfusion* (charts I, V, VII-A, VII-B, XI; chapter 5).

hypothermia: The reduction of body temperature <95° F (<35° C) is commonly observed during severe shock-trauma secondary to the loss of blood, open wounds, burns, multiple blood transfusions, and coagulopathy (charts I, VI-A, VII-D).

hypoxia: Decreased levels of oxygen in the blood and tissues: PaO_2 <75 mmHg (normal PaO_2 = 75-100 mmHg). Cellular hypoxia causes the switch to anaerobic energy production (↓ATP), lactic acidosis, and progressive cellular injury (charts V, VII-D, XI, XII; figures VI, VII).

hypotension: Abnormally low blood pressure (BP <90/60). Jesus suffered severe hypotension caused by multifactorial shock secondary to rapid blood and large water losses, acute cardiac failure, and adrenal fatigue (charts I, V, VII-A, VII-B, VII-C, VIII-B; figures VI, VII; chapter 5).

hypothalamus: An important component of the limbic brain and neuroendocrine system that activates the H-P-A axis in order to regulate, adapt, and prepare the body (charts IV-A, IV-B, V; figure III; chapters 3, 4, 5).

hypothalamus-pituitary-adrenal axis: The H-P-A axis—the connection between the brain and the endocrine system—is vital for homeostasis during afflictions such as fear, stress, conflict and shock-trauma including pain, wounds, bleeding, and hypotension (charts IV-A, IV-B, V; figure III; chapters 3, 4, 5).

hyssop: A small plant with multiple branchlets used to sprinkle blood and water during Levitical purification rites. A "bunch of hyssop" was used to sprinkle the blood of sacrificial Passover lambs on the doorframes of the Hebrew households (Exodus 12:21–23). Around 1,400 years later, a wine-soaked sponge on a "sprig of hyssop" was put to the mouth of Jesus to satisfy His "thirst." Jesus Christ is the "perfect Passover Lamb of God" who fulfilled and perfected the prophetic scriptures (Psalm 22:16; John 1:29, 19:29; chart IX, see 6).

incarnation: The enfleshing (Lat. *caro*, "flesh") of the Son of God was the first step of the passion. Jesus Christ was sent into the world as a divine person wrapped in a human body of flesh and blood; He thoroughly identified with humanity (John 1:1, 14; Acts 2:23; 1 Timothy 3:16; Hebrews 2:14, 17).

instruments of Roman crucifixion: These instruments are displayed on the walls of the Church of the Flagellation in Jerusalem (Barbet 1950; Zugibe 2005).

1. The *patibulum* or crossbar of Palestinian oak was placed across the upper back and shoulders and carried to Mount Calvary; it weighed around 100-150 pounds and was six feet in length and four inches by four inches in width. While flat on the ground the victim's wrists were nailed to the crossbar; the victim and the crossbar were then lifted up together and the *patibulum* was placed over the *stipes*. The *T* (*tau*) cross was assembled by securing the hollowed out "groove" of the crossbar and the "tongue" of the upright with nails and rope.
2. The *stipes* or upright was between 100 and 200 pounds, between eight and ten feet in length (two feet below the surface), and six by six inches in width. The stationary uprights were outside the city gates on a public roadway.
3. The *sedile* or small seat was secured to the *stipes* to prolong the time of survival.
4. The *suppedaneum* or foot plate was commonly used after the first century.
5. The domed, wrought-iron nails were produced by the Romans in a variety of sizes, lengths, and shapes—about five to eight inches in length, four-sided, and tapered. Larger nails were utilized for the feet; the executioner wore a leather apron containing a variety of nails and other tools including a mallet, an auger, and a nail extractor (figure IX).
6. The *titulus* or wooden sign was placed on the *patibulum* publishing the victim's name and crime.

7. A short stool, forks, and a ladder assisted the legionnaires when lifting the victim and crossbar.
8. The forty-pound iron bar was designed specifically for the crucifracture.
9. The Roman lance was seven to nine feet long with a razor-sharp blade twelve inches long and three inches wide (figure X).

International Classification of Psychiatric Disease (ICD-10): The tenth revision of the international classification of psychiatric diseases.

ischemia—ischemic cellular injury during severe shock: Inadequate arterial blood supply to a body part (lower extremities) or a vital organ (lungs, kidneys, heart, and brain). Severe multifactorial shock is associated with ischemic cellular injury characterized by hypoxia, acidosis, decreased energy production, and cellular dysfunction: cellular death causes third-space water loss—a serious complication of hemorrhagic shock (charts I, V, XI; figure VI; chapters 5, 9).

king's game: The unrestrained, barbaric Roman legionnaires amused themselves during this shameless, sarcastic, and cynical charade at the expense of Jesus Christ—the incarnate Son of God was transformed into a ridiculous and impotent counterfeit king. He was relentlessly tormented, mocked, and beaten: His scalp was pierced by the thorns of a royal crown; He was dressed in a royal cloak, and a royal reed was placed in His right hand (Matthew 27:27–31; John 19:1–3). The piercings and defenseless battery resulted in additional wounds, blood and water losses, and a concussion (charts I, V, VI-A; chapters 5, 9, 12, 13).

lesion: A structural abnormality of the tissues, organs, and body parts secondary to trauma or disease. For example, (1) contusions are lesions caused by injuries to small blood vessels (blood loss) and cells (water loss) and (2) ecchymoses are lesions caused by bleeding into the skin (chart VI-A; figure VIII-B).

lethal triad: A life-threatening complication of hemorrhagic shock associated with severe arterial hemorrhage, delayed treatment beyond the golden hour, and multiple blood transfusions. The lethal components include acidosis, hypothermia, and coagulopathy (charts V, VII-D; figures IV, VI).

lifted up: Roman jargon for crucifixion. However, in the fourth gospel, being lifted up served an important divine purpose—the *glorification* of Jesus Christ during His eternal sacrificial death empowered Him to pour out the Holy Spirit on the church and fulfill prophetic scripture (Numbers 21:4–9; John 3:14–15, 7:37–39, 8:28, 12:32–33; chart IX, see 8; chapters 11, 13).

limbic brain or limbic system: The nerve centers—amygdala, hippocampus, hypothalamus, and others—are located in the subcortical region of the brain. They respond to a variety of internal stressors (fear, sorrow, anger, and stress) and external stressors (trauma, blood loss, and shock) by the activation of the autonomic neuroendocrine system to regulate, prepare, and adapt the body (homeostasis; charts IV-A, IV-B, V; figure III; chapters 3, 4, 5).

Longinus: The robust Roman centurion who commanded the violent execution of Jesus Christ—the lethal scourging, struggles and falls on the Via Dolorosa, lifting up on Mount Calvary, declaration of death, and disposition of the corpse. Following the Lord's passion and resurrection, Longinus converted to Christianity, became a bishop in Asia, and was martyred for his faith (Mark 15:39, 44; John 19:33–34).

Macrophage and monocyte: The largest inflammatory WBC located in the tissues and the bloodstream; this cell type provides aggressive phagocytosis as a first responder to traumatic and septic wounds (charts VI-B, XII; chapter 7).

malnutrition: Any abnormality of nutrition (Dorland 2012). In the absence of preliminary agonies, victims of Roman crucifixion survived for several days; they consumed nothing by mouth and developed malnutrition—an early catabolic state consisting of (1) a negative water balance, (2) a negative nitrogen (protein) balance, and (3) a negative calorie (energy) balance (charts II-A, III; chapter 5).

mast cell: A tissue-based inflammatory cell and a first responder to traumatic wounds; mast cells attract neutrophils by chemotaxis and release cytokines that increase blood flow and stimulate diapedesis (chart VI-B; chapter 7).

metabolism: The chemical processes in the human body, for example, growth and repair (anabolism) and energy production (catabolism).

microvasculature and capillary beds: These microscopic capillaries (<100 microns) are present in every organ system for the important exchange of gases, water, nutrients, and toxic by-products. Decompensated multifactorial shock causes severe hypoperfusion, hypoxia, acidosis, and coagulopathy with irreversible cellular and microvascular injuries, third-space fluid loss, and multiple organ dysfunction syndrome (charts V, VII-D, XI; figure VII).

mind: The seat of human consciousness, mental faculties, and the complex functions of thought, cognition, intellect, will, language, memory, and strategy (figure 3; chapter 4).

mitochondria: The preeminent cellular organelles known as the aerobic power plants that synthesize aerobic energy (ATP; chart XI; figure II; chapters 2, 7).

morbidity: A condition or state of disease (Dorland 2012).

mortality: The human quality or state of being subject to death (Dorland 2012).

multiple organ dysfunction syndrome: MODS is an end-stage medical condition with the dysfunction and insufficiency of two or more vital organs. It complicates serious and terminal conditions such as decompensated multifactorial shock, severe dehydration, burns, septicemia, and heat stroke (chart V; figure VII; chapters 5, 12, 13).

myocardial infarction or heart attack: Serious heart condition caused by the inadequate flow of blood and oxygen (ischemia of the muscle) secondary to a coronary arterial thrombosis (blockage).

necrosis: The presence of irreversible cellular injury and cellular death. During decompensated multifactorial shock, ischemic necrosis occurs in multiple organs secondary to hypotension (↓BP), hypoperfusion (↓BF), and hypoxia (↓O$_2$; charts V, XI).

negative nitrogen (protein) balance: The state of nitrogen excretion that exceeds the quantity ingested; nitrogen is the marker used to reflect protein metabolism (Dorland 2012).

negative water balance: The result of fluid losses exceeding fluid intake during a twenty-four-hour period; for example, the absence of fluid intake during one day can result in a negative water balance of 2.0 L and 4.4 lbs. (chart II-A).

neuritis: The injury and inflammation of a peripheral nerve (body) or a cranial nerve (head and neck). Post-traumatic neuritis secondary to stretching, bruising, compressing, and piercing can cause tingling, numbness, burning pain, and weakness. Neuritis was present during the passion as follows: (1) median neuritis (wrists) secondary to the nail, (2) plantar neuritis (feet) secondary to the nail, and (3) trigeminal neuritis (face and scalp) secondary to the thorns (Barbet 1950; Zugibe 2005).

neuroendocrine system: The integrated functions of the central nervous system (limbic brain), the autonomic nervous system (SNS and PNS), and the endocrine system (glands and hormones) that are activated during periods of internal and external stress. The compensatory responses of the neuroendocrine system restore homeostasis (charts IV-A, IV-B, V; figure III; chapter 3).

neuron: The conducting cell of the nervous system that consists of a cell body and nucleus, cytoplasm containing organelles, and an axon or specialized nerve process that conducts impulses to other neurons, muscle cells, and organs. Neurons are particularly sensitive to the deprivation of oxygen and glucose (figures II, III).

neurotransmitter: Chemical compounds that carry the impulses between two neurons (synapse), for example, epinephrine, norepinephrine, endorphin, and serotonin.

neutrophil: The *acute* WBC—vital first responder of the immune system and chief phagocyte—rapidly ingests bacteria, foreign materials, and tissue debris. On the Via Dolorosa, Jesus's WBC count (normal: 5,000-10,000/mm^3) was sharply increased to an estimated >25,000/mm^3 and His neutrophil count (normal: 60% of the WBC count) was elevated to an estimated 85% of the WBC count (charts VI-B; XII; chapter 7).

norepinephrine: An important neurotransmitter and stress hormone that causes vasoconstriction (squeeze the artery) to restore the blood pressure during shock (charts IV-A, IV-B, V).

organelles: Subcellular cytoplasmic structures that provide the important functions for cellular life; for example, mitochondria (energy), ribosomes (proteins), and lysosomes (enzymes; chart XI; figure II; chapter 2).

oxygen: O_2 is nonnegotiable for life—the gaseous element that constitutes 21 percent of the atmosphere. Almighty God instructed His creation, "The life of the flesh in is in the blood" (Leviticus 17:11). The RBCs bind, transport, and deliver O_2 for the production of aerobic energy (ATP). Severe blood loss and hemorrhagic shock cause cellular and microvascular hypoxia ($\downarrow O_2$), acidosis ($\downarrow pH$), coagulopathy, dysfunction, and death (charts I, V, VII-A, VII-D, XI, XII; figures I-A, VII; chapter 7; *Merriam-Webster's Medical Dictionary* 2005).

paralytic ileus: A nonmechanical or functional intestinal obstruction present during the passion causing intestinal swelling, nausea, and vomiting and third-space fluid loss (chart II-B; chapters 5, 9, 12).

passion: The passion (Lat. *passio*, "suffering") consisted of the sacrificial mental afflictions and physical traumas of Jesus Christ that merited eternal salvation and eternal redemption. His profound sufferings included the incarnation (the first step of the passion), the preliminary agonies that caused His rapid demise, and His death on Mount Calvary (Philippians 2:6-8; Hebrews 5:7-8, 9:12; charts I, IV-B, V, VI-A; figures VI, VII, VIII-A, VIII-B; chapters 4, 5, 12, 13).

Passover: The Jewish feast commemorating the mighty deeds of the Lord—the redemption and deliverance of His chosen people. The blood of an unblemished lamb was sprinkled on the doorframe with hyssop. "Seeing the blood" of the sacrificial Passover lambs, almighty God passed over the Hebrew households (Exodus 12:5–7, 13, 21–27, 46). Jesus Christ fulfilled and perfected this preeminent Old Testament event as the perfect and eternal Passover Lamb of God who takes away the sins of the world (John 1:29; 1 Corinthians 5:7; 1 Peter 1:18–19; Revelation 5:6–14; chart IX, see 6).

Passover amnesty: The Roman authorities released a Jewish prisoner each year in commemoration of the Jewish Passover and Exodus. Pontius Pilate vigorously endeavored to obtain amnesty for Jesus

Christ to prevent the execution of an innocent man and to save his own political career. However, the diabolical Jewish mob and defiant temple aristocrats demanded that Jesus be crucified and chose Barabbas—a revolutionary murderer—in preference to Jesus Christ, the Messiah King (Matthew 27:15–21; John 18:38–19:8).

pathophysiology: The disordered and abnormal function of the body secondary to disease and trauma (chapter 5).

patibulum: The heavy crossbar (about 100 pounds) carried by Jesus on the Via Dolorosa from the Fortress of Antonia to Mount Calvary. After being nailed to the patibulum, He was lifted up onto the stationary upright forming a *T* (*tau*) cross (glossary, "instruments of Roman crucifixion").

Pax Romana: "The peace of Rome," the rallying cry of the Roman military, senate, and aristocratic establishment.

pericardial effusion: The accumulation of greater than 30 mL of blood, plasma, or serum in the pericardial sac surrounding the heart. The excessive scourging of Jesus caused an acute pericardial effusion complicated by cardiac tamponade (compression of the heart muscle) and acute cardiac failure (John 19:34;1 John 5:6–8; charts V, VII-A, VIII-B; figures I-C, VI, VII, X; chapters 5, 12, 13).

pericardiocentesis: The needle aspiration of a pericardial effusion (chart VIII-B; figure X).

petechia: A pinpoint, purple-red spot on the skin caused by a tiny hemorrhage. Petechiae and ecchymosis resulted secondary to

(1) the hematidrosis in Gethsemane (Luke 22:44), (2) the Roman scourging and battery (John 19:1), and (3) the falls on the Via Dolorosa (chapter 13).

phagocytosis: Neutrophils and macrophages (WBCs) engulf and destroy bacteria, tissue debris, and foreign materials (charts VI-B, XII; chapter 7).

pit: The dark, damp, and cold dungeon about fifty feet under Caiaphas's priestly palace (recently restored in Jerusalem). During His passion, Jesus was arrested, condemned, and imprisoned overnight in the pit by the Jewish authorities and temple guard (station 6, chapter 13). He was shackled to the floor, suffered from mocking, buffeting, spitting, and pulling His beard, and developed acute dehydration. This underground prison foreshadowed Jesus's descent into the pit—Hades, the place of the dead, and the netherworld; (Psalm 16:10, 88:1–12; Isaiah 50:6; Mark 14:64–65; Ephesians 4:8–10; chart I).

pituitary gland: The preeminent "mother" gland of the endocrine system that regulates many of our basic bodily functions—adrenal, thyroid, renal, cardiovascular, energy, growth, and homeostasis. During the passion, Jesus suffered life-threatening mental afflictions and lethal shock-trauma which necessitated homeostasis by the activation of the hypothalamus (limbic brain), the pituitary gland (ACTH), and the adrenal glands (stress hormones)—the H-P-A axis (charts IV-A, V; figures III, VI, VII; chapters 3, 4, 5).

plasma: The fluid component of blood—50 to 60 percent plasma—transports clotting factors and fibrinogen, immunoglobulins (antibodies), essential nutrients, electrolytes, and hormones. Fresh frozen plasma (FFP) was administered during World War II as a *volume expander* saving thousands of lives. In modern shock-trauma resuscitation, FFP is used to restore blood volume and increase organ perfusion (chart VII-B; chapters 5, 7).

plasminogen and plasmin: Human blood contains a fibrinolytic system of plasminogen (inactive form) and plasmin (activated form). Plasmin dissolves fibrin, which maintains the fluidity of the bloodstream. If an excess of plasmin should result during shock-trauma complicated by coagulopathy, uncontrolled bleeding can occur (charts VII-D, XII).

platelet-activating factor: PAF is an acute inflammatory compound secreted by mast cells for vasodilation (relax the artery) and diapedesis (chart VI-B).

pneumonia: A lung infection that causes inflammation, dyspnea, cough, fever, and hypoxia ($\downarrow PaO_2$). In the absence of the preliminary traumas and sufferings, many victims of Roman crucifixion lingered for days on their crosses and died from dehydration, a catabolic state, pneumonia, and septicemia (charts III, XII; chapter 5).

pneumothorax: A collapsed lung secondary to an air leak in the chest wall or lung.

Pontius Pilate: The Roman governor of Judea (AD 26–36) who adjudicated the civil trials of Jesus Christ. Pilate's insecurity, cynicism, and personal political agenda compromised his pursuit of Roman law and justice. He attempted to release Jesus first by verdicts of not guilty, second by referral to King Herod, third by Passover amnesty, and finally by a strategy of appeasement to pacify the defiant chief priests and furious diabolical mob. Ultimately Pilate condemned Jesus to be "lifted up" and "pierced" on a Roman cross which fulfilled and perfected the prophetic scriptures (John 19:35–37; chart IX, see 8, 19). Sometime later he was recalled to Rome for his brutality of the Jewish people and committed suicide in what is now Switzerland (AD 41).

post-traumatic stress disorder: PTSD is a serious disabling psychopathological condition caused by one or more stressful and violent events. It is complicated by sleep disorders, flashbacks, avoidance of similar stimuli, and recurrent episodes of stress, fear, and anxiety. In my analysis, Jesus Christ and the prophet Jeremiah suffered from PTSD during their ministries (charts IV-A, IV-B, IX, see 16; chapter 4).

preliminary traumas and sufferings: The events during the passion that transpired *prior* to the Roman crucifixion. The PTS included Jesus's life-threatening mental afflictions of Gethsemane, the Jewish religious trials and the pit, the lethal shock-trauma caused during the Roman civil trials, and the struggles and falls on the Via Dolorosa. The preliminary agonies—not Roman crucifixion—were responsible for the rapid demise of Jesus Christ (charts I, III, IV-B, V, VI-A, XI, XII; figures VI, VII, VIII-A, VIII-B; chapter 12; epilogue).

prognosis: The expected outcome of a patient's medical condition. Jesus was in critical condition when he arrived on Calvary and His prognosis was grave.

prostaglandins: An active group of inflammatory compounds released by the mast cells and macrophages (chart VI-B).

psyche: Related to mental function and emotional behavior.

psychopathology: Disordered mental function and abnormal emotional behavior.

psychosomatic disease: Severe fright, stress, anxiety, and conflict can cause mind-body diseases, for example back pain, headaches, and abdominal disorders. Jesus was afflicted by an extremely severe acute stress reaction complicated by psychosomatic sequelae—hematidrosis and adrenal fatigue that influenced His rapid demise on Calvary (charts IV-B, V; chapter 4).

pulmonary contusion, lung contusion: An acute lung injury caused by BFT with characteristic diffuse bilateral lung bruises—hemorrhage, edema, collapse of the alveolar air sacs, and respiratory hypoxia ($\downarrow P_aO_2$; charts VIII-A, XII; figures VI, VII; chapters 5, 12).

pulmonary edema: The abnormal collection of fluid in the alveolar air sacs that obstructs the exchange of O_2 and CO_2 and results in dyspnea, shortness of breath, and respiratory hypoxia ($\downarrow P_aO_2$). Jesus sustained pulmonary edema secondary to pulmonary contusion (scourging, battery, and falls), shock lung secondary to severe hemorrhagic shock, and acute cardiac failure secondary to acute pericardial effusion and cardiac tamponade (charts VIII-A, VIII-B; figures VI, VII; chapter 5).

reactive oxygen species: ROS are oxygen radicals (O_2^-) that injure healthy cells; neutrophils release ROS during the acute inflammatory reactions of shock-trauma and septicemia (chart VI-B).

reconciliation: The restoration of peace and friendship with almighty God by the passion and sacrificial death of Jesus Christ (Romans 5:1, 10–11; 2 Corinthians 5:18–20).

redemption, ransom: The purchase and the freedom from the bondage of sin and death, the devil, and the wrath of God by a ransom—the sacrificial death of Jesus Christ by His *shed blood* (blood loss and severe shock) and His *broken body* (water loss and severe dehydration)—offered to the Father as payment in full (Mark 10:45; John 3:36; Romans 3:24-25, 5:9, 8:1-2; Galatians 3:13; Titus 2:14; Hebrews 9:11–15; 1 Peter 1:18–19; Revelation 5:9).

resuscitation: Emergency trauma care: secure an open Airway, arrest Arterial bleeding, establish normal Breathing, and restore Circulation (A-A-B-C). Cardiopulmonary resuscitation (CPR) and emergency surgery may be necessary.

sacrifice: The offering of something precious to almighty God. Humanity was redeemed by the sacrificial *shed blood* (blood loss and severe shock) and *broken body* (water loss and severe dehydration) of Jesus Christ—the "unblemished lamb of God" (1 Peter 1:18–19). As our great High Priest, He offered Himself to the Father as the perfect, infinite, and eternal sacrifice that fulfilled the prophetic scriptures (Isaiah 53:4; John 10:17–18; Hebrews 5:1, 8:1-3, 10:12-17, 21; chart IX, see 4, 6, 13, 20, 21).

salvation: Humanity has been rescued, delivered, and freed from sin and death, the curse, the wrath of God, and the devil by the passion, sacrificial death, and resurrection of Jesus Christ (John 3:16–17; Galatians 3:13; Romans 5:9, 6:22–23, 8:1–2, 10:9–10, 13; Ephesians 2:8; Titus 3:5–6; Hebrews 5:7–9, 9:11–15, 22, 28; 1 John 3:8).

sanctification: The process of becoming holy, set apart to worship and serve the Lord in the power of the Holy Spirit (Leviticus 11:44–45; John 17:17–19; Romans 6:22; 2 Corinthians 3:18; 2 Thessalonians 2:13).

Sanhedrin: The supreme Jewish tribunal or great council (350 BC–AD 70). The Sanhedrin had legislative, executive, and judicial (ceremonial, moral, and criminal) jurisdictions. Its seventy members consisted of elders (wealthy aristocrats), members of the high priestly families known as the Sadducees (the righteous ones), and temple scribes (Mosaic legal scholars). The presiding officer during Jesus's Jewish trials was Caiaphas, the high priest (AD 16–36). The Sanhedrin condemned Jesus, but crucifixion required Pilate's endorsement: the piercings and lifting up of Jesus Christ fulfilled and perfected the prophetic scriptures (Numbers 21:4–9; Psalm 22:16; Isaiah 53:5; Zechariah 12:10; John 3:14–15, 8:28, 12:32, 18:31–32, 19:6–16, 33–37; chart IX, see 8, 19).

scourging, flogging, whipping at the Roman pillar: The *fear of the whip* was a Roman idiom—the mere thought of Roman flogging evoked gut-wrenching fright, horror, and bloodcurdling terror. Throughout the empire, the citizens were cognizant of the excruciating pain, torn flesh, crushed and lacerated skin, hemorrhage, and respiratory distress of scourging at the pillar (chapters 9, 10).

The fear of deadly complications was in the public eye—the

laceration of a great vessel, the opening of the chest or abdominal cavity, and sudden death (cardiac arrest). Morbid pathophysiology resulted from the blunt force trauma of the flagellum—the leather straps tipped with lead dumbbells which ravaged the flesh and blood of Jesus Christ by crushing billions of cells and lacerating millions of capillaries, arterioles, venules, and sensory nerves.

The magnitude of tissue destruction and rapid losses of blood and water was directly proportional to the number and velocity of the lashes: the potential energy released = mass x velocity^2. My analysis of the scourging of Jesus Christ revealed—not the generally accepted thirty-nine lashes (Deuteronomy 25:3)—but an estimated sixty to seventy lashes that caused an estimated 2.0–3.0 U of immediate blood loss (charts I, V, VI-A; figures VIII-A, VIII-B; chapters 5, 9, 10, 13). The severity of Jesus's scourging also caused internal injuries that consisted of bilateral pleural effusions, diffuse lung contusions, acute pericardial effusion, paralytic ileus, and possibly abdominal injuries, for example contusions of the spleen, kidney, liver, and intestine (charts VIII-A, VIII-B, IX, see 10; glossary, "zone of destruction;" Barbet 1950; Zugibe 2005).

sepsis, septicemia: Severe, systemic infection—the presence of bacteria in the bloodstream which can result in life-threatening septic shock, systemic inflammatory response syndrome, and multiple organ dysfunction syndrome (chart III): however, such lethal infections (blood poisoning) are rarely observed within the first hours after shock-trauma. A large percentage of crucifixion victims who survived for several days, suffered pneumonia or other infections, and fatal septicemia (chapter 5).

sequela: The aftereffect or secondary result of a disease or trauma.

seven words from the cross: The memorable sermon Jesus preached on Calvary; for example, "It is finished" (the sixth word from the cross, John 19:30).

shock syndrome: The failure of the circulatory system to adequately perfuse the vital organs. The hallmark of hemorrhagic shock is *hypoperfusion*—the deficiency of oxygenated blood and nutrients delivered to the vital organs. The pathophysiology of hypoperfusion includes cellular hypoxia ($\downarrow O_2$), acidosis ($\downarrow pH$), decreased energy production ($\downarrow ATP$), coagulopathy, and irreversible microvascular and cellular injuries (charts I, V, VII-C, VII-D, XI, XII; chapter 5).

Shock has several etiologies (chart VII-A; figures VI, VII).

1. blood loss with a decrease in blood volume and oxygen-carrying capacity—hemorrhagic shock (charts I, V, VII-B; chapter 9).
2. water loss and acute dehydration—hypovolemic shock (charts I, II-B, V; chapter 9).
3. cardiac failure with a secondary decrease of the cardiac output and the cardiac ejection fraction—cardiac shock (chart XIII-B).
4. severe vasodilation and collapse of the blood vessels—traumatic shock (sudden, severe pain), adrenal shock (adrenal fatigue and decreased cortisol levels), and septic shock (blood-borne bacteria).

The clinical manifestations of shock consist of hypotension ($\downarrow BP$), weak and rapid pulse rate ($\uparrow HR$), hyperventilation ($\uparrow RR$), cold and clammy skin (↓T), decreased urine output, and mental confusion (charts VII-B, VII-C; figures VI, VII; chapter 5).

Scientific research has documented that hemorrhagic shock causes 60 to 70 percent of traumatic deaths, and 25 percent of these suffered from coagulopathy (chart VII-D; figure IV; Greenfield 2011; Martin and Beckley 2008).

shock—decompensated: The collapse of the circulatory system due to severe hypotension, hypoperfusion, and irreversible cellular and microvascular injuries in multiple organs—the lungs, kidneys, liver, gut, muscle, heart, and brain. The primary cause of Jesus's death was decompensated multifactorial shock secondary to severe blood and water losses and adrenal fatigue with decreased levels of cortisol (charts I, IV-B, V, VII-A, XI, XII; figures VI, VII; chapters 5, 9, 12).

shock—irreversible cellular and microvascular injuries: Prolonged hypotension and hypoperfusion of vital organs results in cellular and microvascular deaths with third-space fluid loss due to the following pathophysiology (charts I, V, VII-D, XI; figure II; chapters 2, 5, 9, 13).

1. the rapid switch from aerobic to anaerobic energy (absence of O_2) resulting in diminished cellular energy production (↓↓ATP), dysfunction, and injury
2. lactic acidosis (↓pH) causing enzyme dysfunction and cellular injury
3. progressive mitochondrial damage
4. the loss of cellular membrane integrity permitting the influx of water, Ca^{++}, and Na^+ (cloudy swelling)
5. the release of ROS resulting in nuclear and membrane injuries

6. the clumping of nuclear DNA and RNA
7. the release of lysosomal enzymes into the cytoplasm results in cellular "autodigestion"

shock lung: An acute respiratory condition secondary to severe blood loss and acute hemorrhagic shock. The pathophysiology includes pulmonary inflammation and edema, alveolar collapse, and coagulopathy (charts I, V, VI-B, VII-D, VIII-A).

shock—multifactorial: Jesus developed severe shock secondary to multiple causes (charts V, VII-A; figure VI; chapters 5, 12, 13): hemorrhagic (blood loss), hypovolemic (water loss), traumatic (severe injuries and pain), cardiac (pericardial effusion with cardiac tamponade), and adrenal ($\downarrow$cortisol secondary to adrenal fatigue).

shock—the lethal triad: A serious complication of severe hemorrhagic shock resulting from severe trauma, massive blood losses, and multiple blood transfusions (chart VII-D). The lethal triad consists of the following: (1) acidosis caused by severe cellular hypoxia ($\downarrow O_2$), anaerobic energy production ($\downarrow$ATP), and secondary lactic acid accumulation ($\downarrow$pH); (2) hypothermia due to the rapid loss of blood and open wounds; and (3) coagulopathy secondary to a hypercoagulable state (trauma), hypothermia and acidosis (shock), and acute inflammatory responses in the microcirculation of multiple organs (chart VI-B; figure VII).

shock-trauma: Major trauma associated with multiple wounds, severe losses of blood and water, and the rapid onset of multifactorial shock. Jesus sustained fatal shock-trauma secondary to the preliminary traumas and sufferings that occurred prior to His crucifixion (charts I, III, V, VI-A; figures VI, VII; chapters 5, 9, 12).

shroud of Turin: The linen burial garment of Jesus Christ displayed in Turin, Italy, since the sixteenth century. The frontal and dorsal photographic negatives of the shroud reveal the miraculous blood markings and body image of a crucified, Hebrew male who had been severely beaten, scourged, and pierced with thorns, nails, and a lance (figures VIII-A, VIII-B; chapter 6). The wondrous shroud reveals evidence that is consistent with the fourfold gospels—the incarnation, passion, sacrificial death, and resurrection of our Lord and savior Jesus Christ.

sign: An objective manifestation of disease or injury observed by the physician; for example, hypotension, an elevated WBC count, bloody sweat, lacerations, and swollen contusions.

soul: The essential nature, the immaterial eternal spirit, and the animating principle of life. The Son of God took for Himself a human soul, intellect, and will and a human body of flesh and blood to suffer and die in solidarity with humanity (John 1:14; Philippians 2:6–8; 1 Timothy 3:16, Hebrews 2:14,17; Revelation 5:6–9).

sovereignty: The sovereignty of the Lord consists of His absolute supremacy, power, independent authority, and infinite control over creation, redemption, and end times. Almighty God is the source, sustainer, and rightful end of everything that exists. Before the foundations of the world, the sovereign Lord predetermined, coordinated, and choreographed the Son's passion and sacrificial death to include

1. the fulfillment and perfection of prophetic scripture,
2. the transcendency of blood and water,
3. the effects of the Christ event, and,
4. the highest standards of modern medical science (Psalm 33:13–15, 66:5–7, 103:19; Isaiah 40:13–14; Daniel 2:44–45, 4:35; Acts 2:23, 17:24–28; Romans 11:36; Ephesians 3:11; 1 Peter 1:20).

space of Destot: The anatomic site used during Roman crucifixion to nail Jesus's wrists to the crossbar. The space consists of four marble-sized carpal bones that form a funnel-shaped depression located directly under the cutaneous palmar crease and transverse palmar ligament on the little-finger side of the wrist joint (figure IX). In my analysis, the space of Destot was easily located by the Roman executioners and provided rigid fixation. There were no broken bones associated with the nails in the wrists of Jesus (Exodus 12:46; Numbers 9:12; Psalm 34:21; John 19:36; chart IX, see 6, 19; figures VIII-A, IX; chapter 9; Barbet 1950).

stipes: The stationary upright of the Roman cross (glossary, "instruments of Roman crucifixion").

stone of agony: During His *greatest agony* in Gethsemane, Jesus said, "My soul is sorrowful even unto death." Under the life-threatening conditions of the acute anxiety reaction, Jesus fell helplessly across this rounded stone, prayed fervently to the Father, and made His *greatest decision*—to drink the cup of the Father's fury and redeem the human race (Mark 14:34–36; Luke 22:43–44; John 3:36; Romans 5:9; chart IV-B; chapter 4; figure VI).

stone of anointing: Joseph of Arimathea, Nicodemus, and other members of the first church on Calvary carried the Roman crossbar together with Jesus's corpse to a flat stone in the close proximity of the Garden of Resurrection—about three feet wide and eight feet long. The nails were extracted, the rigor mortis forcefully broken, and His hands were secured across His groin. Jesus was washed, anointed, and enshrouded "according to the Jewish burial custom" (John 19:38–42; figures VIII-A, VIII-B).

stress and stressors: A circumstance or event that causes a disturbance in normal psychology (mind) and physiology (body): Human stressors may be physical, such as scourging and battery or mental, for instance fear, terror, sorrow, and pain. The sudden, overwhelming afflictions of Gethsemane resulted in an acute stress reaction with severe psychosomatic (mind-body) complications (charts IV-A, IV-B; chapter 4).

stress hormones: Important hormones for homeostasis during the passion—epi, nepi, and cortisol (charts IV-A, IV-B, V; figures III; chapters 3, 4, 5).

symptom: A subjective manifestation of disease or injury perceived by the patient; for example, fear, grief, pain, light-headedness, and weakness.

syndrome (Gr. "concurrence"): A collection of symptoms and signs that together characterize a specific psychological disorder, medical disease, or traumatic condition; for example, the general adaptation syndrome (chart IV-A), the fight-or-flight syndrome (chart IV-B; chapter 4), and the shock syndrome (chapter 5; *Merriam-Webster's Medical Dictionary* 2005).

synthesis (Gr. "the process of combining"): Human cells are capable of combining simpler molecules or chemical elements to produce important substances such as ATP, enzymes, and proteins (figure II; chapter 2; *Merriam-Webster's Medical Dictionary* 2005).

temple aristocrats: Members of the powerful Sanhedrin—the ruling class—included the elite chief priests, scholars of the law, and wealthy elders. These vainglorious leaders of the Jewish religious establishment bear the greatest guilt for the murder of Jesus Christ (Matthew 27:12, 20; John 19:6, 15).

theological effects of the Christ event: The incarnation, passion, sacrificial death, and resurrection of Jesus Christ granted the following Christological results: redemption (Hebrews 9:12), transformation (2 Corinthians 3:18), freedom (Romans 8:2), new creation (2 Corinthians 5:17), salvation (Ephesians 2:8; Hebrews 5:9), expiation (Romans 3:25), reconciliation (Romans 5:10), sanctification (2 Thessalonians 2:13), justification (Romans 3:24, 28), glorification (Romans 8:17), peace (Romans 5:1), access to God (Ephesians 2:13; Hebrews 4:16, 7:19, 10:19–22), and sharing in the divine nature (2 Peter 1:4).

third space fluid loss: The abnormal accumulation of body water (edema) outside the vascular and intracellular fluid compartments (chart I). Jesus suffered large third-space fluid loss secondary to traumatic and ischemic wounds, pleural and pericardial effusions, and paralytic ileus (charts II-B, V; chapters 5, 9).

thoracotomy: The surgical opening of the chest cavity.

tissue: A collection of specialized cells that perform similar functions; for example, muscle tissues contract for movement, and endocrine tissues synthesize and secrete hormones into the bloodstream.

tumor necrosis factor: TNF is a potent inflammatory compound secreted by mast cells and macrophages that causes vasodilation, diapedesis, and local thrombosis (chart VI-B).

tunic: The Levitical high priest wore "a sacred *seamless tunic* next to the skin" (Exodus 28:40; Leviticus 16:4). On Calvary, the legionnaires cast lots for the seamless tunic worn by Jesus Christ, the great High Priest who "offered" His blood and living water to the Father (John 19:23–24; Hebrews 8:1–3, 9:11–15, 10:19–22).

typology (Gr. "image," "foreshadow," "prefigure"): The study of persons, things, and events in the Old Testament that foreshadowed and prefigured their fulfillments and perfections in the New Testament. Typology preserves the sacred unity of scripture—the New Testament is hidden in the Old, and the Old Testament is revealed in the New. Since the Old Testament prefigurements such as shed blood and liquid offerings must be fulfilled, each prophecy provides invaluable evidence for solving the mystery of how Jesus died (chart IX; prologue; chapters 1, 7, 10).

vasoconstriction: To squeeze and narrow an arteriole and artery.

vasodilation: To relax and widen an arteriole and artery.

Veronica: The legendary woman who lived along the Via Dolorosa observed that Jesus had fallen under the Roman crossbar. Heart-stricken and overcome with compassion, Veronica wiped His marred and bloodstained face: The image of His holy face miraculously appeared on the cloth (Isaiah 52:14; station 15, chapter 13).

Via Dolorosa (Lat. "Way of Suffering"): The original fourteen Franciscan Stations of the Cross that trace the sacred journey of Jesus Christ from the Fortress of Antonia (northwest corner of the Jerusalem temple) to Mount Calvary outside the walls (about three-quarters of a mile; Hebrews 13:11–13; chapters 11, 13).

virtue: A standard of moral excellence and righteous behavior. During the worst possible circumstances, Jesus displayed the highest level of virtuous behavior (chapter 13).

vital signs: The objective signs of life that monitor the essential functions of human life: BP (normal: 120/75), HR/P (normal 70–90 per minute), RR (normal: 15–20 per minute), and T (normal: 98.6° F or 37° C). Additional vital statistics include body weight and height, level of consciousness, and percentage of body fat (chapter 5).

Yahweh (Heb. "I AM WHO I AM"): The Lord, the God of Israel. The English translation is "Jehovah." Yahweh is the great "I AM"—self-sufficient, eternal, infinite, perfect, transcendent, sovereign, and all powerful. Throughout the fourth gospel, Jesus unveiled His glorious divinity by His words—the seven "I AM" statements—and His works—the seven miraculous "signs."

zone of destruction—the energy released by the forces of trauma: The amount of tissue destruction secondary to an act of trauma is defined by the following formula: energy = mass x velocity^2. The greater the *velocity* of a bullet or leather strap during Roman scourging, the greater the energy released, and therefore the greater the amount of tissue damage (note that the lead dumbbells on the leather cords increased the velocity which increased the tissue damage). Each of the 60-70 lashes suffered by Jesus resulted in a zone of destruction— His *mortal wounds*: (1) the skin—partial-thickness mechanical burns and lacerations; (2) the subcutaneous tissues, fat, and muscle—crushed cells (third-space water loss) and lacerated blood vessels (blood loss) which resulted in fatal multifactorial shock; (3) the lungs—contusions including hemorrhage and edema (blood and water losses and acute respiratory failure); (4) the pleural sacs around each lung—an acute inflammatory reaction causing bilateral pleural effusions (water loss); and (5) the pericardial sac around the heart—an acute inflammatory reaction causing a pericardial effusion (water loss), cardiac tamponade, and acute cardiac failure (cardiac shock; charts I, II-B, V, VI-A, VI-B, VIII-A, VIII-B; figures VI, VIII-A, VIII-B, X; chapters 5, 10, 12, 13; glossary, "scourging…").